T0305119

# Multi-criteria Analysis in Legal Reasoning

# Multi-criteria Analysis in Legal Reasoning

Bengt Lindell

*Professor of Civil and Criminal Procedure, Faculty of Law, Uppsala University, Sweden*

Cheltenham, UK • Northampton, MA, USA

Published by
Edward Elgar Publishing Limited
The Lypiatts
15 Lansdown Road
Cheltenham
Glos GL50 2JA
UK

Edward Elgar Publishing, Inc.
William Pratt House
9 Dewey Court
Northampton
Massachusetts 01060
USA


A catalogue record for this book
is available from the British Library

Library of Congress Control Number: 2016959930


This book is available electronically in the **Elgar**online
Law subject collection
DOI 10.4337/9781786430205

ISBN 978 1 78643 019 9 (cased)
ISBN 978 1 78643 020 5 (eBook)

Typeset by Servis Filmsetting Ltd, Stockport, Cheshire
Printed and bound in Great Britain by TJ International Ltd, Padstow

# Contents

# Preface

This book explores a structured method for making legal overall assessments and balancing of interests. The method originates from decision theory and is called multi-criteria analysis. The model that is used is additive and is referred to in this book as the simple additive weighting (SAW), which is well known in decision theory and can be used in overall assessments when there are one or more objectives, multiple options and a number of decision-making criteria. However, most people in the legal profession are probably not familiar with decision theory. In an attempt to describe the method in a simple and educational way, this book therefore contains 22 graphic figures and 21 tables as well as a number of concrete examples of the application of multi-criteria analysis and the simple additive model. In addition, simple additive weighting in some examples is used together with fuzzy logic. The book should be seen as an introduction to these decision theory tools, which are intended to be used for problem structuring, analysis and decision support in overall assessments and balancing of interests. My hope is that it will provide inspiration and spark interest in methods that are used in fields of science other than law and which have much to contribute in a legal decision-making context.

Financial support for the book, which was first published in Swedish in 2015 by iUSTUS publishing company in Uppsala, has been provided by the Swedish Foundation for Jurisprudential Research (Institutet för rättsvetenskaplig forskning), to which I would hereby like to express my heartfelt gratitude. For this publication, the contents have been revised somewhat and the book has also been given a shorter title.[1]

---

[1] Translation into English by Chris Kleinman.

# Abbreviations

(all laws and institutions listed refer to Sweden unless otherwise noted)

| | |
|---|---|
| AD | The Labour Court |
| ADR | Alternative dispute resolution |
| AHP | Analytical hierarchy process |
| AvtL | The Contracts Act (1915:218) |
| Bill | Government Bill |
| BrB | The Penal Code (1962:700) |
| CBCA | Criteria-based content analysis |
| DDA | Data development analysis |
| ECHR | European Convention of Human Rights |
| FB | The Parental Code (1949:381) |
| HD | The Supreme Court |
| JT | Juridisk tidskrift (Swedish legal journal) |
| LAK | Act on Public Video Surveillance (1998:150) |
| MADM | Multi-attribute decision model |
| MANOVA | Multiple Analysis of Variance |
| MAUT | Multi-attribute utility theory |
| MAVT | Multi-attribute value theory |
| MB | The Environmental Code (1998:808) |
| MCA | Multi-criteria analysis |
| MCDA | Multi-criteria decision analysis |
| MCDM | Multi-criteria decision method |
| MÖD | The Land and Environment Courts |
| MODM | Multi-objective decision model |
| NCAP | New Cars Assessment Program |
| NIX | NIX registry, Swedish service to block unwanted telephone sales |
| NJA | Nytt juridiskt arkiv, avd. 1 (Journal presenting Swedish Supreme Court cases) 1 |
| NJA | Nytt juridiskt arkiv, avd. 2 (Journal presenting new laws and surrounding issues) 2 |
| PBL | The Planning and Building Act (2010:900) |
| PUL | The Personal Data Act (1998:204) |
| RÅ | Yearbook from the Supreme Administrative Court |

| RB | The Code of Judicial Procedure (1942:740) |
| RF | Instrument of Government (1974:152) |
| RM | Reality monitoring |
| SAOL | Swedish Academy Glossary |
| SAW | Simple additive weighting |
| SMART | Simple multi-attribute rating technique |
| SOU | Swedish Government Official Reports |
| SvJT | Svensk Juristtidning (Swedish journal of jurisprudence) |
| SWEDMA | Swedish Direct Marketing Association |
| TfR | Tidskrift for Retsvidenskap (Norwegian journal of jurisprudence) |
| TJFF | Magazine published by the Law Student Association in Finland |
| TOPSIS | Technique for ordering of preference by similarity to ideal solution |

# Figures

# Tables

# 1. Overall assessments and balancing of interests

## 1.1 INTRODUCTION

The Swedish Academy Glossary (SAOL) does not list a definition for the term 'overall assessment'. However, the term 'overall assessment' refers to a number of factors, aspects or perspectives that are brought together into a comprehensive assessment, an overall assessment. In this book, the word has a more specific meaning. An overall assessment means that a choice must be made between several possible decision options using certain criteria in order to achieve one or more objectives. This definition addresses both the meaning and the purpose of an overall assessment.

Virtually everyone makes overall assessments on a daily basis. This might involve big, important things like purchasing a home: What is our price range? What city/neighbourhood? Running costs (taxes, maintenance, utilities)? Proximity to daycare, school and work? Renovation needs? And so on. Or the assessment might involve where the family should go on holiday. There are a few options (e.g., Spain, Bulgaria or Italy) and a number of selection criteria such as cost, climate and how child-friendly it is. Another example is buying a new car, which will be explored in detail later on. Even in such cases, there are several different options to consider when evaluating the different car models, which have different prices, different environmental performance, different collision safety and comfort levels, and so on.

All overall assessments in this book involve making a decision according to the definition given in the introduction. This also applies for overall assessments made in a legal context. The structured method for overall assessments that will be presented can thus be used in all types of overall assessments, whether these involve buying a house, a holiday or a car, or, for example, assessing if a clause in a contract is 'unreasonable'. In addition, it does not matter which area of law the overall assessment concerns.

Balancing of interests also involves multiple options, criteria and objectives. One important issue that will be examined is if there is any difference between overall assessments and balancing of interests, and if so, what that difference may be.

Legal overall assessments and balancing of interests have great significance for the parties involved and for society at large. Typical examples of such assessments and balancing will be provided later in this chapter. This may involve, for example, the use of land and water, whether an agreement should be nullified, whether camera surveillance should be permitted, what is consistent with 'the best interests of the child' in a custody dispute or on the use of an optional rule in the Swedish Code of Judicial Procedure (hereinafter 'RB'). The decision may concern very large sums of money or an individual's future. Erroneous decisions can furthermore cause major damage – economically, socially and materially. Decisions must therefore be carefully and thoroughly considered. They must also, in every instance involving the exercise of power, be transparent and people affected must have been given an opportunity to participate in the decision-making process. Complicated decisions that require an overall assessment are, however, often informal in the sense that the decision-maker simplifies by not carefully investigating different options, criteria and objectives, either because this takes time and may be costly, or because structured models for decision-making seem difficult to grasp or implement. Instead, shortcuts are taken, which in the literature of the field are often called heuristics.[1]

The structured analysis for decision-making in overall assessments and balancing of interests that will be discussed in Chapter 2 is referred to in this book as multi-criteria analysis, hereinafter referred to by its acronym MCA. This concept is also often referred to as multiple-criteria decision analysis (MCDA). The designation for the methods used in this analysis is multi-criteria decision methods (MCDM). In addition, a distinction is usually made between multi-objective decision models (MODM) and multi-attribute decision models (MADM), which are umbrella terms that encompasses many models. The first of these is used in the planning process that precedes a decision. MADM is used when there are fixed options and formulated criteria for the decision to be made. The basic model described in Chapter 2 includes both. A distinction is furthermore made in MCA between multi-attribute value theory (MAVT) and multi-attribute utility theory (MAUT). The difference between them is that MAVT presupposes that the decision criteria and the outcomes are certain, while MAUT is a model that also handles uncertainty.[2]

---

[1]   For a discussion on shortened decision paths, see Chapter 3.
[2]   About the aforesaid, see Paul Goodwin and George Wright, *Decision Analysis for Management Judgment* (Wiley, 4th edn, 2012) 34, JS Dodgson and others, 'Multi-criteria Analysis: A Manual' <http://eprints.lse.ac.uk/12761/1/Multi-criteria_Analysis.pdf> 50 (retrieved 15 July 2016), also see Valerie Belton

Unlike MAVT, MAUT does not impose a requirement for independence on the criteria. However, it is rather complicated to use. The simple additive model, simple additive weighting (SAW), which is an MADM method, will therefore be used in this book, but simple multi-attribute rating technique (SMART) will also be described. Some uncertainty can be taken into account in these methods, for example by giving criteria less weight in the sensitivity analysis or by assessing uncertainty when selecting options.[3] Another alternative is to add a probability assessment afterwards. The results from the MCA analysis can then be multiplied by the probability of an option occurring.[4] In this way, probability can rather easily be taken into account even when using the additive model. Uncertainty can furthermore be handled with fuzzy logic, which can be combined with MCA. Fuzzy logic, which primarily belongs to the scientific fields of philosophy, mathematics and technology, is used for things like computer programming and the control and regulation of machines. Fuzzy logic is based on set theory and on the premise that language is vague. Water can, for example, be described as 'warm', 'lukewarm' or 'cool', but there is no way to put a precise linguistic label on these states or the transitions between them. When, for example, does 'lukewarm' become 'warm' and how to describe this in words? Fuzzy logic seems to fit well into a legal context because legal language is often vague. The basics of fuzzy logic will be introduced and applied in Chapter 4. Fuzzy logic will also be applied in Chapter 6.

The abbreviation MCA, which is used consistently throughout this book in lieu of the terms MCDA and MCDM, is an umbrella term for a large number of different techniques and models which are used,

---

and Theodor Stewart, *Multiple Criteria Analysis. An Integrated Approach* (Kluwer 2002) 119ff and Freerk A Lootsma, *Multi-Criteria Analysis via Ratio and Difference Judgement* (Kluwer Academic Publisher, 1999) 15ff. Easily approachable literature on the fundamentals of MCA is also available on the Internet. See e.g., Dodgson and others, mentioned above, to which references are made in this book; Vicky Mabin and Michael Beattie, *A Practical Guide to Multi-Criteria Decision Analysis* <http://www.victoria.ac.nz/som/researchprojects/publications/ Multi-Criteria_Decision_Analysis.pdf> (retrieved 5 July 2016) and GA Mendoza, P Macan and others, *Guidelines for Applying Multi-Criteria Analysis to the Assessment of Criteria and Indicators* (1999, The Criteria and Toolbox series, Center for International Forestry Research) <http://www.cifor.org/livesinforests/ publications/pdf_files/toolbox-9c.pdf> (accessed 22 July 2016).

[3]    See section 2.3.8, below.

[4]    Jacek Malczewski, *GIS and Multicriteria Decision Analysis* (Wiley 1999) 214, Ralf L Keeny and Howard Raiffa, *Decisions with Multiple Objectives: Preference and Value Tradeoffs* (Cambridge University Press 1993) 219ff.

for example, in large-scale projects such as the construction of airports, roads, power plants and, not least, in land and environmental planning. When, for example, an airport is to be built, a multitude of factors must be taken into account, such as noise, emissions, safety, and transport routes to and from the airport. In the end, a great number of circumstances must be analysed, considered and weighed before a decision can be made on where the airport will be located. A large-scale project can include such an enormous number of factors that an intuitive overall assessment becomes impossible. Instead, a structured decision model is required, experts must be consulted, and computer support used.

As will be discussed in Chapter 2, two MCA models that have been used for a long time and found to be robust, namely SMART and SAW – which are additive, part of the MAVT family and have the same basic structure – can present difficulties when used in a legal context as direct decision tools. They can, however, be used as analytical tools to structure the decision material and for tentative decision support. It is also possible in a legal context to mathematically combine numeric scoring and weighing. However, it is important to be careful with the results and match these against intuition.[5] Of course, MCA must be adapted to a legal context. This adaptation poses some difficulties, yet also provides relief in other respects. Attempting to make this adaptation has been a key objective in this book.

Deciding on a legal dispute that requires an overall assessment or a balancing of interests is usually easier than determining where an airport should be located – or in any case different. This is true even for complicated disputes with a number of factors to take into consideration. A legitimate question is therefore whether a structured decision model is really needed for legal decision-making. Would it not be just as well to weigh different factors intuitively? Another partially related question is whether a structured decision model – intended primarily for large projects – should be used in legal decision-making. Intuition, which will be briefly discussed in Chapter 3, is both good and necessary. Intuition does not, however, provide transparency, is not structured and is insufficient when the decision basis is too expansive. The other question and possible concern – that MCA might be inappropriate to use in a legal context – is more complicated. As already mentioned, MCA could be used as soon as there is a

---

[5]   Cf Andy Stirling and Sue Meyer, *Rethinking Risk: A Pilot Multi-criteria Mapping of a Genetically Modified Crop in Agricultural Systems in the UK* <http://users.sussex.ac.uk/~prfh0/Rethinking%20Risk.pdf> (1999) (retrieved 1 July 2016). Also see section 3.5 below.

situation with several possible decision options, criteria and goals. When MCA is used for large projects involving, for example, infrastructure or the planning of other public activities, most of the data used is measurable in some way (costs, quantities, distance, volume of different types of emissions, and so on).[6] In practice, however, MAVT and the additive model are also used on factors that can only be assessed subjectively.

In legal assessments, the criteria for decision-making are rarely measurable. The importance of individual legal facts (criteria) is mainly assessed subjectively. 'Importance' here refers to both the strength and the relevance of concrete legal facts as well as their relative weight. In overall assessments and balancing of interests in particular, different relevant and concrete legal facts are not equally important – some carry more weight than the others. This is true also with respect to evidentiary facts, that is, the value of a piece of evidence, which are usually not measurable but are instead assessed subjectively. In addition, the evidentiary value of different evidentiary facts varies. Even though the evidentiary value of an individual evidentiary fact is generally not objectively measurable but is instead decided intuitively, some legal doctrine recommends the use of mathematical methods for the evaluation of evidence. Thus, there are already structured methods for the evaluation of evidence, such as the evidentiary value method and the evidentiary theme method.[7] MCA, such as it is used in this book, can therefore for questions of law be seen as a counterpart to these methods for evaluation of evidence.

Because the importance of concrete legal facts in overall assessments and balancing of interests is assessed subjectively, the results of the analysis naturally become more uncertain than if there had been measurable data.[8] MCA can nevertheless provide valuable decision support, particularly as there are often many factors to take into account in overall assessments and balancing of interests. In any case, using MCA the decision-makers must make a thorough analysis of each individual factor, thus it explicitly forces them to take a position on what they consider important or less important. Presumably, this then leads to a better decision than if

---

[6]   See e.g., *Multikriterieanalyser vid prioriteringar inom hälso-och sjukvården – kriterier och analysmetoder.* Linköpings universitet, Prioriteringscentrum (2013:2) and *Multikriterieanalys för hållbar efterbehandling: Metodutveckling och exempel på tillämpning.* (Swedish Environmental Protection Agency (2009) Report 5891).

[7]   Section 6.1.1, below.

[8]   Dodgson and others (n 2) 27, 124. The problem with subjective assessments is lessened if the decision-maker is a professional, for example a judge who makes decisions on a daily basis.

everything had been assessed intuitively. The above question on whether it is appropriate to use MCA in a legal context can thus be answered in the affirmative. This is true even if the method will be used only to structure and analyse the decision basis and the decision-maker does not want to set numeric values on different criteria and put the effort into conducting a comprehensive mathematical MCA analysis.

How MCA can be applied to overall assessments of legal issues is discussed in Chapter 4. The examples are illustrated with graphic figures in order to show the different stages in MCA and the simple additive model. The premise in the examples is that there are no uncertainties with respect to evidentiary issues (questions of facts), that is, the facts are not uncertain. Consequently, the overall assessments that are made in this chapter concern the legal significance and weight of several different concrete legal facts in the case which together give, or may give, rise to a legal consequence – or at least could be argued to do so (questions of law).

In Chapter 5, certain evidentiary issues with respect to prognostic assessments in law are discussed from the perspective of utility theory, which is integrated into MAUT. There is a clear difference between the entertainment of evidentiary questions in law and according to the utility theory. In law, disputed facts are usually handled separately in the way that legal consequences are attached to facts that have been proven in accordance with the applicable standard of proof. Utility theory, on the other hand, merges probability and utility into an integrated value. This chapter discusses and demonstrates how utility can and should be taken into account in a legal context when the law stipulates prognostic assessments.

The sixth and final chapter of the book provides a short summary of the evidentiary law theories – the evidentiary value method and the evidentiary theme method – which have been the focus of the law of evidence debate in Sweden and Scandinavia in recent decades. This description provides a framework for understanding the subsequent sections in the chapter on different aspects of evidence evaluation and the use of MCA and fuzzy logic in the assessment of oral testimonies and on the burden of proof and standard of proof.

### 1.1.1 Is MCA a Legal Method?

The question of what constitutes a legal method is controversial. A broad definition is that every method used to solve legal problems is a legal method. In this case, MCA is a legal method if it is used for this purpose. Legal method is, however, usually and traditionally associated with different ways of deciding on the meaning of a rule of law, that is, with interpretation and application of law. For example, the German legal philosopher

Philipp Heck advocated a method proposing that all application of law is the result of balancing of interests. Yet, Heck's methodology, which came to be called the jurisprudence of interests ('*Interessenjurisprudenz*'), deals with an entirely different sort of balancing of interests than that discussed in this book. Heck argues that it is not possible to determine the contents of a legislative rule based solely on the aim or purpose of the law. The law is instead the result of a tug of war between different factors and can therefore only be understood as effects of a conflict of interest:

> Es ist nicht möglich, den Inhalt einer Gesetzenorm nur aus ihrem Zweck zu erklären. Das Gesetz ist, wie jede Handlung, die Resultante, gleichsam die Kraftdiagonalen ringender Faktoren, deren Wirkung wir nur als Interessenkonflikt erfassen können.[9]

Teleological interpretation, which was criticized by Heck, is another well-known method that can be used to determine the meaning of a legislative rule.[10]

Both MCA and law application methods are normative. The aim of MCA is to help the decision-maker make the 'best' decision possible. The aim of a law application method is also to help the decision-maker (the legal decision-maker) make the 'best' ruling possible. However, no attempt is made in this book to fit MCA into a law application method, since the methods for the application of law and for decision-making under MCA have different starting points. Regarding, for example, the teleological method, as presented by Ekelöf, the goal of this is to achieve morality and behaviour modification and, from these starting points, make the 'best' decision possible.[11] Even with this objective it is quite appropriate to use MCA, which does not have the aim of indicating from which values individual legal facts in a case should be assessed. The purpose of MCA is instead to provide a structured analysis and decision model. What values the individual decision-maker then wants to insert into the model depends on what he or she considers important and what will lead to a 'good' decision. The scoring and weighting of criteria with regard to the different

---

[9]   Philipp Heck, *Das Problem der Rechtsgewinnung. Gesetzeauslegung und Interessenjurisprudens: Begriffsbildung und Interessenjurisprudenz*. Redigert von Roland Dubischer (Verlag Gehlen 1968) 55.

[10]   Cf n 11 below and Per Olof Ekelöf and Henrik Edelstam, *Rättegång: Första häftet* (8th edn, Norstedts Juridik 2002) 80. Also see Per Henrik Lindblom, *Miljöprocess, Del 1* (Iustus 2001) 81, footnote 20.

[11]   Per Olof Ekelöf, Teleological Construction of Statutes (1958) 2 *Scandinavian Studies in Law* 75. Professor Ekelöf († 1990) was a prominent professor of procedural law at the Faculty of Law at Uppsala University.

decision options is, however, done in accordance with legal requirements. If, for example, a rule of law is to be interpreted restrictively, this may affect the scoring and weighting. If it instead is interpreted broadly, this may correspondingly affect how individual legal facts are assessed. MCA is thus not a law application method, but rather a method that belongs to another science – decision theory. It can be equated with other auxiliary sciences of law, such as semantics or witness psychology.

Concerning the use of MCA as a legal analytical tool, the method can be used in every assessment in which a number of circumstances have been or will be aggregated in a total appraisal. The method therefore has a very broad range of applications. However, while the volume of literature in its own field of knowledge is extensive, there is very little written in legal literature about MCA and fuzzy logic. Even rarer is legal literature in which, as in this book, the method is actually applied.

MCA can be used as an instrument for the planning of negotiations, both before and after a legal dispute has arisen. Howard Raiffa discusses this in *The Art and Science of Negotiation* (2003) and, as co-author, gives an introduction to multi-criteria analysis in *Smart Choices* (2003). From legal negotiations it is then not a big step to, as in this book, use MCA in other areas, such as for analyses of legal situations and decisions. As concerns the use of MCA in Alternative Dispute Resolution (ADR), reference can be made to Nagel and Mills, *Multi-criteria Methods for Alternative Dispute Resolution* (1990). This book shows how computer support can be applied as a tool for using MCA in negotiations and legal disputes.[12] Fuzzy logic seems to receive a bit more attention in the field of evidentiary law than it does in regard to legal assessments,[13] but even here legal literature is sparse.[14] One explanation for the difficulty MCA and fuzzy logic have had in gaining a foothold in the field of law might be that the literature in this subject is written in a different scientific language than law professionals may be used to; a language that is furthermore

---

[12]    Another book about computer support is, for example, Alessio Ishizaka and Philippe Nemery, *Multi-Criteria Decision Analysis: Methods and Software* (Wiley 2013).

[13]    However, see TT Arvind and Lindsey Stirton, 'Explaining the reception of the Code Napoleon in Germany: a fuzzy-set qualitative comparative analysis' (2010) 1 Legal Stud. 1. Also see Odelstad, who is cited in the next section.

[14]    See, for example, Kevin M Clermont, Death of Paradox: The Killer Logic Beneath the Standards of Proof (2013) Cornell Law Faculty Publications, Paper 585 <http://scholarship.law.cornell.edu/facpub/585> and also *Conjunction of Evidence and Fuzzy Logic* (2012) Cornell Legal Studies Research Paper 12-58 <http://papers.ssrn.com/sol3/papers.cfm?abstract_id=2115200> (retrieved 21 July 2016).

often quite formal and may seem at first glance rather unapproachable for a lawyer.

This book is about the use of multi-criteria analysis (MCA) in a legal context with regard to overall assessments and balancing of interests.[15] However, MCA can also be used in other law contexts than judicial processes. For the legislator who is considering different legislative options, the decision-making process includes the creation of alternative options, the selection of criteria and the collection of materials. MCA is also excellent to use in this context, just as legal scholars and legal decision-makers in both the public and private spheres may find the model useful for structuring and analysing a problem and as decision support. Hopefully, this book can, in a way that is more accessible to legal professionals, arouse interest in the possibilities offered by MCA and fuzzy logic.

## 1.2    BALANCING AND COMBINED WEIGHTING

Suppose that a mining company wants to divert a river in order to dry up a part of the riverbed to mine iron ore. Fishermen, indigenous peoples, some residents of the surrounding community and nature conservation advocates are opposed to this for various reasons. The fishermen claim that salmon fishing will be hurt (A) and that their leisure activity will be jeopardized (B). The indigenous people claim that reindeer husbandry will be disturbed and that they will suffer increased costs (C). Local residents claim that the landscape will be destroyed (D) and that tourism will suffer (E). Nature conservation advocates warn that flora and fauna will be disrupted (F) and will be difficult to restore (G). The municipality asserts that mining is important for employment (H). The mining company claims that everything will be restored to its original condition (I).

A court would have great difficulty making an overall assessment or balancing interests of A–I in a case like this without official objectives or guidelines for how this should be done. It would, on the other hand, be possible for the stakeholders involved to, without public guidelines or overriding objectives, come to a privately negotiated solution that looks after their interests. By giving and taking, receiving financial compensation, and imposing various types of restrictions, a negotiated solution might be reached ad hoc. If a court is to make an overall assessment or a balancing of interests, it must at least have one or more

---

[15]    Concerning the use of MCA in the interpretation and application of a rule of law, see section 4.6.2 below.

objectives on which to base the assessment. For example, that it must safeguard the interests of the environment, human health and nature conservation. There may of course also be guidelines for the assessment. Without objectives or guidelines, the assessment will take place in a vacuum. The legal requirements for non-discrimination and foreseeability will thus not be met, which is unacceptable in the governmental exercise of power.

Professor Jan Odelstad has written a book on balancing of interests in the application of planning legislation.[16] In the book, Odelstad analyses the difference between public and private interests using multi-dimensional decision theory, but he also uses another terminology than what is used later on in this book. A short summary of Odelstad's views on balancing of interests is provided below. Those interested in the more detailed and in-depth analyses he makes are referred to his book.[17]

According to Odelstad, a typical decision-making situation often involves a number of options and a set of aspects that may be of significance to how good the options are. He believes that evaluation with respect to aspects is an important step in the weighting of different considerations and in the combined weighting of different aspects into a total appraisal. The total appraisal, says Odelstad, can be seen as a whole consisting of parts that in turn are wholes consisting of smaller parts, and so on. A total appraisal therefore disintegrates into parts, which in turn disintegrate into smaller parts of the same type, but which in a sense are on a different level. The problem, argues Odelstad, consists in determining the 'total goodness' or appropriateness of the options (often for a specific purpose or in a specific context). One should, in other words, make a total appraisal of the options (for that particular purpose or context). The total appraisal (or the 'total goodness', as Odelstad calls it) is achieved through a combined weighting of the original aspects, which then forms a new aspect. The task is therefore to determine what the options are in regard to this new aspect. This entails attempting to determine the ranking of the options with regard to this, that is, establish which of the options is best, second best, good, less good and bad. However, this might not be sufficient. It might also be necessary to identify how much better one option is than another. Based on how the options stand in the total appraisal, the decision, Odelstad says, is often easy to make. This may, for example, mean

---

[16] Professor of Decision, Risk and Policy Analysis, Gävle University College, Sweden.

[17] Jan Odelstad, *Intresseavvägning. En beslutsteoretisk studie med tillämpning på planering* (Thales 2002).

selecting the option that is best overall or establishing a priority order for the options.[18]

Odelstad argues that when we speak of the interests of X, it is more of a question of the value of X. According to Odelstad, it is therefore reasonable to say that X is a private interest if X is valuable or has sufficient value from an individual point of view, and that X is a public interest if X has a large enough value from a general standpoint.[19] According to Odelstad, aspects can be interests, though not every aspect. Every aspect is thus not deserving of the designation of interest. This designation is only given to aspects that are of interest, that is, that have significance or value to the assessment, balancing or weighting in question.[20] Options can also be called interests, according to Odelstad.[21]

Odelstad calls that which is weighted together in a combined weighting, factors or components, and that which these are weighted together into, he calls aggregates. He sees both factors and aggregates as aspects and therefore uses the term 'aggregation' synonymously with combined weighting.[22] This term is common in MCA and is also used at times in this book. Odelstad often uses the term 'aspect'. In MCA, the terms commonly used are attribute or criterion, objectives and options without explicit reference to aspects. This terminology is also used when MCA is discussed later in this book. Aspects will thus not be specifically mentioned, but are of course important to the assessment of different options and criteria.

Odelstad furthermore divides interests into public initial interest aspects, private interest aspects, the joined interest aspect, and the total joined public interest aspect.[23] Odelstad calls the public interest that is considered in planning the 'initial public interest'. The joining of this into a total appraisal Odelstad calls the 'joined public interest' or the 'joined public interest aspect'. This aspect is, according to Odelstad, in a sense the total appraisal from a public standpoint. The combined weighting of all original aspects – both initial public interests and individual interests – into a total appraisal, Odelstad calls the 'total joined public interest' or the 'total joined public interest aspect'. This aspect is also, according to Odelstad,

---

[18]   Ibid., 70ff.
[19]   Ibid., 74.
[20]   Ibid., 75.
[21]   Ibid., 85.
[22]   Ibid., 86. The term 'aggregation' means, in short, that the decision basis is broken down into smaller parts to be analysed and then joined into one or more whole entities. It is this joining of the analysed components in the decision basis that is called aggregation.
[23]   Ibid., 87.

the total appraisal from a public standpoint, but in a different sense than the joined public interest is.[24] Odelstad suggests that the total joined public interest aspect be called the agglomerated public interest aspect.[25]

The terminology that Odelstad uses is complicated, but has advantages. However, should the joined public interest – the agglomerate – really be called public interest? Odelstad, who asks this question himself, says that the interests, whether public or private, are of interest for the 'total goodness' because they contribute to this. According to Odelstad, the 'total goodness' is not, however, an interest because this constitutes the terminus for the assessment.[26] One reason that Odelstad uses this terminology anyway is that he believes that it is not uncommon for the term 'interest' to actually be used to refer to the combined weighting of both public and private interests. Another reason is that Odelstad also views options as interests.[27] The terminology thus becomes symmetrical. However, the crucial question in this context, to which this book several times returns and which Odelstad touches on, though without answering,[28] is whether the 'total goodness' really is a terminus for the assessment or if there is a more total 'total goodness' above this. Perhaps this question is more about control of the assessment made than about adding another level. In such a case control probably belongs to the sensitivity assessment.[29]

Is there, according to Odelstad, any difference between overall assessments and balancing of interests? Odelstad argues that it is often objectives that are weighted together, that the synonymy between 'balancing' and 'weighting' is only partial and that one difference between the words is that 'balancing' is preferable when there are two phenomena that will be brought together. For 'balancing', the idea of scales and weighing plays a role: a typical balancing uses a figurative scale, or more specifically a balance scale, and such a scale has two weighing pans.[30] Another difference in use between 'balancing' and 'weighting' that Odelstad thinks exists is that a balancing more frequently concerns circumstances, whereas a weighting more frequently concerns aspects (viewpoints). Not that it is so, he says, that circumstances are always balanced and aspects are always weighted – in fact the opposite is sometimes done – but Odelstad thinks there is a tendency for this.[31]

---

[24]  Ibid., 84.
[25]  Ibid.
[26]  Ibid., 85.
[27]  Ibid.
[28]  Ibid.
[29]  See section 1.5.1, below.
[30]  Odelstad, 79.
[31]  Ibid.

Odelstad has been given a lot of attention above, and there are two reasons for this. First, his is the only account in Sweden in which a legal balancing of interests has been investigated thoroughly based on multi-dimensional decision theory. Secondly, Odelstad's analysis of what a balancing of interests is stands out as penetrating and well executed. Admittedly, in regard to his terminology, it is rather complicated and it could furthermore be discussed whether a combined weighting of public and private interests should be called a joined public interest. If Peter, Nick and Henry have private interests that are weighted together with a public interest, and these outweigh the public interest, it may seem misleading to call this the 'total joined public interest'. If, on the other hand, this joining is done in the public interest, that is, from a common point of view, it is good if the individual interests are given priority when they weigh more. Naturally, in this case there should be a sufficiently large number of private interests.

Later in this book, examples will be given of overall assessments and balancing of interests. It will be demonstrated that in certain cases, it is not possible to draw a clear line between overall assessments and balancing of interests and that even a balancing of interests may contain an overall assessment. This is also apparent from Odelstad's investigation, even if he does not closely examine the demarcation issue. There are, however, at least sometimes, important differences in the legal conditions for performing a balancing of interests or an overall assessment, which will be discussed. The next question is if the results can differ depending on what type of assessment is made.

## 1.3   EXAMPLES OF BALANCING OF INTERESTS

In the following, a few legislative rules will first be described in which a balancing of interests must be made.[32] A few legal rules that presuppose an overall assessment will then be presented. The aim is not to substantively examine in more detail what a balancing of interests or an overall assessment is in different branches of law and in different situations, but

---

[32]   Weighting norms from a legislative and legal science perspective have been discussed by, among others, Torstein Eckhoff and Nils Kristian Sundby, *Rettsystemer: Systemteoretisk innføring i rettsfilosofien* (2nd edn, Tano 1991). Balancing of interests from a procedural law perspective has been discussed by, among others, Hans Eklund, *Inhibition* (Iustus 1998) 231f and Lars Heuman, 'Avvägningsrekvisit och möjligheten för en domstol att avvisa en fastställelsetalan när käranden kan föra en fullgörelsetalan' (2006–07) JT 837.

rather to try to determine what characterizes these. One overriding question is if there is any difference between balancing of interests and overall assessments. An important question related to this is if the same structured decision model can be used for both balancing of interests and overall assessments. It will also be examined whether, and if so how, the principle of proportionality and prerequisites such as 'extraordinary reasons' or 'special circumstances' (weights) come into a balancing of interests.

### 1.3.1   Planning and Building Act (PBL)

Balancing of interests under this law has, as mentioned above, been thoroughly analysed by Odelstad. The Preamble of the Planning and Building Act (PBL, 2010:900), 1:1, states that the provisions of the law are aimed at, with consideration to individual freedoms, promoting social progress with equal and good social conditions and a good and lasting sustainable living environment for the people of today's society and for future generations. The second chapter of the Act is entitled 'Public and private interests' and in 2:5 PBL, a balancing of interests is directly prescribed:[33] 'Where issues are addressed under this Act, consideration shall be given to both public and private interests.' The Act specifies which interests should be taken into account. PBL 2:3, for example, stipulates a good living environment from a social standpoint, good management of land and water, and good economic growth. It is furthermore stipulated in the Act that certain values must be protected, including the culture-historical and environmental.

It should first be noted that when the Act states that the examination 'of issues under this Act' shall consider both public and private interests, this does not mean that every issue will be subject to a balancing of interests. An issue under the Act could, for example, be whether or not something is a 'building product' or how the term 'property developer' should be interpreted. The intent would not seem to be that such matters should be resolved by a balancing of interests, but rather that planning should be decided after a weighting.

The Act can require an assessment of a great number of factors, which must be categorized and classified according to the terms and designations used by the Act. If there were only two large weighing pans, one for public and one for private interests, there would be a very large amount of data in the pans that would have had to have first been weighted together in some way. For this reason, aggregation would likely be done on several

---

[33]   1:5 in the official translation of PBL (1987:10).

levels. The weighting that the Act stipulates is usually a terminus at the end of a line of many assessments. This is the incremental aggregations and the total appraisal that Odelstad speaks of. As for whether an overall assessment is made on a level above the balancing of interests or if the total appraisal is made within the balancing of interests, we will return to this overriding question later in the book.

### 1.3.2   Environmental Reviews

Stipulations 7:25 and 7:26 of the Environmental Code (1998:808) are provided under the heading 'Review of interests'. These stipulations are as follows, in the order they appear:

> In connection with the consideration of matters relating to protected areas referred to in this chapter, private interests shall also be taken into account. Restrictions on the rights of private individuals to use land or water under safeguard clauses provided in this chapter must therefore not be more stringent than is necessary in order to achieve the purpose of the protection.
>
> Exemptions from prohibitions or other rules issued pursuant to this chapter may only be granted in accordance with sections 7, 9 to 11, 18, 20 and 22 where this is consistent with the purpose of the prohibition or rule.[34]

From 7:25, it is clear that a proportionality assessment must be made. The provision in 7:26, which concerns exemptions, protects the public interest. In the grounds for this, it is stated in 7:26 that exemptions are granted for a private interest that outweighs the public interest;[35] thus a balance-scale mindset and a balancing of interests. The application of the exemption rule is furthermore intended to be restrictive.[36] Exemptions may only be granted if this is in accordance with the aim of the prohibition or regulation.

Balancing of interests in environmental processes has, among others, been addressed by Professor Per Henrik Lindblom. He maintains that the concept of balancing of interests in German doctrine is considered empty and meaningless and that it is difficult to determine quantitatively; at what point do private interests or third-party interests become so numerous that they become public interest? He also mentions something that he calls over-individual interests, which consists of a conglomerate of private

---

[34]   Official translation of The Swedish Environmental Code can be found in Ds (Departemental Serie) 2000:61.
[35]   Governmental Bill 1997/98:45, part II, 98.
[36]   Ibid.

interests and claims that they cannot be individualized, such as people's claim to a good environment.[37]

It is easy to agree with Lindblom that balancing of interests as a legal concept lacks substance. As this book aims to present a structured model for decision support, however, the substantive meaning of the term balancing of interests will, as previously mentioned, not be examined in more detail. The balancing of interests will instead be examined from an analysis and decision perspective. Which factors should be placed in the weighing pans, as well as the weight of these factors, of course raises legal issues, but the weighting itself and the way in which this is done are determined by decision theory and the structured model used. However, some substantive decision aspects will be discussed in this context later in section 1.5.2.

### 1.3.3   Camera Surveillance

On 1 July 2013, a new camera surveillance law came into force, applying instead of the Personal Data Act (PUL, 1998:204) and replacing the Public Camera Surveillance Act (LAK, 1998:150). This Act combines all rules regarding camera surveillance into a single law. Under section 6 of the Public Camera Surveillance Act, permission shall be granted for camera surveillance if interests for such monitoring outweigh private interests in not being monitored. In assessing interests in camera surveillance, special consideration shall be given to whether monitoring is needed to prevent, detect or investigate crime, prevent accidents or for other comparable purposes.

For places where the public has access, permission for camera surveillance shall be granted if interests for such monitoring outweigh private interests in not being monitored. The individual's interest in not being monitored shall be particularly weighed against the area to be monitored and how the monitoring is carried out.[38] Generally speaking, the larger the area to be monitored, the more sensitive the space (for example, toilets) and/or the longer the exposure time, the higher the infringement on privacy will be.[39] The Swedish Data Protection Authority has

---

[37]  Lindblom, Miljöprocess, del 1 (n 10) 77–98. Also see Robert Nordh, *Talerätt i miljömål: Särskilt om vattenrättsliga ansökningsmål samt talan rörande allmänna intressen* (Iustus 1999) 370ff.

[38]  See for example Supreme Administrative Court annuals RÅ 2000, ref. 61 on the weighting itself and RÅ 2010 ref. 22 on the monitoring of streets and public squares.

[39]  Regarding factors to consider, see Kristina Blomberg, *Värt att veta om personuppgiftslagen* (Studentlitteratur 2012) 32.

checklists for employers and for schools considering introducing camera surveillance.

As stated in the Swedish Data Protection Authority's information leaflet of June 2013, permission under the 'The new Camera Surveillance Act' is based on an assessment according to the principle of preponderance of evidence.[40] An important feature of the principle of preponderance of evidence is, according to the Data Protection Authority, that camera surveillance is normally not to be seen as a first-choice option for achieving a particular purpose. It should therefore first be examined if less intrusive options can be considered, such as lighting or the presence of security guards.

Of particular interest from a procedural law angle is the Data Protection Authority's reference to the principle of preponderance of evidence. In procedural law doctrine, this principle is only used in issues of evidence while the Data Protection Authority seems to use this in matters of both evidence and law. See also RÅ 2000, ref. 61:

> Under section 6 of the Public Camera Surveillance Act (LAK), permission shall be granted for camera surveillance if interests for such monitoring outweigh private interests in not being monitored (*the so-called principle of preponderance of evidence*). In assessing interest in public camera surveillance, special consideration shall be given to whether this is needed to prevent crime, prevent accidents or for comparable purposes. In assessing private interests in not being monitored, special consideration shall be given to how the monitoring is conducted and to the areas to be monitored. (My emphasis, my translation)

It is evident from this quote that the Supreme Administrative Court uses the principle of preponderance of evidence not only in the existence of facts, but also to weigh the legal implication of the factors that are in each figurative weighing pan. The question of what the term 'privacy' entails and if, and to what extent, the monitoring is an invasion of privacy, is unquestionably an issue of law. From a procedural angle, it is thus about a different use of the principle of preponderance of evidence than the usual. This indicates that the principle of preponderance of evidence in camera surveillance is used as a decision rule for the entire weighting operation. We will return to this use of the principle of preponderance of evidence later.[41]

---

[40]  <http://www.datainspektionen.se/press/nyheter/2013ny-kameraovervakn-ingslag-fran-1-juli/> (retrieved 15 August 2014).

[41]  Section 1.5, below.

The right to privacy is protected in article 8 of the European Convention on Human Rights (ECHR). However, ECHR permits exceptions because there are times when the individual must tolerate infringement on the person's private life if this is needed to, for example, prevent crime and if the intrusion is reasonable in relation to the interests of society. The principle of proportionality must therefore be considered in the application of the Camera Surveillance Act.

### 1.3.4   Tenancy Act

In chapter 12 of the Swedish Land Code – the 'Tenancy Act' – there are a number of provisions that refer to balancing of interests. Section 46, section 1, clauses 1–10; for example, specify when a tenant's legal protection of tenancy may be withdrawn. Clause 10 – the general clause – provides for a balancing of interests. A prerequisite for this is that there must be substantive grounds for moving out. On weighting, the Tenancy Act Committee states:

> Of importance should also be how the weight of the substantive grounds relates to the weight of the tenant's interest in retaining the flat. A substantive ground should, for instance, not entail the sacrifice of an urgent interest in maintaining the residence. The substantive grounds must have such weight that it appears reasonable or fair that the tenant must move. It is quite natural that a balancing of interests of this type, which is required here, must in situations with troubling housing shortages normally tip the scales in favour of the tenant. In such market conditions, the matter at hand is, for the tenant, of such vital interest as having a roof over one's head. Even if the tenant also, in a reasonably balanced market, has a major interest in retaining the leased rental unit, this interest is, however, not one of such magnitude that it should, to the same extent as in a noticeable housing shortage, tip the scales in favour of the tenant. This assessment is consistent with the statement at the inception of the Tenancy Act, that the Act's extension rules in housing shortages should to a certain extent protect the tenant even against terminations for reasons that would otherwise be considered fully legitimate. What this matter, in market conditions without housing shortages, chiefly entails for the tenant is the idealistic interest in keeping one's home intact and continuing to live in the place where one has grown into the environment and become comfortable in it. For a family with children, the interest in remaining undisturbed in the home of course carries particular weight. This idealistic interest, which is thus linked to the preservation of the home in the leased residence, is, however, not the only factor, which more generally can be considered to speak in favour of allowing the tenancy to continue. Consideration must also be given to the fact that a move generally involves expenses for the tenant, which are often considerable in comparison to the tenant's economical resources, in any case if expenses for alterations and acquisitions of furniture, fixtures and similar are also to be taken into account. Even other factors, such as the distance between home and work, could at times

play a role when it comes to assessing the tenant's interest in maintaining the rental unit. [42] (My translation)

The Committee's statement is a good and clear example of balance scale thinking (see reference to 'weighing pans'). In other words, there must be substantive grounds. The weight of these substantive grounds must then be weighed against the tenant's interests. If these substantive grounds have a low weight, the interest in maintaining the residence must not be sacrificed. The Committee further differentiates between a situation in which there is a housing shortage and a situation in which there is not a housing shortage. In the latter, the tenant's idealistic interest in remaining in the residence and the costs of a move are mentioned.

In NJA 2011 p. 27, concerning the application of 12:57, paragraph 1, clauses 2–4, it is stated that the landlord in cases of demolition and renovation does not need to give reasons for demolition or renovation, and that this therefore represents a type of legal balancing of interests. This expression thus means that the balancing of interests is set out on beforehand in the law.[43] Later on in this book this will be referred to as legal balancing of interests, in contrast to, as in the Committee's example above, law-based balancing of interests.

### 1.3.5 Optional Rules – Procedural Weighting

That the court, in accordance with an optional provision in RB, 'may' do something usually means that there is a balancing of interests. An example of a 'classic' procedural weighting rule is the provision for declaratory claim in 13.2 RB.[44] The declaratory claim may be admissible for examination if it is deemed appropriate. The plaintiff's interest in having an uncertain legal situation determined must be weighed against the defendant's interest in not suffering 'prejudice' by the uncertainty being removed. Even in the production of a document pursuant to 38:2 RB a balancing of interests must, in some cases, be conducted. To begin with, the prerequisites in the provision on identification, relevance and evidential significance of the required document must be met. If the opposing party alleges that

---

[42]   SOU 1961:47, 90, also see SOU 1966:14, 209, Government Bill (1968:91) and Leif Holmqvist and Rune Thomsson, *Hyreslagen. En kommentar* (10th edn, Norstedts Juridik 2010) 507ff. Also see Bertil Bengtsson, Richard Hager and Anders Victorin, *Hyra och annan nyttjaderätt till fast egendom* (8th edn, Norstedts Juridik 2013) 60ff.
[43]   Bertil Bengtsson and others, ibid., 110.
[44]   Heuman (n 32).

the documents contain trade secrets, 'extraordinary cause' is furthermore required for disclosure of the documents. The evidentiary value of the documents must then be weighted against the risk of injury.[45] Because the effort involved in disclosing documents can be burdensome, involving, for example, months of work to find data files, the effort must also be proportional to the claimant's interest in obtaining the documents.

A balancing of interests must also in certain cases be done in the use of preliminary seizure in accordance with 15:1–3 RB. The provision in 15:3 RB may thus require a balancing of interests.[46] In RH 2001:10, the Court of Appeals rejected, after a proportionality assessment, a motion for sequestration, even though the prerequisites specified in 15:1 RB were met. The Court of Appeals, however, found it possible to conduct a balancing of interests even in the decision on sequestration, referring to NJA 1993, p. 182, which provides that this is possible.

Balancing of interests can be triadic. In the application of the above-mentioned 13:2 RB, two private interests – the plaintiff's and the defendant's – can be weighed against each other, but public interests for expedient proceedings must also be taken into account. It is perhaps for this reason that the Supreme Court used the word 'appropriate' in this context.[47] In such a case it is not a balancing of interests such as is done when decisions are made on camera surveillance, where public interests are weighed against private interests. On the other hand, public and private interests are included in virtually all types of interests. In a document production dispute amenable to out-of-court settlement, the individual claimant's interests in obtaining the document are placed against the individual possessor's interests. Could there be a public interest in producing the documents that should also be considered so that the weighting becomes triadic? It could be argued that there is a public interest in effective and expedient litigation or arbitration, but this interest is so general that it then applies to the application of all rules in RB or in the Arbitration Act. In principle, it should therefore not have influence on the balancing of two private interests in a dispute amenable to out-of-court settlement.

Trade secrets are protected by law because there is a public interest in protecting them.[48] For this reason, 'extraordinary cause' is required for

---

[45] See for example NJA 2012 p. 289, concerning the court's examination of an application for a subpoena for the production of a document in arbitration.
[46] Eklund, Inhibition 235 (n 32) and Peter Westberg, *Det provisoriska rättsskyddet i tvistemål. En funktionsstudie över kvarstad och andra civilprocessuella säkerhetsåtgärder*, Bok 1 (Jurisförlaget Lund 2004) 18.
[47] NJA 2005 p. 517, NJA 2007 p. 108.
[48] Act on the Protection of Trade Secrets (1990:409).

the production of documents which the adversary claims contain trade secrets. However, this might well be the case even with regard to the party petitioning for disclosure; it depends on what law is invoked.[49] Anyway, as soon as an overall suitability assessment comes into the picture for a balancing of interests, the question clearly arises as to whether another level is added to the assessment: an overall assessment on top of a balancing of interests.[50]

## 1.4   OVERALL ASSESSMENTS

Overall assessments typically include a variety of circumstances and considerations. While it is claimed that balancing of interests would seem to require support in law or preparatory work[51] – which seems doubtful – the same does not apply to overall assessments. The reason for this is that it is inherent in its very nature that an overall assessment must be made when there are several factors to be weighted together. The word 'overall assessment' is not always used in court practice as a designation for this combined weighting. Other common expressions are 'in a collective assessment', 'all in all, we find. . .' and similar formulations. However, if it is expressed in the preparatory work that an overall assessment must be made, these tend to be referred to in the reasons for the judgement.

That an overall assessment will be made does not necessarily mean that this is difficult or that it includes a large number of factors. It may be that there is a circumstance that is prominent and significant, a single circumstance that knocks out all the others or at least achieves dominance.[52] In such cases, the overall assessment is easy. There are also overall assessments in which the same type of event has occurred several times and must be assessed once again along with the previous, for example if an employee is dismissed because of repeated inappropriate behaviour. When similar things have happened previously the overall assessment aims at putting the events together to determine if they are sufficient for a dismissal. For the use of MCA, however, it does not matter if it is the same event or several different types of events that need to be assessed, because

---

[49]   For example, the party petitioning for disclosure claims that the defendant has infringed on his or her right to a patent.

[50]   Cf Odelstad (n 18) and the 'total goodness'.

[51]   Kent Källström, 'Arrendators ersättningsrätt vid uppsägning av anläggningsarrende. Om ändamålstolkning av avvägningsnormer' (1988) SvJT 622. However, as will be discussed later, there are different types of balancing of interests.

[52]   See section 4.4.6, below.

an overall assessment in both cases means that a choice has to be made between dismissal and non-dismissal according to a number of criteria.

### 1.4.1   Best Interests of the Child

A typical example of when an overall assessment must be made can be found in the provision of 6:2a FB on 'the best interests of the child', even if this is not actually stated in the wording of the law. According to *Utredningen om barnets rätt* (Investigation on Children's Rights), which was started in 1977 and completed with the report SOU 1979:63, children need:

- care and protection;
- people who they can receive love from and give love to;
- a stable and lasting relationship with their parents;
- to develop in an environment that meets their needs for stimulation;
- parents' help setting boundaries for their actions;
- to feel that they are needed and that they can take responsibility;
- to be able to influence their situation;
- to gradually free themselves from their dependence on their parents;
- togetherness with both parents even if they are in conflict with each other.[53]

These criteria, which are based on what a child typically needs, still largely apply today.[54] In addition to the above needs, the official report states that in the assessment of 'the best interests of the child', 'particular importance should be attached to' the risk that the child or another person in the family is being abused or that the child is unlawfully taken away or kept or otherwise mistreated, and of the child's need for close and good contact with both parents. It has been argued that these factors constitute *presumptions*.[55] In a structured overall assessment, it is more likely a question of factors that are given greater *weight* than others. The child's need for participation has further been emphasized through a reminder in the provision that the child's wishes must be considered, taking into account the child's age and level of maturity, when decisions are made on custody, residence and visitation (6:2a, paragraph 3 FB).

---

[53]   SOU 1979:63, 56.
[54]   Anna Singer, *Barnets bästa. Om barns rättsliga ställning i familj och samhälle* (6th edn, Norstedts Juridik 2012) 27.
[55]   Göran Ewerlöf, Tor Sverne and Anna Singer, *Barnets bästa: om föräldrars och samhällets ansvar* (5th edn, Norstedts Juridik 2004) 79.

## 1.4.2 Contracts Act, Section 36

Another typical example of a provision that requires an overall assessment is section 36 of the Swedish Contracts Act (AvtL) and the assessment of whether a condition in an agreement is 'unreasonable'. This general clause, which is mandatory, has been called the Contracts Act's perhaps most important provision.[56] It can be applied in virtually any property law agreement. According to the legal doctrine, unreasonable is a relational concept.[57] In the preparatory work, no method is given for how the provision should be used and there is, according to von Post, no definitive ruling from the Supreme Court or the appellate courts where a term has been found unreasonable in itself.[58]

The formulation of the general clause makes it possible to consider all factors that may be significant to the contractual relationship. Even if the provision is aimed at the terms of a contract, it is an overall assessment that is conclusive.[59] Regarding the content of the agreement, the starting point for the assessment should, according to the preparatory work, be what without the term would be normal. Furthermore, an assessment is needed of how large the deviation from the normal must be for the term to be considered unreasonable.[60] Concrete factors that according to the preparatory work can be significant include, for example, that the ruling is put in a superior party's hands or disproportion between the benefits the agreement gives the parties (particularly if the agreement is not commercial).[61] Furthermore, the relationship between breach of contract and the consequences of this can be significant, as can attempts to circumvent existing law.[62] As regards circumstances at contract inception, sections 28–31 and 33 of AvtL can, depending on the circumstances, be applied instead. In such circumstances, either the provisions mentioned or section 36 of AvtL can be used. This last rule can, however, also be applied to certain circumstances that do not fall under sections 28–31 or 33 of AvtL, such as the withholding of important information or poor language

---

[56]   Kurt Grönfors and Rolf Dotevall, *Avtalslagen. En kommentar* (4th edn, Norstedts gula bibliotek 2010) 237.

[57]   Jan Ramberg and Christina Hultmark, *Allmän avtalsrätt* (Norstedts 2000) 192, Grönfors and Dotevall, ibid., 246.

[58]   Claes-Robert von Post, *Studier kring 36 § avtalslagen med inriktning på rent kommersiella förhållanden* (Jure AB 1999) 97.

[59]   Government Bill 1975/76:81, 106.

[60]   Ibid., 166 and Ramberg and Hultmark (n 57) 192.

[61]   SOU 1974:83, 132.

[62]   Government Bill 1975/76:83, 120.

skills.[63] Other circumstances that can be considered are whether a party has abused their negotiating position through surprise tactics or has behaved aggressively. Consideration can also be given to incorrect or misleading information provided by a stronger party, even if this was done in good faith, or if the party provided information on a future action that did not occur due to unforeseen circumstances. A lack of knowledge with respect to the weaker party can also be taken into account. According to this argument, circumstances of this type should be able to be considered even in commercial relationships, but they are given particular importance in consumer relationships.[64] Particularly in long-term contractual relationships, subsequent events[65] can lead to modification and in exceptional cases nullity, unless these changes could not be foreseen or the parties have built some mechanism into the agreement that compensates for this.[66]

Other circumstances refer to factors that can be significant in the assessment of reasonableness. This could be good business practice in the industry or the parties' earlier practices.[67] If it concerns a situation in which the parties have previously signed several agreements, terms from previous agreements can affect the assessment of a subsequent agreement.[68] Consideration of third parties should not affect the assessment.[69] If a distinction is made between the parties on the basis of gender, age, ethnicity or nationality, this is a matter of discrimination. This should, according to the preparatory work, be invokable as grounds for modification. Financial differences are not deemed to be discriminatory.[70]

The possibility of taking into account inferior status enables a generous application in relation to the weaker party; a consumer-friendly interpretation, according to Hultmark and Ramberg.[71] In a dispute between business owners, one of them may hold an inferior position in relation to the other, which in this case can be taken into account.[72] With the support of the provision, the term can be modified, the agreement modified in another respect, or the agreement nullified. It should also be possible to set aside a term and modify the entire agreement if there are

---

[63]   Axel Adlercreutz and Lars Gorton, *Avtalsrätt* (Norstedts Juridik 2011) 300.
[64]   SOU 1974:83, p. 132ff. See von Post (n 58) 159.
[65]   Adlercreutz and Gorton (n 63) 300.
[66]   Ramberg and Hultmark (n 57) 90. In consumer relationships, there is greater potential for modification on this ground, Government Bill 1975/76:81, 127.
[67]   Adlercreutz and Gorton (n 63) 300.
[68]   SOU 1974:83, 158.
[69]   Ibid., 160.
[70]   Ibid., 147f.
[71]   Ramberg and Hultmark (n 57) 91.
[72]   Government Bill 1975/76:81, 117, 137.

several unreasonable terms. The court has full freedom to choose the most suitable solution, provided that this is possible with regard to the party's claims and allegations.[73] Modification can be better than nullification if the parties wish to maintain a good business relationship.[74]

When a term is modified, its content is changed. This may concern terms on deadlines, penalty reduction or damage compensation amounts. This may particularly be the case in unforeseen circumstances.[75] The aim of the adjustment is to make the term acceptable. It does not need to mean that the contractual relationship between the parties has to be equal.[76] Setting aside the term means that the agreement is applied as though the term were not there. If this is impossible or inappropriate, other terms in the agreement can be modified so as to remove or mitigate the unreasonableness of the term. If it is not possible to divide the agreement up in this way, it can instead be declared completely null and void.

It is not intended that any of these solutions should prevail as a standard solution, but the courts should first seek to modify a contract term so that an inappropriate dispositive rule does not come to regulate the contractual relationship between the parties instead.[77] In practice, however, it is most common to completely set aside a term.[78] von Post says that there is no cut-and-dried case in which an agreement has been modified in parts other than the term in question and that there is no case in which an agreement has been declared null and void.[79]

### 1.4.3 Other Overall Assessments

Overall assessments are often made in sentencing. Sentencing will be analysed in Chapter 4 using multi-criteria analysis. Regarding procedural stipulations, the choice between attendance in person and participation through video conferencing also requires an overall assessment. A structural analysis of this type of situation is provided in Chapter 4. Another classic example of an overall assessment can be found in the provision on the free evaluation of evidence; after an assessment of everything that has occurred in the case during the main hearing, the courts will determine what has been proven. There are also situations where there seems to be

---

[73] SOU 1974:83, p. 121.
[74] Ibid., 133.
[75] Ibid., 120.
[76] Ramberg and Hultmark (n 57) 91.
[77] Government Bill 1975/76:81, 110.
[78] von Post (n 58) 256.
[79] Ibid., 258.

both a balancing of interests and an overall assessment, for example under the Personal Data Act.[80] This will be discussed in more detail later in the book, where it will also become clear that the terms balancing of interests and overall assessment are not used consistently. Overall assessments are made, when necessary, in many other cases than those mentioned here. See, for example, NJA 2013 p. 689 and the application of 5:2 of the Swedish Bankruptcy Act (1987:672), which provides that the payment of clearly unreasonable salary claims can be refused and where in the preparatory work, Government Bill 1986/87:90 p. 228, it is stated that the question is to be answered after an overall assessment. In NJA 2008 p. 457, which concerned the question of whether a so-called mixed gift would constitute the recipient's private property, the Supreme Court cited 'in an overall assessment. . .'. On the whole, overall assessments appear often and in diverse branches of law. It would be virtually impossible to give a full account of when these occur.

## 1.5   WHAT ARE THE DIFFERENCES BETWEEN BALANCING OF INTERESTS AND OVERALL ASSESSMENTS?

The example above demonstrates that there are some differences between balancing of interests and overall assessments. The starting point for the first of these is often – but not always – that there is a legally protected interest, for example, shoreline protection, tenure, or right to privacy. I call these law-based balancing of interests. They should be differentiated from legal balancing of interests, which are characterized by the fact that balancing of interests is already laid down on beforehand in the law.[81] If a legally protected interest were absolute and inviolable, a balancing of interests would not be possible. A balancing of interests thus presupposes that the protected interest may give way if there is a strong enough counter-interest. The weaker the protected interest is, the easier it will be to counterbalance it.

Other characteristics of balancing of interests are that the real and practical measure through which the protected interest is set aside usually lies in the future and that the court or decision-maker at the time of the decision must take a position on whether the protected interest should be preserved intact or if the action which is being sought or otherwise

---

[80]   See section 1.3.3, above.
[81]   See section 1.3.4, above.

actualized should be permitted and allowed to encroach on the protected interest. The action that the balancing of interests concerns thus requires an approval, in the examples above by the municipality (initially), rent tribunal or Data Protection Authority. Sometimes the examination of the matter coincides with the action itself. For example, the question of whether a declaratory claim will be entertained and a declaratory judgement rendered are examined in the same lawsuit. It is common, however, that there is an interval of time between the approval of action and the execution of it. If, for example, a petition for disclosure under 38:2 RB is approved, the claimant normally will not receive the documents immediately; it may take a while.

If the balancing of interests is supported by an optional rule in RB, it can be said to be law-based, because the law prescribes, or in any case implies, that a weighting is to be done between the different interests. The optional procedural rules, however, do not concern legally protected interests. The balancing of interests is due only to the fact that there are two parties standing against each other with different interests in the case. However, they are – with respect to procedure – equally protected by the law. It is furthermore typical of balancing of interests that, regardless of whether it is legal or law-based and affects a legally protected interest or otherwise, there should be a basis for this; certain necessary conditions must be met. Returning once again to the example above with law-based balancing of interests, there must be a shoreline protection, tenure and a right to privacy. If this were to be contentious, the examination of the prerequisites would be a preliminary issue in the case. As far as the application of 13:2 RB is concerned, there should be a legal relationship and this should be uncertain. It would seem, however, that the prejudicial prerequisite should be included in the balancing of interests. Regarding the obligation to produce a document pursuant to 38:2 RB, it is unclear to what extent the necessary conditions of identification, evidential significance and relevance must be met.[82] If they are met, there seems to be no need for a balancing of interests because the petition for disclosure should be approved. In NJA 1998 p. 829, however, a weighting was done between relevance and the counterparty's interest in not having to disclose the requested documents. Thus, a proportionality assessment may also need to be done. This can be made independently or be included in the balancing of interests.

---

[82] It should be noted that 38:2 RB does not explicitly state that a balancing of interests should be done, but has support in precedents, see for example NJA 1977 p. 254.

The example demonstrates briefly that law-based balancing of interests are typically aimed at a future action which is characterized in that it may cause harm or inconvenience, that there is a conflicting interest that the measure should not be taken, and that certain prerequisites must be met for the action to be permitted. The point of doing a balancing of interests is removed when permission for the action has been finally granted, because the protected interest has then been set aside and cannot be appealed.

The balancing of interests is often typified, that is, it is singled out in the determination which factors should generally be accorded weight and these are described in a general way; see above on camera surveillance and that some actions normally threaten privacy for the majority.[83] No assessment is usually made on the individual level because camera surveillance affects everyone who comes in proximity of the camera. An individual assessment can, however, be considered in the balancing of interests that is done under the Tenancy Act. One factor mentioned in the statement above is that a move is costly. If the tenant is wealthy, however, this does not play the same role as it does if the tenant is poor. The tenant's financial status is presumably not significant, but it should be significant what economic potential tenants have collectively to withstand the costs of a move. If it is just a single tenant, it is of course only their financial situation that becomes relevant.

There are examples of balancing of interests being done also when a mix of past, present and future events must be considered. In NJA 2012 p. 715, the question arose on the termination of trusteeship under 11:7 FB and the right of trustees to resign. The following is stated in paragraphs 14–16 in the Supreme Court's decision:

> This means that a trustee, even if the need for trusteeship remains and even if no replacement has been appointed, is entitled to resign his post if he has reasonable cause to do so. In the assessment of what is reasonable cause, a *weighting* may be done between the trustee's motives for terminating the assignment and the need for a trustee to be continuously available. In some cases, the circumstances can be such that the trustee shall be deemed to be entitled to immediately resign his post, for example when an illness gives cause to presume he has a limited time to live. It may also be that there is a final deadline after which the trustee shall not need to remain, such as when he assumes a post that prevents continuing the assignment. The actions of a person who is put under a trusteeship may in some cases also be so severe that an immediate right to vacate the post should exist. In general, however, the trustee must accept certain and perhaps not entirely insignificant inconvenience, as the need for trusteeship must be met

---

[83]   Section 1.3.3, above. For a discussion of what can be deemed an encroachment on privacy, see Blomberg (n 39) 31.

while awaiting the appointment of a new trustee. Among the factors to consider in the assessment of what can be reasonably demanded of the trustee is how difficult it is for the chief guardian to find a replacement. Of significance in the *balancing of interests* is also the time it takes for the chief guardian to find a replacement. The longer it takes to appoint a new trustee, the lower the requirements should be for the grounds that shall be deemed sufficient for the trustee to be entitled to resign. (My emphasis, my translation)

This case concerns a decision on trusteeship and the question was whether or not it could cease. The balancing of interests comes into the legal case in retrospect. The need for trusteeship is weighed against the trustee's right to resign. From the beginning, before the trustee was appointed, there was a need and a law-based interest in a trustee so that a trustee could be appointed. A balancing of interests must then be done afterwards to terminate the trusteeship. The termination of trusteeship thus becomes a mirror image of the appointment of a trustee.

As discussed, overall assessments do not require any support in law or other legal sources, as these must be done when there are several factors to take a position on. Overall assessments most often come into play in cases where the necessary conditions of the law are open, particularly when they refer to a standard referencing socio-ethical benchmarks ('unreasonable', 'unjust') or where there is otherwise a concept with a broad and undetermined content, such as 'the best interests of the child'. However, overall assessments can also occur in situations where the applicable prerequisite at first glance seems to be descriptive but at a closer look refers to a complicated legal concept. For example, what are the necessary or sufficient legal conditions for being an 'employee'? In addition, it may concern the choice between different options (legal consequences), which could be difficult to decide on. The question of consequence in a certain case could, for example, be imprisonment or suspended sentence.[84] On the whole, overall assessments in criminal cases are rather often made in the determination of sanctions as well as in the determination of the offence.

In contrast to the balancing of interests, which are targeted on future events, overall assessments seem to usually launch from a past event that must be evaluated with respect to a legal consequence. This situation is by and large the most common situation in the application of the law, because the administration of justice or judicial examination is generally retrospective and not prospective. To connect to the legal cases and the example above: Was an agreement entered? Is the agreement 'unreasonable'? Was the paid salary 'unreasonable'? Was it a gift? Was the gift a mixed gift?

---

[84] See the example in section 4.5, below.

Something has thus occurred that needs to be classified in retrospect. In other cases, a past occurrence is a prerequisite for something that will occur: the accused has embezzled funds and admitted the crime. Should the sanction be imprisonment or a suspended sentence? This is a matter then of legal remedy. Thus, overall assessments can with respect to the foregoing, be explained with the traditional legal fact-legal consequence model. The agreement is a legal fact and can of course not be revoked only after a balancing of interests (pacta sunt servanda). A legal counterfact is required in order to revoke it.[85] Or there is, as in 5:2 KL, a wage claim – legal fact – which is not fully sustained because it is 'unreasonable'. The question of how something can be legally qualified can also, as in NJA 2008, p.457, be determined after an overall assessment, in which the nature of the legal fact is decided.

The attentive reader has already noted that 'the best interests of the child' does not fit into this explanatory model. In this case, it concerns a legal fact that projects into the future. Should not then the question of 'the best interests of the child' be determined after a balancing of interests instead of an overall assessment?[86] The answer is no. 'The best interests of the child' can of course be said to be a protected interest, but it is of a different nature than the protected interests provided in the examples above: shoreline protection, tenure and right to privacy. These interests have been protected by law, but in another way than as 'the best interests of the child'. If both parents want sole custody and shared custody is not an option, the law does not favour either parent at the start, but rather it is an open question of who should get custody. In contrast, shoreline protection, for example, is already present from the start. The custody issue is furthermore not about the parents' interests, but instead about what is best for the child, although it could be debated whether in this case the issue should be regarded to concern a law-based balancing of interests – in this case between the child and the parents. Such a model, however, would risk being conflict-driven, although on the other hand put the child's interests in focus in a clearer way than an overall assessment. This issue, which will not be investigated here, may perhaps merit a closer examination.

NJA 2008 p.55, which concerns permission for water activities, states that:

---

[85]   A legal counter-fact, if proven, means that another alleged legal fact does not have the legal consequence it otherwise would have had.

[86]   As noted above, an overall assessment shall be made in accordance with the preparatory work.

Under chapter 11, section 6 of the Environmental Code, water activities may be conducted only if their benefits from a public and private perspective *outweigh* the costs, damage and inconvenience of these. The review shall consist of *an overall assessment of the water activities* and the primary objective shall be to prevent water activities that are not justified in terms of public finances. As the Swedish Land and Environment Court of Appeal has found, the benefits from a public and private standpoint *outweigh* the costs, damage and inconvenience, and therefore, the decision of Swedish Land and Environment Court of Appeal to permit water activities shall be established. (My emphasis, my translation)

This case deals with permission to conduct water activities. A weighting was done in which the benefits were weighed against the costs, damage and inconvenience, that is, the drawbacks. In the grounds for the judgement, the expression 'outweigh the costs' is used, which indicates a weighting. The purpose of the weighting is to prevent water activities that are harmful from a perspective of public finances. The interest meriting protection is thus public finances. Why is it then said in this case that the review should be an overall assessment? The case can be compared with NJA 2013, p. 441, in which the claimant was demanding a utility easement for a 30-metre wide corridor. Under section 6 of the Swedish Utility Easements Act (1973:1144), utility easements may not be granted if the objective should more suitably be met in another way, or if public or private inconvenience of granting such outweighs the benefits that can be gained. The Supreme Court stated the following:

As regards *the balancing of interests under section 6*, the preparatory work does not provide any strict direction for the application of the law (see Government Bill 1973:157 p. 100 f. and 131 f.). Nor is there any guiding case law. It is, however, clear from the preparatory work that the provision has been designed on patterns from the corresponding rule in chapter 2, section 12, first paragraph of the Expropriation Act (1972:719). It can be concluded from this that the *weighting* shall take into account all relevant interests and that consideration shall be given not only to financial but also idealistic value (see Government Bill 1972:109 p. 219). (My emphasis, my translation)

The assessments in these cases are similar, but in the one an overall assessment was made and in the other a balancing of interests. In essence, the same sort of assessments have certainly been done, but there is reason to discuss two aspects of them. The first case (NJA 2008 p. 55) concerns protected interest, this means, simplified, that the assessment does not start in a substantively neutral position. The same is true with respect to the second (NJA 2013 p. 441). Compare: 'water activities may only be conducted if' and utility easement may 'not be granted if the objective should more suitably be met in another way'. Anyone petitioning for water activities under 11:6 MB or for a utility easement thus has an uphill battle as the opposing interests are protected by law. This would also manifest itself if the facts were uncertain; the burden of proof would then probably fall on the party petitioning to conduct water activities or be granted a utility easement.

NJA 2008 p. 55 speaks of benefits from public and private perspectives and assesses whether these outweigh the costs, damage and inconvenience of the water activities. Five factors are thus named. Using the weighing pan analogy, these five factors would need to be combined into two categories, which is fully possible if benefits from public and private perspectives are put in one pan and the costs, damage and inconvenience in the other. In this case, however, the factors must first be weighed together, which presupposes an overall assessment, which is then done before the balancing of interests. Alternatively, several weightings are done, which end in an overall assessment. In the second legal case, NJA 2013, p. 441, it seems that the assessment was preceded by overall assessments and concluded with a combined balancing of interests. These two legal cases demonstrate what was discussed previously, that aggregations are done on several levels in the balancing of interests and overall assessments. If, in a legal case, it is stated in the reasons for the judgement that weighting has been done, but at the same time in the closing remarks it is stated that an overall assessment was made, this is not a contradiction but instead depends on the number of levels in the assessment and how the aggregations were done. However, when it is stipulated in law or is apparent by law that a balancing of interests must be done, it is inappropriate to write in the reasons for the judgement that an overall assessment has been made, even if the weighting actually ended with the weightings being combined after an overall assessment, because this can lead to misunderstandings.

When the court decides on whether video conferencing will be used in a hearing, an overall assessment must, under the Government Bill, be conducted of all relevant circumstances.[87] The importance of the person appearing in the courtroom must be weighed against the circumstances suggesting that he or she should appear in another way.[88] When, on the other hand, it concerns the taking of evidence outside the main hearing and questioning by telephone – where basically the same type of assessment must be made – it is stated in the Government Bill that a balancing of interests must be made between the examination and the importance of

---

[87]   Government Bill 2004/05:131, 95.
[88]   Ibid., 92ff.

the case on one side, and on the other, the costs for the appearance of the witness in the hearing and the inconvenience of appearing at court.[89] Also see NJA 1998 p. 862, where the Supreme Court stated:

> Under the provision of chapter 46, section 7, paragraph 2 of RB, examination in the main hearing of a criminal trial may be conducted by telephone only if one of two conditions exist [. . .] Under the second alternative, examination may be conducted by telephone if the taking of testimony under the usual rules would result in costs or inconvenience that are not reasonably proportionate to the importance of hearing the testimony in such a way. Under that alternative, a *balancing of interests* shall be done, leaving some room for questioning by telephone, even if such a questioning does not seem fully equivalent with examination directly before the court. For questioning by telephone to be acceptable, however, the objective of taking evidence orally must be substantially met even by telephone (referred Government Bill, ibid). Of importance with respect to the balancing of interests is, among other things, the nature of the case and the weight of the evidence in the assessment of the case. (My emphasis, my translation. The Government Bill referred to is Bill 1986/87:89 p. 220, the relevant provision is now 5:10 RB).

Today, the same conditions for using telephone conferencing apply as for video conferencing, albeit that the conditions in each case can be applied somewhat differently. This means that the courts in their position on questioning by telephone must make an overall assessment. Thus, what was previously deemed to be a balancing of interests has now become an overall assessment. However, the different designations of overall assessment and balancing of interests made by the lawmaker do not seem to have any difference in substance. They are in these contexts exchangeable.

### 1.5.1 Final Overall Assessment or Balancing of Interests?

As already discussed, an aggregation process means that both balancing of interests and overall assessments can exist in the same decision-making process. This will be illustrated in more detail in this section. Section 11 of the Personal Data Act (PUL) contains a provision under which personal data may not be processed for purposes directly related to marketing, unless the registered person has declared in writing that he or she is opposed to such processing. As in several other cases under PUL concerning protected interests, a balancing of interests must be done. What is interesting is that the Data Protection Authority in the publication

---

[89] Ibid., 95.

'Intresseavvägning enligt personuppgiftslagen' ("Balancing of interests under the Personal Data Act" (2009) writes the following:[90]

> *In the overall assessment made in the balancing of interests*, consideration should be given to the following:[91]
> The purpose (aim) of the processing.
> Who the marketing is directed at (for example, private individuals or businesses, or if the target group needs special support, such as in the case of children).
> The scale of the marketing.
> What type of personal data will be processed (for example, information that under the Personal Data Act is deemed sensitive or innocuous information such as address details).
> If the processing entails detailed knowledge about the registered person.
> How the information is processed.
> If the information requires special protection.
> If there is a right to oppose processing under section 11 of PUL (for example, through the Swedish service to block unwanted telephone sales, the NIX registry).
> The security and sorting procedures in place for the collected data.
> If there are special provisions in laws or regulations that must be considered, such as confidentiality stipulations.
> If company agreements in the area are complied with (for example, Swedma's rules for the use of personal data in direct marketing).
> The information provided to the registered person.
> (My emphasis, my translation)

Before continuing this discussion, it should also be noted that the Swedish Labour Court in judgement 2010 no. 87 (breach of collective agreement) states that:

> In a judicial review under section 10f of the Personal Data act, a *balancing of interests* shall be done *after an overall assessment* has been made of all circumstances in that particular case. (My emphasis, my translation).

The legal case indicates the order in which the Swedish Labour Court has performed the reviews: an overall assessment is first made, and then a balancing of interests. When the Data Protection Authority says that an overall assessment shall be made in the balancing of interests, it would seem to mean the same thing. These decisions indicate that what is primary and decisive is the balancing of interests, regardless of whether it is done before or after an overall assessment or if the overall assessment

---

[90] <http://www.datainspektionen.se/documents/faktabroschyr-intresseavvagning.pdf> (retrieved 5 October 2014).
[91] The same is stated in the Data Act Committee's report, see RÅ 2001, ref. 68.

is done along with the balancing of interests. This is essentially because it is about law-based protected interests and that the balancing of interests therefore also has significance as a *decision rule*, which will be discussed further below.

The 13 conditions listed on the Data Protection Authority website contain various types of factors. Naturally, all 13 will not occur in one particular case, but a number of them are always included in the assessment. Each point on the list may involve several concrete circumstances and these may overlap each other so that one single factor occurs on more than one point on the list. An aggregation is done on several levels, meaning that some factors are sorted and packaged into groups into which they are deemed under some principle to belong, thereby obtaining a number of overall-assessed 'packages' for and against what is placed in each weighing pan. After the overall assessments have then been made, the balancing of interests comes in because such is stipulated in the law. The balancing of interests becomes the final station and thus functions as a decision rule. Of course, it is not certain that the decision-maker needs to go the entire distance. Some preliminary assessments can provide the answer at an earlier stage in simple cases.

The idea that an overall assessment should be done alongside balancing of interests or within it may signify that overall-assessed circumstances in the weighing pans that are balanced according to interests then, finally, become subject to an overall assessment. In such a case, this total appraisal is made on a level above the balancing of interests. However, even if this is true, the law-based balancing of interests must function as a decision rule; the overall assessment then represents a reconciliation of what has already been assessed and a final control of the balancing of interests and possibly a final fine-tuning of it.[92]

As discussed above, the difference between an overall assessment and a balancing of interests emerges in the decision-making situation, in any case if it is a law-based balancing of interests. Suppose that it had been stipulated in section 6 of the Camera Surveillance Act that the issue should be decided after an overall assessment and not through a balancing of interests. Would this make a difference in the way the issue was assessed or in the results of the assessment? And would it, to take another example, similarly make a difference in the assessment under the Environmental Code if an overall assessment had been stipulated instead of a balancing of interests? If the answer is that it makes no difference, it becomes a matter of indifference how the lawmaker expresses itself. If the answer is instead

---

[92]   Cf the sensitivity analysis described in section 2.3.8, below.

yes, it does or may have significance for the results, there is an important difference.

According to Odelstad, a weighting often concerns factors, while a combined weighting more often concerns aspects. But, as mentioned above, he also believes that objectives are weighted together. An aggregation, however, begins on the factual level. If I, for example, were going to buy a car and the objective was to buy a car that was economic and safe, repair and insurance costs, taxes and fuel consumption would be important economic factors. These costs can be determined for different car models and they therefore constitute concrete factors at the bottom of a decision tree. The same applies for safety. Data on safety can be obtained from crash test findings. Data is also available on the active and passive safety of various models. For each objective, there are now a number of concrete factors and these should be weighted together. So what is the next step? Should the factors favouring economy and those favouring safety be weighted against each other? Or should they be weighted together? Because I want the model I choose to be good in terms of both economy and safety, it could first appear that economy should not be weighted against safety. Yet, at the same time, there are two objectives that should somehow be weighted together. But it is not certain that I value the factors that favour economy as much as those that favour safety.

According to MCA, a weighting is done in the overall assessment by giving different weight to different factors for economy and safety.[93] When MCA is used, it thus does not become evident if it is a matter of balancing of interests or overall assessment, but rather this question comes into play when – after the analysis – a decision should be made. In addition, whether I call the car purchase the result of a balancing of interests or an overall assessment, I may choose the same model of car. If, however, the car's safety were to be a prioritized interest, corresponding to an interest protected by law, the compared safety factors of the cars will be accorded relatively more weight than other factors and in any case, when the final position is taken, the prioritized interest will tip the balance between the competing car models if they are otherwise equivalent. In an overall assessment, the car that received the highest points in all factors would instead be the winner if there was no prioritized interest. For this reason, a balancing of interests concerning a legally protected interest should therefore be seen as a decision rule. Thus, overall assessments and balancing of interests can then be performed with the same model, but the decision or judgement and the direction it goes can be influenced by whether it is an

---

[93]   See section 2.3.5 below for further discussion on this.

issue of a legal or law-based balancing of interests or a 'neutral' overall assessment.

An overall assessment thus concerns factors, while a balancing of interests relates specifically to interests. If it is stipulated by law that a balancing of interests must be done, the objective is to channel factors to the stated interests; this is the weighing pan. In addition, in an overall assessment a factor does not generally have a particular weight from the start.[94] Furthermore, and as shown above, there could very well be a difference with respect to the outcome if the law prescribes a balancing of interests instead of an overall assessment, albeit this conclusion at a first glance might be deemed as somewhat tempered by precedent (NJA 2008 p. 55 and NJA 2013 p. 441) and the reasons given for video conferencing and the taking of evidence/testimony cited above. One hypothesis is that this can be due to the balancing of interests concerning more than two interests. If the balance scale metaphor is to be used in such cases, it seems clear that it can be unimportant whether we are talking about a balancing of interests or an overall assessment. If there are several interests, these must ultimately either be weighted together through an overall assessment or else several interests be combined, if this is possible, into two interests so as to facilitate the use of the balance scale as a substantive decision rule, which would seem to be necessary if this concerns a law-based balancing of protected interests. Another explanation for inconsistencies is that the terms balancing of interests and overall assessment are used synonymously without further reflection. Presumably, this happens sometimes and perhaps even often.

### 1.5.2 The Principle of Proportionality, 'Special Reasons' and Other Markers

The balance scale metaphor suggests the notion that a weighting is mechanical; factors that speak for or against something are placed in each weighing pan. The decision-maker then reads the scale – quite simply looks to see if the advantages of an action are heavier than the disadvantages and then makes a decision. Figure 1.1 below illustrates that circumstances and aspects are sorted in under public and private interests which are weighted against each other. On the top of the decision tree, an overall assessment is made in order to fine-tune the balancing.

However, the principle of proportionality (for example, under the Environmental Code), makes the balancing of interests more complicated.

---

[94]   An exception is the abovementioned 6:2a FB, where particular importance should be attached to certain risks.

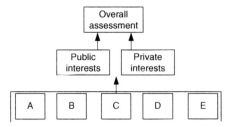

*Figure 1.1    Balance of interests*

In addition, there are prerequisites with different contents relating
to the weighting. Thus, exemption from protection pursuant to the
Environmental Code requires 'special reasons'. Another example is, as
mentioned above, that duty to disclose trade secrets requires 'extraordinary cause'. For duty of disclosure, it means that it may not be enough
that there are sufficient grounds for the document to be produced and that
the scale tips slightly in favour of the party petitioning for disclosure; the
weighting must be significantly in favour of the petitioner. Weights can
also be found in overall assessments; for example, special consideration
must be given to ensuring that the child is not 'mistreated'. This weighting is, however, not general but instead refers to a preselected factor that
must, when there are reasons, be included in the overall assessment.

The principle of proportionality exists on different levels: between states,
groups or individuals or in the state against the individual. In principle,
if there is a right that is considered fundamental, usually a constitutional
right, and this right is restricted in some way, there must be 'special reasons'
or similar for such a measure. The worth of the right or interest in upholding it will then be weighed against an opposing interest. In European Union
law, a proportionality test must be done, consisting of three criteria that
must all be met for a measure to be considered proportional. These are:
is the measure suitable to achieve a legitimate aim? Is the measure necessary to achieve that objective or are less restrictive means available? Is the
utility the measure provides in reasonable proportion to the harm that
the measure can cause for those involved? Measures must not exceed that
which is necessary with regard to the aim, for example society's requirements for safety against the individual's right to privacy. The principle of
proportionality is thus also a principle of law and order, in that it means
that there must be a balance between the ends and the means.[95]

---

[95]    Regarding balancing of interests in EU law, see TJFF 2012, 5th booklet.

Westerlund argues that there is not only one, but rather three principles of proportionality in the Environmental Code. One concerns the political proportionality assessment. As I interpret his argument, this is about the deliberations conducted when certain legislation is introduced. The second is about the substantive proportionality assessment that is done in this specific case. The third, which Westerlund calls instrumental, is used, he says, to assess how already established goals and objectives should be achieved in the least intrusive manner.[96]

According to Westberg, a proportionality assessment generally means that a risk assessment and a risk distribution must be performed. He says that one of the parties in an uncertain decision-making situation must bear the risk for the damages that can arise as a result of a decision.[97] This formulation is reminiscent of a burden of proof rule, yet the principle of proportionality is not considered to be a burden of proof rule and Westberg does not claim this, not even mentioning burden of proof rules in this context. However, if Westberg is right in that one of the parties in an uncertain decision-making situation must bear the risk for the damages that can arise, it seems like the principle of proportionality also could function as a burden of proof rule. One objection could possibly be that the principle of proportionality is a substantive rule. The burden of proof rules are, however, also considered to be substantive.[98] If both the burden of proof rules and the principle of proportionality are substantive, wherein lies the difference? It could be argued that the burden of proof rules concern uncertainty regarding factual elements in the case while the principle of proportionality concerns a weighting between opposing substantive interests. In this case, the burden of proof rules are substantive in a different way than the principle of proportionality; the former are substantive as a counterpart to the substantive regulation in question, because the assignment of the burden of proof must be based on this. From this aspect, the burden of proof issue is already settled when the proportionality issue is assessed. The proportionality assessment thus becomes a substantive weighting issue. This can be an important difference, but the distinction does not seem entirely convincing. It is in any case difficult to see how the boundaries between the burden of proof and the proportionality test could be more specifically defined.

The principle of proportionality finds expression in many rules of law.

---

[96] Staffan Westerlund, *Proportionalitetsprincipen: verklighet, missförstånd eller nydaning* (1996) Miljörättslig tidskrift (2) 254.
[97] Westberg (n 46) 194.
[98] Lars Welamson and Johan Munck, *Processen i hovrätt och Högsta domstolen* (4th edn, Norstedts Juridik 2011) 115.

Shoreline protection in accordance with 7:25 MB was previously used as an example of balancing of interests. The shoreline protection entails a restriction of the individual's right to have free recourse to his or her property, a right that is prescribed in 2:18 RF. Because exemption is required to build in shoreline-protected areas pursuant to 6:18 MB, conservation and environmental interests in the law are given precedence over the individual interest in using the shoreline-protected area.[99] It is this initial balancing of interests that Westerlund calls political. MB lists the factors that may be considered 'special reasons' for exemption from the prohibition against building on shoreline-protected areas. According to a ruling by the Land and Environment Court, exemption cannot be granted for factors other than those listed in MB 7:18 c–d.[100] It is therefore a legal balancing of interests.[101] If 'special reasons' in the case do not exist, exemption may not be granted with reference to the principle of proportionality. What significance does the principle of proportionality have, then? If there are 'special reasons', the principle has no significance at all. An approval means of course no further restriction on the individual's rights. On the other hand, an approval means a restriction on public interest, which is, however, already protected in the law through the requirement on exemption.[102] It is thus not possible, after conditions for exemption are found, to give a refusal with reference to the principle of proportionality, just as exemption cannot be granted with reference to the principle of proportionality after it is established that there are no grounds for exemption. It would seem, in view of the foregoing, that the principle of proportionality could be used in borderline cases in favour of the property owner, that is, if it is uncertain if there are legal grounds for exemption.

If a property owner wants to build a pier in the shoreline-protected area, exemption may be granted if its function requires that it must be located at the water and the construction cannot be built outside the area. If the property owner claims he must be able to dock at his property from the water and the area is inhospitable and not used by the public, and the alternative for the property owner would be to travel 100 kilometres by car instead of 200 meters by boat, it can still be said that the pier is not needed, but at the same time a refusal with reference to these factors would seem disproportionately severe against the property owner. Furthermore,

---

[99] See cabinet minister's statement in Government Bill 1997/98:45, Part 1, 321.

[100] MÖD M 5451–13.

[101] See section 1.3.4 above for a discussion of the difference between law-based and legal-based balancing of interests.

[102] Under this notion, the principle of proportionality seems to in this case only go in one direction.

assume that the property owner has two suggestions for the design of the pier (for the sake of simplicity, we can call the suggestions the 'big pier' and the 'little pier'), and the small pier has less impact on the public interest than the big pier.[103] It would seem that the proportionality assessment should be made along with balancing of interests and within the list of special reasons provided in the law of situations for which exemption can be granted. However, the principle of proportionality does thereby not become visible in the decision, or at least risks not being. Because the principle of proportionality is a self-contained legal principle, it is obviously desirable that, for reasons of transparency, visibility and clarity, it is made clear in the decision.

For duty of disclosure in the case of documents containing trade secrets, there must be, as mentioned above, 'extraordinary cause'. The implication of this necessary condition is not specifically commented on in case law or the literature. The starting point is that the documents are sufficiently identified and that they can be assumed to have relevance and evidential significance. It would seem reasonable that 'extraordinary cause' means that the information cannot be obtained in another way and that sufficient investigation has been conducted in this regard. The requirements for identification are, however, not set in stone. These requirements can probably be granted a bit of leeway in the balancing of interests.

A trade secret concerns an interest protected by law and hence the high requirements for granting a duty of disclosure. Similar to the example with 'special reasons' for exemption from shoreline protection, the proportionality assessment in this case exists in the legal condition for the right to infringe on the protected interest, that is, in the examination of the prerequisite 'extraordinary cause' in 38:2 RB and in the balancing of interests. Just as in the example with exemption from shoreline protection, the principle of proportionality must be assumed to only work in one direction in this case. Thus, if it is assumed that the very restrictive necessary condition 'extraordinary cause' is met, a proportionality assessment will not be made in respect of the already protected interest to the detriment of the party petitioning for disclosure; if so, it would be practically impossible to be granted disclosure. In other cases (that is, in cases that do not concern trade secrets), the petition for disclosure may, however, be refused because the requested measure is disproportionate to the costs and inconvenience this poses to the other party to produce the documents.

Concerning all coercive measures in criminal procedure, to take a final

---

[103]   The size and design of the pier seem to belong to what Westerlund (n 96) calls the instrumental principle of proportionality.

example, the principle of proportionality is prescribed in RB: the reasons for the measure must counterbalance the infringement or other detriment to the suspect or another opposing interest. The principle of proportionality in detention is established by law in 24:1, paragraph 3 RB. In the case of detention, it must first be determined if the necessary conditions for detention are met, that is, that imprisonment for one or more years is prescribed and that one of the grounds for detention have been met.[104] If the prerequisites are met, detention may be carried out under 24:1, paragraph 1 RB. Detention is thus not mandatory under this provision, nor is there a presumption of detention as in the second paragraph. One might think that the optional provision provides for a proportionality assessment, but this is, as discussed, specifically regulated in paragraph 3.

The interests that are in conflict with each other in the case of detention under RB 24:1, paragraph 1 are the individual's interest in not being deprived of liberty and the public interest in preventing new crime, impeding the suspect from fleeing and in being able to prosecute without important evidence being tampered with or destroyed. When the balancing of interests is formulated in this way, without concretion, it is initial. If advanced age and failing health are invoked as reasons against detention, and if the crime is just over the minimum of one year in the range of punishment and the crime was provoked, these circumstances may be weighted together after an overall assessment and then form the basis for the balancing of interests. The prosecutor can then plead, for example, that the crime concerned violence against an official, a serious classified crime. It then becomes clear that in the end, a combined weighting of the factors must be done from various perspectives, and that the initial assessment must be moved to another level where an overall assessment is made along with the balancing of interests, and finally, on top to fine-tune the assessment.

## 1.6   SUMMARY AND CONCLUSIONS

From this chapter, it is clear that the book is about a structured way of making overall assessments and balancing of interests. Various decision theory premises and classifications have been presented. The simple additive model has been selected as a model for the forthcoming analyses.

---

[104]   These conditions are that the suspected person will: (1) flee or otherwise evade legal proceedings or punishment; (2) impede the inquiry into the matter at issue by removing evidence or in another way; or (3) continue his criminal activity.

An overall assessment means that a choice must be made between several possible decision options using certain criteria in order to achieve one or more objectives. Balancing of interests also involves multiple options, criteria and objectives. In this chapter, it has been examined whether there is any difference between overall assessments and balancing of interests, and if so, what that difference may be. It is not an easy task to examine this question, but the same structured decision support can be used for both. There is, however, one important difference. A law-based balancing of interests is not just a weighting. It also functions as a decision rule or at least as a part of a decision rule. Substantive markers, such as 'special reasons' or 'extraordinary cause' mean that the scale is out of balance at the onset. In the example of shoreline protection, the public interest outweighs the private interest right from the start. Let us say that it weighs 15 kg and the private interest weighs 10 kg. The property owner must therefore not only add special reasons weighing 5 kg to put the scale in balance, but rather must add 30 kg or maybe more in order to get an exemption. The balance scale metaphor illustrates what I call a vertical decision-making situation. The overall assessment, on the other hand, is horizontal, that is, flat. For example, the plaintiff alleges five circumstances, legal facts (criteria) to support the argument that the agreement is 'unreasonable'. Let us say that these weigh 10, 15, 9, 7 and 6 kilos. These are not placed in any weighing pan because no interest has been designated priority from the start. Consequently, this is not a situation where different interests are balanced against each other. The decision-maker can therefore not use a balance scale as decision support. It may therefore be significant to the decision's contents if an overall assessment is made or a balancing of interests is done.

Another question is whether Odelstad is right in that a total appraisal (overall assessment) is also done in a balancing of interests. In complicated balancing of interests, a total appraisal is probably made at the end, which also seems consistent with common practice. Even if such an overall assessment is made, this does not change the fact that this basically concerns a weighting in law-based balancing of interests and that the balancing of interests is primary because it functions as a decision rule or as a key element in a decision rule. The overall assessment that is made, where appropriate, in the balancing of interests, should therefore be regarded as a final check of the balancing that has been done.

Overall assessments may need to be done on several levels leading up to the total appraisal. In simpler cases, the decision-maker does not need to make this total and final appraisal because it becomes clear on a lower level which decision will be made. This also means that the principle of proportionality sometimes is not relevant or that it is clear that there are not 'special reasons' or 'extraordinary cause' or similar. Another question which has been discussed in this chapter is whether there is any space for public interests when two private interests are in conflict with each other in a dispute amenable to out-of-court settlement. If there are no law-based interests involved, it has been argued that the weighting should only concern the parties' interests. If law-based interests are involved in a dispute amenable to out-of-court settlement, the assessment becomes more complicated.

# 2. Multi-criteria analysis

## 2.1 INTRODUCTION

How are decisions made? How is an overall assessment made? Studies on decision-making processes have been conducted in various academic disciplines, for example in economics theory, where game theory, among other things, has been used to study market situations; in the social sciences, where it has been examined how public decisions are made; and in psychological research, where the studies often deal with cognitive processes in individuals who make or should make decisions. Good decision conditions have been described and discussed.[1] Bad decisions have also been investigated.[2]

A decision problem can be generally described as a discrete problem that is also continuous, which means that the decision space is made up of an undetermined number of possible decision options. This occurs when there is a difference between the current and the desired state, the need for change is identified and there are at least two different courses of action.[3] The different courses of action may include choosing one of these, ranking the options from the best to the worst, or putting them into a group of predefined classes.[4]

---

[1]   About decision-making in general, see literature referred to in Chapter 1 (n 2) and, furthermore, Bernard Roy, *Multicriteria Methodology for Decision Aiding* (Kluwer Academic Publisher 1996), Jon Elster, *Reason and Rationality* (Princeton University Press 2009) and James G March with the assistance of Chip Heat, *A Primer on Decision Making. How Decisions Happen* (Simon & Schuster Ltd 1994).

[2]   See Peter G Hall, *Great Planning Disasters* (University of California Press 1982). Case studies in the book include London's third-largest airport (Stansted), San Francisco Arena, Concorde and the Sydney Opera House. Cf Herbert A Simon, *Administrative Behaviour. A Study of Decision-Making Processes in Administrative Organization* (4th edn, The Free Press 1997) on well-structured and poorly-structured problems, 128.

[3]   Malczewski (Ch 1 n 4) 96.

[4]   Wassila Ourdane, Nicolas Maudet and Alexis Tsoukiàs, 'Argumentation Theory and Decision Aiding' in Mattias Ehrgott, José Rui Figueira and Salvatore Greco (eds), *Trends in Multiple Criteria Decision Analysis* (Springer 2010).

Sometimes a decision-making process is described as a three-step process. In the first stage, the problem and possible changes are identified, and in the second, possible options. The third step means that the selected options are valued in terms of what impact each of them will have in regard to each decision criterion. This stage may include strategies aimed at reducing the number of possible options. The decision-making process may take place in turns, which means that it may become necessary to jump back and forth between stages.[5]

The decision-making process begins with the discovery of a problem and the decision-maker starting at 'square one' by acquiring information on the situation and then, based on certain objectives that must be decided, working out options and criteria. It is clear that this description does not fit into a judicial process. The parties have already done the work preparing documentation, the plaintiff has also chosen options (legal consequences) that are expressed through the claims. The foundation for the claim, that is, different concrete legal facts, comprise criteria for the various options. Although a process is usually defined through the claims and their foundations in the summons application and during preparations, it may happen that the decision basis changes somewhat right up until a judgement is rendered, for example new process material may emerge during the main hearing or even in a higher court. The possibility of presenting new claims and adding new process materials is, however, considerably limited once the preparations have been completed. The decision basis is thus normally finalized through the preparations.

By using MCA, the analysis becomes transparent and clear. The method forces an open report of the standpoints on decision options and criteria in relation to the stated objectives. Clarity results from the scoring and weighting of options and criteria required by the method. This need not be numerical. The decision-maker can instead construct a performance matrix, in which mathematical calculations have been omitted. An informal decision method (intuition) does not meet requirements for clarity and transparency. In addition, complex issues are at risk of not being properly analysed with intuition.

MCA can be used by a sole decision-maker or by a group. If it is used by a group of people, it also involves negotiations on which objectives, criteria and options should be included and how they should be valued. MCA simplifies the decision-making process and the efforts preparing the decision basis, which becomes particularly evident if MCA is used for planning large projects. One aim of MCA is to help the decision-maker to

---

[5]  Malczewski, (Ch 1 n 4) 96–8.

develop coherent preferences. The decision-making process is furthermore not started with these in planning processes, but rather they are created during the course of the decision process. Once this has been done, it is easier to make complicated decisions. MCA thereby makes it possible to take into account different possible solutions and develop 'trade-offs' between different decision criteria and alternatives. The selection of criteria, as well as scoring and weighting, becomes open in planning processes for dispute and discussion. Changes can be made continuously until the decision framework is completed.[6]

As noted in the introduction to Chapter 1, a distinction is usually made between Multi-objective decision models (MODM) and Multi-attribute decision models (MADM). MODM comprises the planning process that precedes a choice; MADM is used when there are set options and outlined criteria for the decision to be made. MADM is therefore the model that fits into overall assessments and balancing of interests in judicial processes. The simple additive model, Simple additive weighting (SAW), can then be used. The basic model of MCA, which will be presented below, also includes the planning stage.

MCA can also have drawbacks. If expert assistance is required, MCA is not a good model for legal problem structuring, analysis or decision support. The model should also be such that legal decision-makers can understand and use it without too much exertion. It is for many reasons important that lawyers feel that they are on secure ground for them to use a method they are not used to. It must also not be too time-consuming for them to use. The relative simplicity is emphasized here because many structured methods for decision-making may be difficult to understand for non-experts in the field, who have a completely different education than lawyers.

The methods described in this book, which are intended for problem structuring, as analysis tools and decision support, are based on the general basic steps in MCA. These methods or models, which are easy to understand intuitively, are SAW and SMART. Both models have proved to provide robust and good results. Of these two, it is, as mentioned in Chapter 1, SAW that will be used in the analyses made later in this book.[7]

---

[6] See Lootsma (Ch 1 n 2) 139ff, Belton and Stewart (Ch 1 n 2) 268ff, Marc D Kilgour, Ye Chen and Keith W Hipel, 'Multiple Criteria Approaches to Group Decision and Negotiation' in Ehrgott, Figueira and Greco (n 4).

[7] Regarding the reason SAW was chosen over SMART, see section 4.3, below.

SMART has been widely applied because of its relative simplicity and transparency, which means that decision-makers from many different backgrounds can easily apply the method and understand its recommendation. Although SMART may not always capture all the detail and complexities of a decision, it can be an excellent method for illuminating the important aspects of the problem and how they relate to each other. Often this is sufficient for a decision to be made with confidence and insight.[8]

Most MCA approaches use this additive model [. . .] Models of this type have a well-established record of providing robust and effective support to decision-makers working on a range of problems and in various circumstances. (statement primarily applies to SAW, my note)[9]

Simple additive weighting (SAW) methods are the most often used techniques for tackling spatial multiattribute decision-making. The techniques are also referred to as weighted linear combination (WLC) or scoring methods. They are based on the concept of weighted average. The decision maker directly assigns weights of relative importance to each attribute [. . .]. A total score is then obtained for each alternative by multiplying the importance weight assigned for each attribute by multiplying the importance weight assigned for each attribute by the scaled value given to the alternative on that attribute, and summing the products over all attributes.[10]

MCA is thus a tool for problem structuring, analysis and decision-making for complex, multi-dimensional problems.[11] Without a tool for the decision-making process that makes it logically structured, there is a risk of it being unclear.[12] No special knowledge is required to apply the simple additive model. Incorrectly used, it can naturally provide results that are not reliable, but this applies to all models or methods and should be compared with the risks of an intuitive overall assessment or balancing of interests.

To make an appraisal, the decision-maker must, according to MCA, choose a set of criteria (attributes), which in turn can be linked with some form of measurement, either directly or indirectly, or the criteria can be assessed subjectively. The selection and weighting of criteria is perhaps the most difficult in a valuation process, because the selected criteria and weighing of these shows the focus or starting point for the assessment.[13] The following very simple examples illustrate this:

---

[8]   Goodwin and Wright (Ch 1 n 2) 33–4.
[9]   Dodgson and others (Ch 1 n 2) 25, 121–30.
[10]  Malczewski (Ch 1 n 4) 199.
[11]  Belton and Stewart (Ch 1 n 2) 1ff, Lootsma (Ch 1 n 2) 1ff.
[12]  Cf Roy (n 1) 4, which states that it is not possible to separate the term 'decision' from the decision-making process.
[13]  Goodwin and Wright (Ch 1 n 2) 31ff.

Two thirsty people are trying to decide whether to buy a can of Cola or a bottle of Orange Juice. The two Criteria being used to make this decision are the cost and health benefit of each drink. The first person is concerned by the small amount of money they have and wants to buy the Cola as it is cheaper. The second person is more concerned with living a long healthy life and is willing to pay for the more expensive, but healthier Orange Juice.[14]

To reach a decision in this situation, the importance of the criteria (cost and health) must be valued relative to the decision to be made. If cost is considered to have a greater relative weight than health, the soft drink should be chosen. Deciding the relative weight of different criteria can be difficult, as can choosing which criteria should be used. Using MCA makes it possible to value the relative weight of all decision criteria and assess their impact on the final decision. To link back to the discussion in Chapter 1 on the distinction between balancing of interests and overall assessments, we can say that the concrete circumstances that are weighted in this example are money against health, or more specifically, the sugar, calories, colourings in soft drinks against a pure natural product, which, however, is more expensive. The options of soft drink or juice also represent different interests: cost and health. Just putting these interests onto a balance scale is not enough to determine which option should be chosen; they must also be assigned weight.

A fundamental starting point in decision-making is that the decision-maker wants to be consistent and non-contradictory in their evaluation and decision-making process. MCA is based on this basic assumption and ensures coherency through the principle of transitivity: if A is preferable to B and B is preferable to C, then A must also be preferable to C. By treating these rather obvious principles as axioms, it is possible to prove theorems that are not manifestly false as valuable guidelines in decision-making. The axiom establishes a logical equivalence between coherent preferences and numerical systems. If preferences are coherent, two things automatically follow: probability and utility, both associated with the consequences of a decision. Preferences and criteria establish the probability of the consequences occurring and the subjectively determined utility value and they also demonstrate the decision-maker's risk attitude. From this also follows a recommendation on which decision option to select, namely that which is associated with the highest sum of probability-weighted benefits.[15] This is the expected utility rule, which has existed in various

14    Mendoza, Macan and others (Ch 1 n 2).
15    Dodgson and others (Ch 1 n 2) 37, 47.

forms for more than 200 years.[16] To apply this, probability and utility for each possible consequence of an option must be multiplied by each other. The totals are then added together to provide the expected utility for that option. This process is repeated for each option. The option that has the highest expected utility is then chosen. This approach has been used since the 1960s in many decision analyses and given rise to the scientific theory called decision theory.[17]

Keeny and Raiffa subsequently extended the number of axioms so that decisions with multiple objectives can be analysed. They first presented the complete model in 1976, the aforementioned Multi Attribute Utility Theory (MAUT). Their book,[18] which is still used today, built on decision theory, which most associate with decision trees, handling uncertainties and expected utility. By expanding the common decision prototype of probability and expected utility with multi-dimensional consequences, Keeny and Raiffa succeeded in creating a robust theoretical model that integrates the uncertainty connected with future consequences to the objectives that these consequences realize.[19]

MCA is often used when decisions are made in interdisciplinary and multidisciplinary expert groups or groups composed of people with different perspectives and values.[20] In such situations, which may concern sustainable development or evaluation of social and economic progress, it can be difficult to reach agreement.[21] However, if MCA is used, participants in the decision-making process do not need to be in agreement on the relative weight of different criteria or how different decision options should be ranked. Each person makes their own assessment by making concrete evaluations and thereby contributing to a recommendation emanating from the entire group. How this is possible using MCA will be discussed below in section 2.2. MCA is furthermore usually used to evaluate something that is intended to be implemented and not for things that have already happened. However, it can also be used to evaluate decisions that have already been taken.[22] In this case, the stage in which criteria are determined and negotiated is omitted,

---

[16]  A brief introduction to the history of the utility rule is provided in James M Joyce, *The Foundations of Causal Decision Theory* (Cambridge University Press 1999) 9ff.
[17]  Dodgson and others (Ch 1 n 2) 84.
[18]  Keeny and Raiffa (Ch 1 n 4).
[19]  Dodgson and others (Ch 1 n 2) 25.
[20]  Lootsma, (Ch 1 n 2) 139ff.
[21]  Cf Dodgson and others (Ch 1 n 2) 64–6.
[22]  Ibid., 49.

because these are already specified in the decision or in the supporting data for this.

To summarize, the main purpose of MCA is to assist the decision-maker in choosing the best option from a number of possible alternatives. The last stage involves a final recommendation with a ranking of the options from best to worst. It should be emphasized that MCA is just a method. As such, it disregards a number of circumstances in order to highlight what is characteristic in a decision-making situation. Because the method, which must be simplified and therefore becomes a sort of caricature of reality, should represent what is important in a decision-making situation, its purpose is to help the decision-maker make the most informed decision possible in accordance with certain assumptions and certain premises.[23] MCA does not provide the 'right' answers, an objective solution, freeing the decision-maker from the responsibility of making a well-considered decision in a complex situation.[24]

## 2.2  DIFFERENT FORMS OF MCA AND OTHER METHODS – AN OVERVIEW

There are many different types of MCA methods. All of these, if the planning phase is included, contain the various basic steps that will be described below in section 2.3.1. The differences between methods or models that can nevertheless be found can be significant and are due to additions or modifications of various kinds. For example, as already discussed, risk can be built into the model, making the model different and more difficult to apply.

The simplest model of MCA is the performance matrix, which means that mathematical scoring and weighting are not done. The decision options are instead put into a matrix in order to make these and the decision criteria transparent and clear. The performance matrix is a starting point in the use of MCA and SAW. The prevailing option is then selected through a direct evaluation of the different options and criteria in the matrix.[25] The method works adequately when there are only a few options and criteria. In such cases, intuitive combined weighting generally works just as well. The mathematical calculations are thus omitted in the performance matrix, though they can relatively easily be connected.

23  Cf Roy (n 1) 8ff.
24  Belton and Stewart (Ch 1 n 2) 3.
25  Dodgson and others (Ch 1 n 2) 21.

*Table 2.1    Example of simple performance matrix*

|  | Economy | Safety | Design | Total |
|---|---|---|---|---|
| **Volvo V70** | *** | ***** | **** | 12 |
| **Ford Mondeo** | **** | **** | ***** | 13 |
| **Kia Ceed** | **** | **** | *** | 11 |

The performance matrix can be useful in providing an overview of the problems even in more complicated cases.

Common examples of performance matrices are easy to find in newspapers and magazines. If, for example, cars in a certain price class are examined and compared with each other in an automotive magazine using specific criteria, symbols such as plus signs or stars are often used to indicate how good the tester or test panel considered each car to be after an overall assessment, as in Table 2.1.

In the simple performance matrix, the numbers of stars represent how well the options (car models) meet the designated criteria. In this example, Ford Mondeo was the winner. It should be noted that this result does not build on any advanced studies of the cars' characteristics.

Multi-Attribute Utility Theory (MAUT), which is discussed several times above, stems from the work done by von Neumann, Morgenstern and Savage in the 1940s and 1950s.[26] The theory was developed and became more usable through the aforementioned work of Keeny and Raiffa in 1976. The performance matrix discussed above was used as the starting point. There are then procedures to determine whether or not the criteria are mutually independent. The third step consists of estimating the parameters in a mathematical function, which makes it possible to express an index, U, showing the decision-maker's overall assessment of the utility value of an option in light of its consequences for each of the separate criteria. The model is rather complicated to use and can therefore, depending on the nature of the problem, require experts and time. What makes the model particularly complicated is that it takes into account uncertainty, that it permits the criteria to interact and affect each

---

[26]    John von Neumann and Oskar Morgenstern, *Theory of Games and Economic Behavior* (Princeton University Press 1944), Leonard Savage, *The Foundations of Statistics* (New York: Dover 1954).

other and that it is not based on the mutual independence of the preferences with regard to criteria.[27]

The simple additive model, SAW, can be used if it is deemed that the
criteria per preference are mutually independent and if neither the criteria
nor the outcomes are uncertain.[28] SAW shows how the value of an option
with respect to a number of criteria can be weighed together to an overall
value. As discussed, this is done by taking the value score for each option,
on each of the relevant criteria, and multiplying it by the weight of each
criterion. All of these weighted scores are then added together.

SMART was presented in 1986 by Ward Edwards.[29] The aim of introducing SMART was to create a simpler model than, for example MAUT,
so that it could be used by decision-makers without special training in
decision theory. Because the first model of SMART could in certain cases
yield remarkable results, it was expanded with a swing method to assess
the relative importance of weights.[30] SMART now exists both with and
without swing. SMART with swing is usually called SMARTS.[31] SAW
also uses swing and the methods are basically the same. One difference
is that SMARTS does not use a relative method to standardize the raw
values, such as the actual price, to a normalized scale. Instead, a value
function defines how each value should be translated to the used scale.
The value function converts mathematical rankings under a normalization process to a consistent internal scale from 0 (lowest) to 1 (highest).
SAW, on the other hand, works directly with numerical values that the
decision-maker may specify. The differences are discussed below in the
examples in section 2.3.6 and 2.3.7.

The Analytical hierarchy process (AHP), which is well known in decision theory, also contains linear addition. It is based on comparing two
options with each other at a time, which is problematic in itself. One criticism that has been directed at the model concerns the reverse ranking. This
phenomenon occurs if a new option is added. In this case, the ranking of
two other existing options, which are not at all related to the new option,

---

[27]   Dodgson and other (Ch 1 n 2) 25.
[28]   According to Belton and Stewart, (Ch 1 n 2) the multiattribute utility
theory is used less in practice than the multiattribute value theory because of its
complexity, 6–7, 123.
[29]   Ward Edwards, 'How to use Multiattribute Utility Measurement For Social
Decisionmaking' (1977), IEEE Transactions on Systems, Man, and Cybernetics,
SMC-7, 326.
[30]   For further discussion on the swing method, see below section 2.3.5.
[31]   Goodwin and Wright (Ch 1 n 2) use SMARTS yet refer to it as SMART.
There is also a model called SMARTER that uses a special weighting process.

can be reversed. It is for this reason that it has been questioned whether AHP is a rational method for evaluating options.[32] However, the reversed ranking does not seem to be a serious problem with the theoretical foundation of AHP since it is frequently used in practise.

Outranking Methods is another way to compare options with each other given certain criteria.[33] The option that meets the most criteria beats the next, and so on. However, the method is more difficult to use than would appear from this simplified description, particularly as there can be disagreement about what it specifically means that one option is better than another.

Concordance Methods are also based on comparisons in pairs of options and outranking. ELECTRE II, III and IV and PROMETHEE are software for these models that enable sophisticated data processing of scores and weights in very large projects.[34] Multi-objective decision rules also include models for analysing how effective different options are. Noted methods for this are Data Development Analysis (DDA) and the Technique for Ordering of Preference by Similarity to Ideal Solution (TOPSIS).[35] Besides these, there are a range of different methods for ranking and evaluating options and for determining weights.

After Keeny and Raiffa, the number of MCA methods and variants has seen an almost explosive development. In selecting an MCA model for use in legal contexts, the writing of this book involved studying a large number of MCA techniques based on two main criteria. The model must be able to be used without prior knowledge and understood intuitively, which applies to the simple additive model, which incidentally is also recommended for use in public decision-making and has widespread use.[36] In addition, SAW can be applied relatively quickly.

There are decision-making methods other than MCA.[37] Some are financial, the most famous being the cost/benefit model, which presupposes that the expected costs for an option can be calculated. If these cannot be provided, benefit/effectiveness criteria are used instead. In procedural law, it is common to seek solutions that are process-economical. Because the overall procedural costs are difficult to calculate with exact

---

[32]   Belton and Stewart (Ch 1 n 2) 109, Malczewski (Ch 1 n 4) 223.
[33]   AHP entails a sort of elimination process, but is not considered an outranking method because it provides a hierarchical order that is then assessed in total; see Malczewski, ibid., 220.
[34]   See for example Ishizaka and Nemery (Ch 1 n 12).
[35]   Malczewski (Ch 1 n 4) 197.
[36]   Dodgson and others (Ch 1 n 2) 47; also Belton and Stewart (Ch 1 n 2) 339.
[37]   Dodgson and others, ibid., 23ff.

numerical values, this therefore involves benefit/effectiveness reasoning, though this is actually quite close to pure cost/benefit analyses. Cost/benefit analysis are often made alongside MCA analyses.

## 2.3   THE STEPS OF MCA

### 2.3.1   The Basic Model

The following describes the general basic model, which contains the different basic steps that are found in a range of different variants of MCA. As mentioned in Chapter 1, the models can, however, vary significantly, even though the basic model is the same. These differences include, for example, the methods for weighting and rating or what type of scale is used. Generally speaking, more advanced models probably seem complicated, in any case for the average lawyer. They do not, however, provide significantly more reliable results, at least not in a legal context where scoring and weighting are subjectively determined anyway.

The basic steps in the general model are described below. The presentation is theoretical and may be a bit difficult to take in for those who are not familiar with decision theory and multi-dimensional analysis. A few simple examples are therefore provided after the introduction to help illustrate the theory. The basic model consists of the following steps: [38]

- establish the aims and the decision context;
- identify the options to be assessed;
- identify objectives and criteria for the assessment. Make a decision tree;
- scoring. Check the consistency of the scores for each criterion;
- weighting. Assign weights to each criterion to reflect their relative importance to the decision;
- combine the weights and scores for each option and calculate its total value;
- examine the results;
- sensitivity analysis. Do other preferences or weightings affect the overall ranking of the options? Look at the advantages and disadvantages of the selected options and compare them in pairs. Develop possible new options that could be better than those first chosen.

---

[38]   For further discussion on these steps, see Goodwin and Wright (Ch 1 n 2) 34ff, Lootsma (Ch 1 n 2) 15ff and Belton and Stewart (Ch 1 n 2) 52ff.

## 2.3.2   Aims, Decision Context and Options

The first step is to determine the aims of the analysis, identify key decision-makers and other significant participants and arrange a system for performing the analysis. It is important to carefully define the purpose of the analysis – what should be achieved. The aim or aims determine the following steps and their specific formulation and contents. If the aims are incorrectly defined, the rest of the analysis will also be flawed. The aims in the decision-making process and other steps in this can, however, be reformulated during a planning phase – which is quite common – and are thus not set in stone from the start.

An important factor in the use of MCA in governmental planning and decision-making is the participation of interest groups and policy-makers in the decision-making process. As previously noted, MCA is often used in the planning of large public-sector projects such as the construction of airports and new roads. When using MCA for planning a new airport, a lot of time needs to be devoted to defining the current conditions and the aims to be achieved, potential obstacles, if reformulating the objectives could make the decision-making process simpler, what weaknesses may exist, and so on.

The participants in the decision-making process discuss and determine together what the objectives should be, which options should be included and what the decision criteria will be. Participants sometimes have different interests and may therefore assess scores and weights differently. In the environments in which MCA is often used, this is natural and not infrequently dependent on political agendas. In the final combined weighting, however, different valuations will be counted and will affect which option is selected. MCA can also, as discussed in the beginning of Chapter 1, be used in simpler decisions, such as when a family is considering buying a new car or house. The interest group in such cases consists of the entire family, who can together discuss what requirements they want to set on a new car or house. A car, for example, should be safe, environmentally friendly and inexpensive to purchase and to own. The purpose of the analysis then becomes to find the car that best meets these criteria, which also becomes the aim of the analysis. Those with an interest in the matter are usually called 'stakeholders' in the literature in this field.

## 2.3.3   Criteria for Assessment of the Options

MCA illustrates the decision-maker's preferences and subjective evaluations of different decision options by showing the estimated scores and relative weight of each criterion with respect to the various decision options (preferences). Different criteria can thus be clearly compared with each other while a final aggregation provides an answer on the best option. A decision tree is usually built to structure the problem and simplify the analysis.[39] This decision tree can be subsequently changed in light of new circumstances, which is often the case in planning processes where new information gradually comes in. The overall goal is listed at the top of the decision tree. Also listed at the top is the greatest potential for trade-off, which often involves an exchange of options against costs. By organizing objectives and criteria in a decision tree, the decision-maker can more easily detect conflicting objectives.[40] He or she can then return to an earlier step in the analysis, which is common when the MCA model is used in a project planning stage.

Criteria express how the options create value. Under MCA, it is strictly speaking not the options that are assessed, but rather the consequences of the different options with regard to selected criteria.[41] Only factors with consequences that are relevant for the set objectives are called criteria (or attributes). As far as the consequences are concerned, the easiest approach is to formulate a qualitative description for the options, taking into account each criterion. If the options are already given and the criteria are fixed, a 'bottom-up' method can be used to compare criteria by asking how one option differs from another with respect to an important criterion. A 'top-down' method means that the decision-maker sets goals and then compares the options with different possible criteria to see if the overall goal can be reached.[42] For complex problems, it can be necessary to make separate consequence tables for each option.[43]

Determining which criteria to use may include grouping these into units relating to their ability to meet the overall goals that have been set. This grouping is made in the decision tree. A grouping of criteria should reflect a clear and logical compilation of criteria that can then be combined into coherent groups, each of which is relevant to the problem to be solved.

---

[39] For a discussion of problem structuring, see Belton and Stewart, 'Problem Structuring and Multiple Criteria Decision Analysis' in Ehrgott, Figueira and Greco (n 4); OI Larichev and HM Moskovich, 'Unstructured Problems and Development of Prescriptive Decision Making Methods' in Pantos M Pardalos, Yannis Siskos and Constantin Zopounidis (eds) *Advances in Multicriteria Analysis* (Kluwer Academic Publishers 1995).

[40] Ibid.

[41] Dodgson and others (Ch 1 n 2) 55, Belton and Stewart (Ch 1 n 2) 55–6, Roy (n 1) 170.

[42] Belton and Stewart, ibid., 58–60.

[43] Dodgson and others (Ch 1 n 2) 55.

The grouping may also include organizing the criteria into high-priority and low-priority goals.[44]

Some criteria groups will usually be identified as more effective than others. This will then form a hierarchy of criteria. Organizing criteria and objectives in this way makes it easier to assess the options. The grouping may also include identifying sub-criteria for a main criterion.[45] Because the criteria must be mutually independent (see below), such a grouping may be important in order to avoid double counting. A grouping of criteria is, however, only relevant if the criteria are numerous, disparate or difficult to assess. Criteria should be:

- complete;
- relevant;
- operational;
- precise or concrete;
- mutually independent.[46]

If the decision tree is complete, all relevant criteria are included. For the criteria to be complete, no important criterion may be omitted. If a new criterion is discovered, this must be incorporated into the model. In a judicial process, the legal facts the parties refer to become criteria if the process is amenable to out-of-court settlement, even if there are other legal facts that have not been referred to that may be important. If the process is not amenable to out-of-court settlement or if it is a criminal case, the court can on its own motion enrich the decision basis by, after consulting with the parties, taking into account legal facts that have not been alleged.

The criteria must furthermore be needed for the decision, that is, they must be relevant. This involves downscaling and stripping away everything that is not necessary or superfluous. If there are two criteria that mean the same thing, one should be taken out. This process of downscaling can be labour intensive if there are a lot of criteria. And it can also be difficult.[47] It is particularly important to note in this context that MCA under the additive model is compensatory, which means that good performance in

---

[44]   Ibid., 34.
[45]   Belton and Stewart (Ch 1 n 2) 139, Roy (n 1) 184.
[46]   For a discussion of these requirements, see Belton and Stewart, ibid., 55–6, 88, Goodwin and Wright (Ch 1 n 2) 36, 52–4, Malczewski (Ch 1 n 4) 107–9 and Dodgson and others (Ch 1 n 2) 35.
[47]   Roy (n 1) 170ff. The meaning of a criteria and how it differs from another can be difficult to determine if it is vague, cf section 4.4.7.

a criterion may compensate for or even eliminate a weak criterion.[48] The requirement that criteria must be operational means that all criteria at the bottom of the decision tree must be sufficiently precise for an evaluation and comparison. If not, attempts must be made to make further clarifications. Criteria must also be concrete and preferably measurable (though measurability is not a requirement). In a legal context, criteria must be as concrete and clear as possible and – of course – comprehensible. In practice, MCA often involves a mix of measurable and non-measurable criteria.[49]

> Although the MCDA model is not difficult to apply, for some time researchers have sought ways of using linear additive choice models that require less precise data inputs than the basic model. Of course, with less precise information input, the recommendations output by the model will be less precise too and less likely unambiguously to identify a best option. However, it may be that this is a price worth paying, if the input demands on the decision-maker are less, or if the model can be constructed and applied more quickly.[50]

In law the basic input as well as the recommendations output by the model will be less precise. However, as Dodgson and others says, this could be a price worth paying, in particular compared to the use of pure intuition.

If the preference scores for a decision option on one criterion can be assessed independently of the preference scores for each of the other criteria, the requirement for independence has been met. If it is not met, the criteria in question may need to be combined into one criterion.[51] Another possibility may be to remove the criterion if it falls below a minimum level, that is, it has very little importance.[52] A third alternative is of course to try to more precisely clarify the criteria.[53] If the requirement for independence is not met, the results will be, as noted above, misleading due to double counting.[54]

According to Dodgson and others, the requirement for independence is simpler and less restrictive than statistical or empirical ('real-world') independence.[55] They provide several examples. Two criteria can be empirically linked and provide a statistic relationship between two factors

---

[48] Dodgson and others (Ch 1 n 2) 22.
[49] Goodwin and Wright (Ch 1 n 2) 38.
[50] Dodgson and others (Ch 1 n 2) 123.
[51] Ibid., 36.
[52] Ibid.
[53] Goodwin and Wright (Ch 1 n 2) 36.
[54] Dodgson and others (Ch 1 n 2) 36.
[55] Ibid., 66, also Roy (n 1) 224.

while still being independent with regard to the decision options: cars with nice interiors are generally more expensive than cars with simple interiors. Price and nice interior are thus empirically joined. Most car buyers, however, prefer a nice interior and a lower purchase price. Preference scores can be given for the interior without knowing the price of the car and for the price without knowing how luxurious the interior of the car is. These preferences are thus mutually independent even if there is a correlation between the factors in the real world. Another example is that most people choose a main course at a restaurant without first looking at the wine list. Preferences for main courses are thus independent of the wine list, while preferences for wine can very well depend on the choice of main course.[56]

### 2.3.3.1   A few examples of structuring and decision trees
In this section, a few simple examples are given to concretize the use of MCA with regard to problem structuring and decision trees.

The objective in the first example is – to return to and in certain aspects reuse the previous car example – to buy a car that should be economical, safe and have an attractive design.[57] The word objective is used here, just as in other places in this book, synonymously with aim. One can just as well say that the aim is to buy a car that should be economical, safe and have an attractive design. Economy, safety and an attractive design are thus criteria for the choice of car model, which are more precise objectives on a lower level (than 'buying a car'). At the bottom of the decision tree are concrete circumstances, which are a breakdown of these criteria: economy, safety and attractive design into more concrete criteria (except 'design'). Economy is thus broken down into purchase price and operating costs. Operating costs include taxes, insurance, fuel consumption, and repair costs. For the sake of simplicity, all details on this level have not been included in Figure 2.1 below. Safety includes active and passive safety.

When assessing how far the sub-grouping can or should go, one might ask the question: why is this important? How concrete the bottom level of the decision tree can be made depends on what it concerns. There is no set answer to how specified the criteria should be. If economy is deemed important, and the question of what this means is asked, and the potential car buyer's answer is 'purchase price' and 'operating costs', then a new

---

[56]   Dodgson and others, ibid., 66. For a discussion on whether criteria (legal facts) should be legally independent, see sections 4.2.1, 4.4.7 and 4.5.2.
[57]   See section 1.5.1, above.

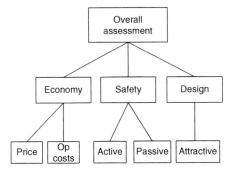

*Figure 2.1    Decision tree – overall assessment*

level has been created in the decision tree. Economy can then be seen as a more precise objective and price and operating costs as criteria. If the buyer is then asked why these specific criteria have been chosen, they might think of new ones, and so on. This process ends when the potential buyer is satisfied with the clarifications and cannot think of any more.[58] If a car should have an 'attractive design', this assessment is purely subjective. However, this requirement can, in the assessor's own perception, exclude some models, for example estate cars, which then shortens the list of possible car models. If the buyer furthermore is asked why 'passive safety' is important and the answer is that it reduces certain injuries, an objective is to reduce such injuries in a collision. Different safety details in a car are furthermore tools for achieving safety and not the goal itself. It is easy to list these: seatbelt tensioners, airbags and anti-intrusion bars. One might also use NCAP's crash test ratings.[59]

The selection of criteria needs to be reviewed; some can be measured, some are subjectively assessed. In the example, the assessment of 'attractive design' is purely subjective. A simple decision tree for the discussed example is shown in Figure 2.1.

As discussed, criteria should be operational. They should thus lead to or, to put it better, help the car buyer purchase a car with the characteristics he or she wants and result in the achievement of the decided objectives. The more clearly the criteria are related to the desired characteristics, the better. In this example, it is easy to see that there is an objective relationship between economy and safety and the criteria set for these objectives. There are no objective standards for 'attractive design', which means that

---

[58]    Dodgson and others (Ch 1 n 2) 56, Belton and Stewart (Ch 1 n 2) 136.
[59]    European New Car Assessment Programme.

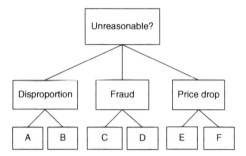

*Figure 2.2 Decision tree – unreasonable*

how this subjective criterion is assessed depends entirely on the individual car buyer. This does not mean that this criterion is unimportant. On the contrary, for the car buyer in the example, it is important. The buyer must therefore evaluate each car's design and weigh this assessment together with the others. Similarly, the car buyer must decide what relative weight he thinks 'attractive design' should be given (compared with safety, for example).

Figure 2.2 above illustrates a simple legal example. It is stylized and intended only to illustrate the basic principles of MCA. Substantive details in 36 AvtL are thus completely bypassed. The plaintiff alleges that a clause in an agreement should be modified or be set aside entirely (options) because there is a significant disproportion between the performances of the parties, the defendant intentionally withheld important information and that after commencement of the agreement there was a steep and unexpected drop in prices that makes the claimant's performance a considerable burden. The legal facts are specified through the allegation of concrete legal facts A–F. Just as in the car example, the criteria must be operational and thus relevant for the assessment of whether or not the agreement is 'unreasonable'. Thus, a legal relation must be deemed to exist between each legal fact and the prerequisite 'unreasonable'. If such a legal connection exists, the legal facts have what in this book is called a legal value. That the alleged factors given in this example can have a relevant legal value would seem to be obvious. They belong to the type of factor mentioned in the preparatory work for section 36 of AvtL. It should also be clear that they can have different weights, that is, that the legal values of the various factors may differ from each other and with regard to the different options. The assessment of scores and weights in this case is, unlike in the car example, subjective throughout.

If an objective is to buy a safe, environmentally friendly and 'attractive' car, the criteria related to safety, environmental friendliness and 'attractive design' are important. The car that best fulfils these criteria is the car that should be selected. Similarly, if a court determines that an agreement is 'unreasonable', only the criteria (legal facts) that are legally commensurate with 'unreasonable' are relevant. The court should choose the option (modify or set aside) that has the highest legal value with regard to the alleged legal facts (criteria). I will set out a simple calculation that illustrates this below.

### 2.3.4 Scoring and Weighting

Scoring and weighting mean that the decision-maker assesses how an option works with regard to a relevant criterion.[60] The assessment system thus consists of two components and can therefore be said to be dualistic. In scoring, an option is rated on a scale according to selected criteria. The other component is the assessment of the weight of the criteria. For mathematical calculations to be possible, both scores and weights must be given numerical values. As discussed above, the mathematical calculations are not included in the performance matrix and sometimes this is sufficient. If the criteria are structured in a decision tree, the criteria should be scored and weighted according to the option on the lowest level on the decision tree. The scoring of options with regard to criteria is discussed first in the following section. The following section describes weighting.

#### 2.3.4.1 Scoring
In MCA, the use of preferences is fundamental because these help to obtain valid results. The initial evaluation of scores for options often reveals contradictions, both within and between criteria. Several modifications can be necessary before the participants in a planning process feel that there is sufficient consistency in their preferences. Consistency thus does not need to be in a planning process right from the beginning, but rather the modelling process helps the assessor structure the material so that consistency arises. The scores for each criterion are usually checked for consistency when the scores are evaluated. The way consistency is checked depends on the type of scale used.[61]

Scoring is usually done on an interval scale, that is, a scale in which the difference between the options is relevant, see Figure 2.3 below. To construct a scale, it is necessary to define two reference points and then set numerical values for these. These numbers usually represent the top

---

[60] Belton and Stewart (Ch 1 n 2) 12ff.
[61] Belton and Stewart, ibid., 141, Dodgson and others (Ch 1 n 2) 6.

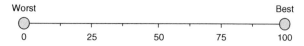

*Figure 2.3    Interval scale*

and bottom of the scale, usually 0 and 100, but other numbers can be used, such as 0 and 10.[62] The minimum and maximum of the scale can be determined in different ways, but it is common to use a local or global scale.[63]

A local scale is defined by the options that are under consideration in the concrete decision-making situation. If the endpoints on the scale are 0 and 100, the options with regard to the criteria are given scores that reflect their importance in relation to these two endpoints. The local scale allows relatively rapid assessment of the values.[64] The global scale has the same endpoints, but in this scale 0 represents the worst and 100 the best in the type of problem to be solved. A global scale is thus hypothetical because it is based on taking account of other options and other criteria than just those that are significant for the actual problem in the moment of decision. Consequently, the endpoints of the scale are defined by the optimal and the worst performance for a given criterion. Because the scale is hypothetical, it requires more work to create than a local scale, since it is difficult to determine the implications of the scale's endpoints.[65] The global scale is preferable if new options can arise because these will not affect the scale. If a local scale is used and new options arise, the entire assessment procedure must be restarted from the beginning.

Valid value functions can be decided under both the local and the global scale. Whichever scale is used, it must be consistent with the weighting that is later done. For the ranking of the options, it does not matter whether the scale is global or local.[66]

Once the reference points on the scale have been determined, on either a local or a global scale, it must be decided how the options will be scored with regard to the criteria.[67] This can be done through the definition of a partial value function, the construction of a qualitative value scale or

---

[62]   Belton and Stewart, ibid., 121, Dodgson and others, ibid., 60.
[63]   Belton and Stewart, ibid., 121, Dodgson and others, ibid., 42.
[64]   Belton and Stewart, ibid., 121.
[65]   Belton and Stewart, ibid., Dodgson and others (Ch 1 n 2) 42.
[66]   Ibid.
[67]   Belton and Stewart, ibid., 123. There are computer programs for the use of constructed scales, for example MACBETH, see above section 2.2.

through a direct rating of the options.[68] The use of a partial value function requires that the criteria that are relevant for ranking are measurable (compare, for example, fuel consumption as a criterion for selecting a car or office space for selecting an office building). Because the criteria in a legal context are rarely measurable, the partial value function is not used. The construction of a qualitative value scale is done in advance and contains descriptions of what the criteria should be compared against; compare Beaufort's scale for wind speed.[69] This option will not be used either because legal decision-makers will use the legal facts the parties have alleged.

Unlike the construction of a qualitative scale, which can be compared with the creation of a criterion, in direct rating no attempt is made to define a scale with properties characterizing the function independently of the options being valued.[70] The decision-maker instead specifies a score or a point in an analogue scale that reflects the value of an option (with regard to a criterion) in relation to a specified reference point.

### 2.3.4.2  Closer examination of direct rating

A relative preference scale is a simple scale that at one end has the least preferred and at the other end the most preferred with respect to an option on a criterion. As also shown, a selected preference value of 100 points represents an option that is best and 0 for that which is worst. Points are then given to the remaining options so that differences in points represent differences in consequences, which are often easier to assess than giving absolute judgements. Relative scales are particularly suitable for comparing options that occur at the same time.[71]

It is not possible to compare numerical values with qualitative judgements such as 'good', 'less good' and 'bad' and then arrive at a combined overall weighted score. For a meaningful comparison to be made, a translation must be performed to a common and uniform scale so that

---

[68]  Belton and Stewart, ibid., 84. Three different models have been identified for solving multi-criteria problems. Value Measurement Theory, Satisficing and Outranking, Belton and Stewart, ibid. If the criteria are measurable, a linear scale can be created. If, for example, a company wants to acquire a new office, office space can be an important criterion. Because the cost of office space increases by the number of square metres, the scale will be linear, though only to a certain point. At a certain area, the increase in office space becomes irrelevant. On a scale, a rising curve suddenly turns downwards. A mathematical limit can be set through so-called bisection.

[69]  Belton and Stewart, ibid., 130.

[70]  Ibid., 129.

[71]  Dodgson and others (Ch 1 n 2) 62.

the options can be compared. Celsius and Fahrenheit as different ways to measure temperature can be used as analogy. The Celsius scale covers a larger temperature scale because one degree Celsius represents 95 per cent more temperature change than a degree on the Fahrenheit scale. One can, however, not say that a water temperature of 80 degrees Celsius is twice as hot as 40 degrees Celsius, which becomes apparent when these figures are converted to Fahrenheit, which are 175°F and 104°F.[72] If Celsius and Fahrenheit are used, the units must be weighted against each other to determine the relative importance of Celsius versus Fahrenheit or vice versa.[73] If qualitative judgements are used, these can be translated to numerical values, such as 100 points for 'very good' and 0 points for 'very bad'. 'Good' might be given 80 points and 'acceptable' 50 points. Numerical values can be translated to qualitative judgements by reverse conversion. It does not really matter how it is done, as long as a translation is performed that makes a meaningful comparison possible.[74] In this book, direct rating and a relative scale is used throughout, with one exception. As such, no translation between the different scales is needed (however, in the car purchase below in section 2.3.7 the purchase price is inverted). This simplifies the procedure; scoring and weighting become less complicated.

If, for example, safety is considered an important property in a car, safety is a criterion that should be given high value on a scale (provided, of course, that the car model in question – the option – is a car model with a high level of safety). Should two options be equivalent with respect to a certain criterion, it is hardly likely that this criterion is important for the choice to be made, even if the decision-maker thinks that the criterion is important in itself.[75] Note, however, that the latter relates to weighting and not scoring, to which I will return.

As shown, the score represents the value associated with the option's consequences with regard to a certain criterion. The strength of a preference should not be confused with preference itself. This is due to what was discussed above, that in decision theory coherent preferences logically implicate two measurable units, probability and utility. Thus, A can be preferred over B if they have the same value because A is more probable. If strength or preference is only an expression for values, A and B must be considered to be equally probable. If they are not equally probable, the uncertainty associated with A and B must be handled somehow.[76]

---

[72]   Goodwin and Wright (Ch 1 n 2) 39.
[73]   Goodwin and Wright, ibid., 38, Dodgson and others (Ch 1 n 2) 62, 82.
[74]   Compare the use of fuzzy logic, in Chapters 4 and 6.
[75]   Dodgson and others (Ch 1 n 2) 56, Goodwin and Wright (Ch 1 n 2) 29.
[76]   Dodgson and others, ibid., 61.

### 2.3.5 The Swing Method

To measure how attractive an option is in comparison with others and to be able to combine the preference scales for different options, each criterion must be given a weight in order to make it possible to compare the relative importance of the criteria.[77] The weighting thus relates the score for one criterion to the score for all other criteria. If criterion A is given double the weight of criterion B, it should be understood that the decision-maker rates 10 weight points for criterion A as the same as 20 weight points for criterion B and therefore would be willing to trade A for B.[78] The purpose of the weighting is thus to reflect the relative importance of a criterion across all criteria to be able to make an overall assessment of scores and weights.

If the overall assessment concerns, for example and again, a car purchase, the car's safety, comfort and fuel consumption (three different criteria) are probably not equally important to the car buyer. This means that a criterion that is considered very important, such as safety, can be given a lower relative weight than another criterion, for example repair costs, if the car models have about the same level of safety, but differ in regard to repair costs. If, on the other hand, there is a large difference in safety between the cars, the safety criterion would be of considerable importance. The same applies if, for example, the purchase price of the car is important but the price difference between the various possible models is marginal. In this case, the price differences are given relatively little importance. On the contrary, they have considerable importance if they differ greatly between the models.[79] This also applies to legal decisions. Some legal facts have greater weight than others. On the other hand, if one concrete legal fact is equally important for two possible legal alternatives, this legal fact will not be decisive because it will be given little relative weight in the comparison. The weight of a criterion thus reflects both the difference in preferences and how much this difference means in the specific decision-making situation.[80]

In order to put values on the weights, the decision-maker must make comparisons between the criteria with respect to the different decision options. In the weighting, a swing method is often used.[81] How does a swing from 0 to 100 on a preference scale for a criterion stand in comparison with

---

[77] Goodwin and Wright (Ch 1 n 2) 42.
[78] Belton and Stewart (Ch 1 n 2) 135.
[79] Dodgson and others (Ch 1 n 2) 56.
[80] Ibid., 63.
[81] Belton and Stewart (Ch 1 n 2) 134ff, Dodgson and others, ibid.

a swing for another criterion?[82] To determine this, the decision-maker should consider both the difference between the least and the most preferred and how much the decision-maker cares about this difference.[83]

If the MCA only covers a few criteria, the greatest swing can usually be quickly discovered. If the decision tree is small, the decision-maker can then consider all the criteria on the bottom level at the same time and determine which swing produces the greatest upwards variation.[84] This criterion is given the value of 100 and will continue to be the reference point or standard against which the other criteria are compared. If there are many criteria, it may be necessary to compare the criteria in pairs: two criteria at a time are compared with regard to swing and the one with the largest variation is saved. Some reference points can, as already discussed, be expressed in linguistic expressions, such as 'good' or 'neutral'. This can make it easier for the assessor if the swing is significant.[85] If numerical calculations are done, these expressions must then be translated to numerical values, unless a simpler performance matrix is used.

Dodgson and others describe the weighting process when decisions are made by a group of people. First, the criterion with the greatest swing is selected, which becomes the most important criterion and the standard against which other criteria are assessed. This criterion is given the weight of 100. The participants are then asked to write down, without any prior discussion, the weight of the next criterion. If the criterion is assessed to represent half of the variation of the standard (100), it is given a weight of 50. The participants are then asked to enter weights for the rest of the criteria in the same way. The results are then written down as a frequency distribution (for example, 100, 90, 80, 70 and so on).[86] Participants with extreme weightings, high and low, are asked to explain their reasoning, after which there can be a general discussion. This last step means that a group of selected participants makes the final determination of the weights for the criteria.[87] Who then decides the final weight of the criteria? In public planning, this is often a political issue. In other situations, it could be senior members of the decision group with expertise and extensive experience who make the decision.

Determining weights is fundamental for the effectiveness of MCA. The

---

[82]   Goodwin and Wright (Ch 1 n 2) 44.
[83]   Dodgson and others (Ch 1 n 2) 63, Belton and Stewart (Ch 1 n 2) 135, Goodwin and Wright, ibid.
[84]   Dodgson and others, ibid., 64.
[85]   Belton and Stewart (Ch 1 n 2) 136.
[86]   Dodgson and others (Ch 1 n 2) 64.
[87]   Ibid.

weight often arises from the opinion of a group of people. They may meet other stakeholders or people who can articulate the key players' values and the weights are then compared. With space and time for reflection, a broad or at least broader consensus will hopefully follow. If a consensus is not reached, it may be best to take two or more criteria for a parallel comparison. It is also sometimes possible to select options even without consensus on weighting. Even if an agreement cannot be reached, the awareness of different assessments can facilitate the search for acceptable compromises.[88]

The simple additive model and SMARTS are, as mentioned, compensatory. This means that high scores on one criterion can compensate for low scores on another. All MCA models are not compensatory, but in a legal context, a compensatory model is an advantage because legal facts are often compensatory in balancing of interests and overall assessments, or at least most of them.

### 2.3.6 SMARTS: An Example

To concretely exemplify scoring and weighting, suppose a Swedish-based company wants to move its head offices and the assessment of the new premises will be based on the following criteria: size, image, parking facilities, comfort, visibility and proximity to customers. To these criteria are added costs and benefit. To simplify the example, these are not included here. Furthermore – also for simplicity – only one criterion will be selected to illustrate the assessment. The total appraisal, which covers all options and criteria, is not difficult to understand after the different stages have been described in the following.

Goodwin and Wright, who use SMARTS, differentiate between the assessments of criteria that are not measurable, such as 'image' and other criteria that are measurable, such as office space. With a legal context in mind, just this non-measurable criterion, 'image' is used in the example. According to Goodwin and Wright, the owner should be asked to specify the premises that have the best and the worst images. The premise with the best image is given the value of 100 and the premise with the worst value is given 0. Other values could have been used, such as 80 or 20, but as Goodwin and Wright point out, the calculation will be easier to do with the values 0 and 100.[89] To give the example, Figure 2.4 below, a Swedish

---

[88]  Belton and Stewart (Ch 1 n 2) 134.
[89]  Goodwin and Wright (Ch 1 n 2) 38. Belton and Stewart, ibid., 136ff also establish a ranking first. Concerning the use of SMART and the direct ranking of options, also see Lootsma (Ch 1 n 2) 15ff.

| | |
|---:|---|
| 100 | Dragarbrunnsgatan |
| 90 | |
| 80 | Sysslomansgatan |
| 70 | Svartbäcksgatan |
| 60 | Kungsgatan |
| 50 | |
| 40 | |
| 30 | |
| 20 | Tycho Hedéns väg |
| 10 | |
| 0 | Boländerna |

*Figure 2.4     Results of direct scoring using a local scale*

and local connection, the example has been modified so that it refers to possible locations in Uppsala.

Dragarbrunnsgatan is, in the owner's view, the best location with regard to the criterion 'image' and Boländerna the worst. Other options are placed in-between. Scoring thus means that points are given to the options so that the difference in points represents the difference in strength of the preferences. Note that what is then being investigated is how each option performs with respect to each criterion. It should also be noted that what is being compared is the interval between the reference points on the scale.[90] The scale therefore does not show that Kungsgatan is three times better than a location on Tycho Hedéns väg. It shows that the improvement is increased three times within the interval. This is because the scale is discretionary and in no way absolute.[91] Consequently, 0 for Boländerna is also discretionary.[92]

Once the owner has set point values for each criterion, the criteria must be weighted so that they can be combined into the various location options. The purpose of this step is to be able to make a total appraisal of all options on all criteria. The simplest approach, according to Goodwin and Wright, is to ask the owner to envision an office that least meets all

---

[90]   Goodwin and Wright, ibid., 38.
[91]   Belton and Stewart (Ch 1 n 2) 132.
[92]   Options can also be compared in pairs, which is done if the decision-maker uses AHP (Analytic Hierarchy Process), a method in which comparison in pairs is made explicit and systematic. One drawback of this method is that it can be cumbersome to use because many assessments are needed if there are several criteria. In a way, a comparison is made in all models that require scoring, because the scoring is done in relation to reference points.

of these criteria, that is, one that is remote with a bad image, few parking spaces, and so on. The decision-maker is then asked which criterion could be moved to the highest level, if only one could be chosen.[93] If the decision-maker then chooses proximity to customers, this is given 100 weight points as proximity to customers is deemed to be the most important. The decision-maker is then asked which is the second most important, and so on. The ranking can then be as follows:

1  proximity to customers
2  visibility
3  image
4  size
5  comfort
6  parking facilities

Proximity to customers is thus therefore given a weight of 100. The decision-maker should then compare a swing for the option with the worst and the best visibility with a swing for a location with the worst and the best proximity to customers. Suppose that the decision-maker determines that a swing for visibility is 80 per cent as important as a swing for proximity to customers. In that case, visibility is given a weight of 80. In the same manner, it is determined that a swing from the worst to the best image is 70 per cent as important as a swing from the worst and from the best location for proximity to customers. The weight for this will then be 70. The decision-maker continues in the same way until all criteria have been given a weight.[94] Figure 2.5 shows how the weighting might be for one location option, Svartbäcksgatan.

In accordance with SMARTS, it is then customary to normalize the weights so that the total sum becomes 100 because this simplifies the analysis. The normalization is done by dividing each weight by 310 and then multiplying by 100. The aggregated value for Svartbäcksgatan is thus 3200 + 2080 + 1610 + 300 + 120 + 30 = 7340/100 = 73.4.[95] Note that this total sum is then compared with the total score for the other options, which are Dragarbrunnsgatan, Sysslomansgatan, Kungsgatan, Tycho Hedéns väg and Boländerna, with regard to other criteria (proximity to customers, visibility, size, comfort and parking facilities). These options have, as indicated, been omitted to simplify the description.

---

[93]  Goodwin and Wright (Ch 1 n 2) 44, Belton and Stewart (Ch 1 n 2) 136.
[94]  After Goodwin and Wright, ibid.
[95]  Ibid.

| Weighting for a location option | | |
|---|---|---|
|  | Original weight | Normalized weight |
| Proximity | 100 | 32 |
| Visibility | 80 | 26 |
| Image | 70 | 23 |
| Size | 30 | 10 |
| Comfort | 20 | 6 |
| Parking | 10 | 3 |
| Total | 310 | 100 |

*Figure 2.5    Weighting for a local option*

### 2.3.7   SAW: An Example

The use of SMARTS has been illustrated above. SMARTS, like SAW, is an additive model. The models have the same structure, but differ in some ways, such as in the normalization process.

In this example, a family wants to buy a new car. The family consists of Hugo and Elsy and their two children Hans (age five) and Lisa (age ten). Hugo thinks that he knows what the family needs – a sports coupé. It might be a bit crowded, but the road handling is fantastic. The decision, however, will be made by the entire family. They will sit down together and discuss what requirements the car should meet and what properties are most important. The majority immediately decide that the car should be a large- or medium-sized estate car. A sports coupé is out of the question, says Elsy, and a small car would not work. The size class of the car thus does not even need to be discussed. This simplifies the decision, which will still be rather difficult because there are around 20 possible cars to choose from. They therefore limit themselves to the following cars:

- Volvo V 60
- Renault Laguna
- Toyota Avensis
- Ford Mondeo
- VW Passat
- BMW 520
- Audi A 6

The family agrees that the car should have the following properties:

- low operating cost
- comfortable

- reliable
- eco-friendly
- collision-safe
- spacious

The scoring is shown in Figure 2.6 below. In this case, a total of 100 weight points have been distributed (fixed budget) on all criteria, of which there are seven. This weighting differs from that done with SMARTS in the location example, where 100 points were used for each criterion. Because fewer points are distributed than in the location example the assessment will be thicker and blunter. On the other hand, it also becomes easier. However, there may be a risk of bias and misleading results because knowing that there are a limited number of points may affect the distribution of them. Of course, it is even easier to use SAW if the assessment is made without using the swing method, that is, if the assessment is done without the control provided by the swing method. Presumably, professional legal decision-makers can make reliable intuitive assessments of each individual criterion. However, the swing method offers pointers for this.

The family agrees on the following weighting:

- purchase price, 30
- comfort, 10
- reliable, 15
- eco-friendly, 20
- collision-safe, 15
- spacious, 10

This provides the following table:

| Car purchase | | | | | | | |
|---|---|---|---|---|---|---|---|
| | Cost | Comfort | Reliability | Eco-friendly | Collision-safe | Spacious | Total |
| Volvo V 60 | 84 | 80 | 70 | 90 | 90 | 90 | 84 |
| Renault Laguna | 94 | 80 | 60 | 80 | 80 | 80 | 81 |
| Toyota Avensis | 100 | 70 | 90 | 80 | 80 | 80 | 87 |
| Ford Mondeo | 99 | 70 | 70 | 80 | 80 | 80 | 84 |
| VW Passat | 58 | 80 | 90 | 90 | 90 | 90 | 79 |
| BMW 520 | 28 | 90 | 80 | 90 | 90 | 80 | 69 |
| Audi A 6 | 0 | 90 | 80 | 90 | 90 | 90 | 62 |

*Figure 2.6   Car purchase*

Because the purchase price is important for the family, it has been given a weight of 30. Audi A 6 costs SEK 354000 and is most expensive, which gives it 0 points. The Toyota Avensis has the lowest purchase price at SEK 213000, and has therefore been given 100 points. The scores for the different cars are based on their price, which is inverted to obtain a value that enables a comparison. The basis for the assessment of each criterion can be obtained from car tests in motor magazines, which include results from crash tests, fuel consumption, comfort, and so on. The final calculation of points is then done using the formula shown below. As Figure 2.6 shows, the winner is Toyota Avensis with 87 points. The Audi A 6 comes in last at 62 points.[96]

### 2.3.7.1  Combine weights and scores

With scoring and weighting, the decision-maker gets a measurement of how each option works with respect to each criterion and a weighting that makes it possible to compare the relative values of different criteria. The next step will be to calculate how well each option works overall. This is done by using SAW and the formula:

$$S_i = w_1 s_{i1} + w_2 s_{i2} + \ldots + w_n s_{in} = \sum_{j=1}^{n} w_j s_{ij} \qquad (2.1)$$

Expressed in words, the formula is: multiply the score for an option with the weight of a criterion. Do the same for all criteria. Then add up all of these totals to get the overall preference for the option. Repeat the procedure for all of the options.[97] The formula might look complicated, but it is actually easy to use.[98]

---

[96]  I wrote this example about four years ago, with the car prices prevailing then. The inverted value is based on these car prices. A car purchase is a common example in literature of multi-dimensional analysis to illustrate the use of SAW or SMARTS. In Lootsma (Ch 1 n 2) 36ff is another such example, but with other values and calculations than in this example. Overall, the literature shows that the calculations can differ somewhat, which then means that certain deviations have been made from the basic model, often with the aim of refining it. The results with different models, however, show little difference.

[97]  Dodgson and others (Ch 1 n 2) 65, Goodwin and Wright (Ch 1 n 2) 51 and Belton and Stewart (Ch 1 n 2) 120.

[98]  Vincent Mousseau, 'Eliciting Information Concerning Importance of Criteria' in Pardalos, Yannos and n Zopounidis (n 39).

### 2.3.7.2 A simple judicial example

The interested reader who has managed to read this far, may be wondering how SAW could be used in a legal context. To demonstrate this, I will once again refer to the example at Figure 2.2 above with 36 AvtL.[99]

The options are to set aside (A) or modify (B) the clause. These options will be ranked on a scale of 1–9, where 9 is the best and 0 is the worst. It should be reiterated here that it does not matter if the scale is from 0 to 9 or 0 to 100 or whatever else is preferred. As long as it is used consistently and the scales are comparable, the calculations will be correct. Again, a total of 100 weight points will be distributed.

It should be emphasized that this simple example is only intended to show how the simple additive model works or can work formally, structurally and mathematically in a legal context. In the example, fraud and disproportion (legal facts) have been given nine points each on option A (set aside the clause) and eight and seven points respectively for option (B) modification. The weights are given at the bottom of the matrix. The relative weight of disproportion is 0.4. Disproportion has thus been deemed to be manifest. Had the relative weight of disproportion been deemed to be 0.15 and the price drop to 0.55, this would show that the price drop had been assessed to be the heaviest criterion. The decision-maker can change the input values and work interactively with the figure until he or she is satisfied with the assessment that has been made. As Figure 2.8 shows, the totals are obtained by multiplying the weight with the score for each criterion $0.4 \times 9 + 0.3 \times 9 + 0.3 \times 7 = 8.4$ and the same procedure for option B.

It can of course be seen as a major problem that 'unreasonable' as a prerequisite is vague because it can be difficult to determine both what concrete

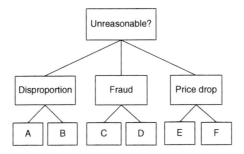

*Figure 2.7    Decision tree – unreasonable*

---

99   See section 2.3.3.1, above.

| Unreasonable | | | |
|---|---|---|---|
| | Disproportion | Fraud | Price drop | Total |
| A | 9 | 9 | 7 | 8.4 |
| B | 8 | 7 | 8 | 7.7 |
| Weight | 0.4 | 0.3 | 0.3 | |

*Figure 2.8    Unreasonable*

circumstances (legal facts) are relevant and what weight these should have. In this way, this assessment differs from many of the criteria in the car purchase, which are measurable. However, it is similar to criteria such as 'image' in the location option in the office acquisition example or 'nice design' as an important criterion in a car purchase. The opinion expressed in this book is that a structured and numerical assessment is better than an intuitive total appraisal, even if the input values are entirely based on subjective assessments. In the structured method, each criterion must be carefully assessed and then the criteria must be investigated to determine whether they are mutually independent. This helps ensure a fair impact of all factors in the overall assessment. When the input values are subjectively assessed, the results are admittedly more uncertain than if the data is measurable, but the combined weighted result is not intuitively determined but based on mathematical rules. Because of this, intuition will have its impact only on one stage in the analysis and not affect the overall assessment of them.[100]

### 2.3.8   Examine the Results – Sensitivity Analysis

Belton and Stewart give three perspectives on the sensitivity analysis: the technical, the individual and the group perspective. In the technical perspective, the weights and scores input into the model are compared with the results. The comparison will show which input values are significantly important for the results. A minor modification of these can change the ranking order that has been set for the options. The sensitivity analysis can thus give the decision-maker cause to more closely consider the input values.[101] In the individual perspective, the results provided by the model can be compared with the decision-maker's intuition. Do they seem to match, or not? If not, perhaps something has been miscalculated and scored or weighted too high or too low.[102] If decisions are made in a group, the

---

[100]   See also section 3.5, below.
[101]   Belton and Stewart (Ch 1 n 2) 148.
[102]   Ibid.

participants' scoring and weighting can be compared, which can lead to the incorporation of additional decision options and criteria into the model.[103]

In judicial processes, the legal values are usually subjectively determined and the decision basis on the whole is often not measurable. This can lead to the results seeming uncertain, which can mean that the criteria should be further clarified.[104] If a somewhat modified assessment of points and weights leads to the same decision options coming up all the time (though perhaps not in the same order) and the difference between the options is not significant, it may not matter much which option is chosen. Another important observation, which will be shown in the sentencing example,[105] is that a slight change in the score and/or weight of some criteria does not have any impact on the final results (in that example). This makes it clear which criteria are the most important.[106] The sensitivity analysis can then be focused on these and other criteria, in that one can try to change the scores and weights to see how much is required for the results to change. This can make it easier to 'calibrate' an assessment that seems reasonable.

## 2.4  SUMMARY AND CONCLUSIONS

Because MCA is intended for decision problems with multiple objectives, options and criteria, the premise is that it can also be used for balancing of interests and overall assessments in a legal context. Multi-criteria analysis, MCA, simplifies problem structuring and analysis and constitutes decision support. The last stage in MCA involves a final recommendation with a ranking of the options from best to worst. Because MCA is a method to facilitate good decisions, it disregards a number of circumstances in order to highlight what is characteristic in a decision situation. Furthermore, MCA does not provide an 'objective' solution, freeing the decision-maker from the responsibility of making a well-considered decision in a complex situation.

There are several MCA methods, which are briefly described in this chapter. There are also other decision-making methods besides MCA, such as the cost/benefit model. In addition, different MCA models can provide different results. For example, outranking can give a different result than the simple additive model because it is based on the comparison

[103]  Ibid.
[104]  Cf Dodgson and others (Ch 1 n 2) 68, Keeny and Raiffa (Ch 1 n 4) 100.
[105]  Below, section 4.5.
[106]  Cf Dodgson and others (ch 1 n 2) 69.

of criteria and options in pairs. This, in turn, can provide a different result than the analytical hierarchy model. Even if the final results do not differ much from model to model, it is important to see MCA as an analysis tool and decision support. If the results seem strange, the reasons for this can usually be discovered by performing a sensitivity analysis. It might, for example, be so because the objectives or criteria have not been defined well enough or that there is dependence between the preferences for the various options with regard to the selected decision criteria.

The general MCA model contains a number of steps which have been described: determine the objectives and decision context; identify the options to be assessed; identify criteria for assessment, scoring and weighting; add up the scores and weights; and perform a sensitivity analysis. In this chapter, several simple examples of the application of SMARTS and SAW have been provided in order to concretize MCA, particularly in regard to scoring and weighting.

If the input data is not carefully analysed and thought out, the results of the analysis will be misleading. The difficulty in using MCA does not lie in the mathematics (at least not if the simple additive model is used), but rather in the analysis that precedes the input of values into the decision model. This difficulty relates to the fact that law is not a measurable science. However, MCA can be used even if scoring and weighting are based only on subjective ratings. It becomes easier to identify these subjective ratings if they are given numerical values. The basis for differences in opinion then also emerges more clearly and the decision-making process becomes transparent and open. The subjective appraisals of the decision-makers, even if they differ, will be reflected in the final position, and different appraisals for the scores and weights of criteria do not necessarily mean that the decision-makers are divided on what the final results should be.

The primary aim of MCA is to help the decision-maker gain insight into the problem situation and into his/her own and others' appraisals and attitudes regarding the problem in order to make an informed decision. To summarize, the method has the following merits (listed in no particular order):[107]

- it is a tool for handling multiple criteria pointing in different directions;
- it allows the decision-maker to structure a complex problem;
- it provides a special language for the discussion that may be formal or not formal;

---

[107]   Cf Mendoza, Macan and others (Ch 1 n 2).

- it integrates subjective values in a structured model;
- it makes it possible to handle subjective judgements in a structured decision model;
- it provides transparency because the decision-maker is forced to take a position on his or her own values as well as on others';
- it leads to more thoroughly considered decisions that can be more easily explained and justified than when using intuition;
- it is relatively simple to use.

# 3. Intuition

## 3.1 INTRODUCTION

Earlier in this book, intuition was compared and contrasted with the use of a structured decision-making method. The following chapter provides a brief overview of intuition.

Virtually everyone uses what is commonly referred to as intuition. However, there is no definitive answer on what intuition actually is. Instinct, on the other hand, is different than intuition. If someone puts their hand on a hot stove, they will pull their hand back instinctively, in self-preservation. If a box of matches is emptied out onto the floor and a person is asked to estimate the number of matches, they will make a rapid intuitive assessment. If the person is instead asked to count each match, it is a completely different thought process. In all likelihood, the result of the assessment will be correct if each match is counted, while a rapid intuitive estimate can lead to serious misjudgements. If, however, the person is asked to repeatedly intuitively assess the number of matches emptied onto the floor, and these are then counted, the intuitive estimate will improve after each experience. Gradually, the intuitive assessment therefore will become quite reliable because of the past experiences. At the end of the chapter, abbreviated decision paths, heuristics, are described. These are, among other things, based on that practice or past experiences leads to intuitive skill.

A court sometimes makes discretionary assessments. If, for example, under a prerequisite in a legislative rule, it will be determined if two courses of events essentially correspond, the judge can count how many factors in each course of event are the same and how many are different. If each course of events consists of five factors and three are the same, the judge may, based on this, determine if the courses of events essentially correspond to each other or not. This distinction, which has a concrete basis, is discretionary because there is no exact measuring stick. It is made intuitively within vague boundaries, but cannot be said to be arbitrary. Thus, in an assessment that is arbitrary there is more room to manoeuvre. Even if such an assessment is not completely free, at least the decision context will set some boundaries. However, in both cases, the intuitive elements in the assessments are based on an inference from the facts in the case or otherwise. As will be shown, 'pure' intuition is not inferred or is at least not considered to be.

In the Swedish Academy Glossary (SAOL), intuition is described approximately as follows:[1]

> *General description.* Philosophical and psychological term for contemplation; a particular type of perception and source of knowledge contrary to thinking and employing symbols; in terms of both regular sensory contemplation and, usually, of a perception that corresponds with or is deemed to correspond with the sensory contemplation in that what is perceived is immediately given.
> *Mystical and religious intuition.* An experience of the absolute or the divine; also perception where something appears as axiomatic or a priori essential; in Bergson's philosophy of a kind of spiritual incorporation in an object.
> *Genius intuition.* Vivid imagination replacing observation; more or less brilliant inspiration; ability to instinctively understand something correctly.
> *Artistic intuition.* The artistic imagination occurs in the strict scientific field with a divine-like gaze, like an inner clarity.

According to SAOL, there are thus different types of intuition, which will be described in more detail below.

## 3.2 DIFFERENT TYPES OF INTUITION

As shown above, intuition has, depending on its object, been described in different ways. Bergson's perception of intuition is not easy to explain. Bergson defines intuition as an independent mental function that makes it possible to understand life itself and its events. In addition, he compared the human with other animals and even with insects, which exist and survive without possessing intellect. Bergson believed that humans, unlike animals, use concepts and categories to understand the world and events in it. Furthermore, he argued that this understanding requires intuition and that the human being can make that intuition accessible.[2] For Bergson (and also Kant), intuition is the mental tool that makes it possible to translate reality into something objective or at least comprehensible.

---

[1]   The definitions provided in the dictionary have been shortened and divided into headings.

[2]   See GRS Mead, *Bergson's Intuition* (Kessinger Publishing 2010), which is a 34-page article taken from a book published in 1913, *Quests Old and New,* by the same author.

Generally speaking, one can say that the well-known philosophers usually mentioned in connection with intuition, such as Bergson, Kant, Spinoza and Husserl, to name a few, devoted their contemplations to attempting to explain our understanding or perception of reality and the relationship between how we perceive reality and the concepts we use to describe it. Although we know much more today about how our brains work than we did when these philosophers were writing, the old questions remain.

From the examples in the dictionary it is apparent that intuition can be divided into aesthetic intuition, religious intuition, genius intuition and moral institution. Aesthetic intuition is about beauty, perfection and rapture for the beautiful and perfect, whether it is the beauty of nature, a painting or a musical composition. The perception of beauty requires a high level of mental ability of the type that is sometimes attributed to intuition. The same applies to the artistic creation where the artist wants to depict or convey something.[3] Even religious intuition is discussed in the literature. The writings often return to the conviction of ascension to or an understanding of the spiritual or the absolute. This feeling is based on some type of spiritual experience that cannot be explained with intellect. What this feeling is, or more specifically, consists of, is the subject of much debate, at least among sceptics.[4]

Geniuses, that is, those with an intellect considerably greater than the masses and a higher intelligence than even highly intelligent people, have been the subject of considerable fascination and attention in studies on intuition. These studies show that several of known geniuses throughout history have toed the line between genius and madness. Some intellectual giants have even written themselves about how they think, Goethe and Spinoza for example. Wild, who refers to studies in the subject, argues that geniuses often become preoccupied with the problem they want to solve, that nothing exists for them other than this problem and that they become completely absorbed in it, often for a long period of time. Because all of their mental energy is focused on the problem, of which they cannot let go as 'normal' people would do, they develop a narrow intellectual focus that displaces the rest of reality. So suddenly, one day, they not only solve the problem, but maybe even advance an entirely new theory, provided of course that they do not go insane.

Spinoza gives the following examples on intuition:

---

[3]  KW Wild, *Intuition* (Cambridge University Press 1938) 133ff.
[4]  Ibid., 104ff.

Let three numbers be given to find the fourth, which is in the same proportion to the third as the second is to the first. Tradesmen without hesitation multiply the second by the third and divide the product by the first: either because they have not forgotten the rule which they received from the schoolmaster without any proof, or because they have often tried it with very small numbers, or by conviction of the proof of Prop. 19, Bk. 7 of Euclid's *Elements*, namely, the common property of proportional. But in very small numbers there is no need of this, for when the numbers 1, 2, 3 are given, who is there who could not see that the fourth proportional is 6? And this is much clearer because we conclude the fourth number from the same ratio which intuitively we see that the first bears to the second.[5]

Very rapid comprehension can be perceived as an intuitive ability. In such cases, all people with a very high intelligence would automatically be intuitive. This is, however, not what Spinoza would seem to be saying. Even if he is not explicit, his example raises questions on whether intuition, as with Bergson, is a priori and absolute, whether it is an immediate and aesthetic form of knowledge, or whether it is moral or intellectual.[6] In the quote above, Spinoza asks the rhetorical question: who cannot see that the fourth number is a proportion? People generally have a sense for proportions. This sense, which may be genetic, is important not only in art and mathematics, but also in moral judgements.

In modern literature, intuition has through empirical research become more connected with rationality and logic than with mysticism. The premises for intuition that we encounter with philosophers such as Kant, however, remain. Robert Audi accordingly specifies the following four criteria for intuition:

- it must not be inferred, that is, grounded in premises;
- the feeling must be strong and clear, an unshakable conviction;
- the object of the feeling must be understood;
- intuition is not dependent on hypotheses or theories.[7]

---

[5] Spinoza, I Everyman edition, Wild, ibid., 21.
[6] Wild, ibid., 22.
[7] Robert Audi, *The Good in the Right. A Theory of intuition and Intrinsic value* (Princeton University Press 2004) 35. Cf Thomas Baldwin, 'The Three Phases of Intuitionism' in Philip Stratton-Lake (ed.) *Ethical Intuitionism. Re-evaluations* (Clarendon Press 2006), who writes that: (1) the concepts involved should be clear and distinct; (2) the principles should be reflectively self-evident; (3) the principles should be consistent; and (4) the principles should command general consent. The premises of the intuition should thus be obvious and not require any proof.

That intuition must not be inferred does not, according to Audi, exclude that an intuitive conviction can be based on a premise. However, at the moment the intuitive conviction arises it may not be inferred.[8] The intuitive conviction must furthermore be strong enough to form a judgement that something must be a certain way. As Audi himself points out, there could however be a grey zone where an intuitive feeling can turn into an intuitive conviction.[9] For example, if I see shapes in the fog of what looks like a dog, I may become convinced that it is a dog when the fog lifts, or else I may become convinced that it is a large cat. In this example, the intuitive feeling is based on some vague premises. It also implies that an intuitive conviction can disappear if something emerges that makes me doubt my conviction.

The question on premises and inference recurs in the determination of moral intuition. Sinnott-Armstrong has defined moral intuition as follows:

> I define a 'moral intuition' as a strong immediate moral belief. 'Moral' beliefs are beliefs that something is morally right or wrong, good or bad, virtuous, and so on for other moral predicate [. . .] Moral intuitions in this sense might arise after reflection on the facts of the situation. They might result from moral appearances that are not full beliefs. Nonetheless, they are not inferred from those facts or appearances. The facts only specify which case the intuition is about. The appearances merely make acts seem morally right or wrong.[10]
>
> There are only two ways for moral intuitions or any other beliefs to be justified:
> A belief is justified inferentially if and only if it is justified only because the believer is able to infer it from some other belief.
> A belief is justified noninferentially if and only if it is justified independently of whether the believer is able to infer it from any other belief.
> Whether a belief is justified inferentially or noninferentially depends not on whether the believer *actually* bases the belief in an actual inference but instead on whether the believer is *able* to infer that belief from other beliefs.[11]

Michael Huemer has stated on ethical (or moral) intuition:

> Reasoning sometimes changes how things seem to us. But there is also a way things seem to us prior to reasoning; otherwise, reasoning could not get

---

[8]   Audi, ibid., 33.
[9]   Ibid., 34, 66–77.
[10]   Walter Sinnott-Armstrong, 'Framing Moral Institutions' in Walter Sinnott-Armstrong (ed.) *Moral Psychology Volume 2, The Cognitive Science of Morality: Intuition and Diversity* (The MIT Press 2008).
[11]   Ibid. Also see William Tolhurst, 'Moral Institutions Framed' in *Moral Psychology Volume 2* (n 10), who says that 'in the absence of adequate reasons to believe they are reliable, suspending belief is the best response'.

started. The way things seem to reasoning we may call an 'initial appearance'. An initial, intellectual appearance is an 'intuition' [. . .] An ethical intuition is an intuition whose content is an evaluative proposition [. . .] Here are some examples in ethics:

Employment is better than suffering.

If A is better than B and B is better than C, then A is better than C.

It is unjust to punish a person for a crime he did not commit.

Courage, benevolence, and honesty are virtues.

Here are some examples of ethical claims that, I take it, are not intuitive, even for those who believe them:

The United States should not have gone to war in Iraq in 2003.

We should privatize Social Security.

Abortion is wrong.

Though these propositions seem to be true to some, the relevant appearances do not count as 'intuitions' because they depend on other beliefs.[12]

The quotes, which are taken from modern literature, describe views that frequently recur, with smaller or larger modifications. They include examples that most would agree with, such as that it would be wrong to punish someone for a crime the person did not commit. However, they also contain stumbling blocks. The idea that intuition is a conviction that something is true or right without it being possible to infer this feeling from empirical facts begs, for example, the question of how it is possible to determine if intuition is inferred. Because an intuitive feeling that something is true or right is a subjective feeling originating from the assessor's own unconscious, there are no criteria from which it can be determined if intuition is inferred or if it is 'standing on its own feet'. Moreover, it seems surprising that Huemer attributes the axiom of transitivity to ethics.

In the administration of justice, valuations have been encapsulated in laws that may seem unjust. 'Abortion is wrong', Huemer says is not an 'intuition' because the valuation is based on other convictions. If abortion is prohibited by law, however, this is not a conviction but a fact. Virtues such as 'courage', 'benevolence' and 'honesty' are furthermore created by people, that they have had different connotations throughout history and that the meanings of these words are culturally conditioned. They are also contextual, just as ethics in general appear to be contextual. The woman who kills the man who beat and tortured her for years is in a way courageous, but, of course, she is not honoured for this courage. And the right thing to do may be to withhold an unpleasant truth rather than to reveal it.

A specific issue is addressed below, which deals with whether the

---

[12]   Michael Huemer, *Ethical Intuitionism* (Palgrave Macmillan 2005) 101–2.

assessment of cause-effect can be kept separate from moral assessments. This question is illustrated with the following example:

> Lauren and Jane work for the same company. They each need to use a computer for work sometimes. Unfortunately, the computer isn't very powerful. If two people are logged on at the same time, it usually crashes. So, the company decided to institute an official policy. It declared that Lauren would be the only one permitted to use the computer in the mornings and that Jane would be the only one permitted to use the computer in the afternoons. As expected, Lauren logged on the computer the next day at 9.00 am. But Jane decided to disobey the official policy. She also logged on at 9.00 am. The computer crashed immediately.[13]

In this case, most people would say that Jane caused the computer crash by logging on in contravention of the official policy, although her behaviour is otherwise essentially the same as Lauren's. It seems then that normative human judgements may have implications in the assessment of causality.[14] Below is another example.

> The receptionist in the philosophy department keeps her desk stocked with pens. The administrative assistants are allowed to take the pens, but faculty members are supposed to buy their own. The administrative assistants typically do take their pens. Unfortunately, so do the faculty members. The receptionist has repeatedly emailed them reminders that only administrative assistants are allowed to take the pens. On Monday morning, one of the administrative assistants encounters Professor Smith walking past the receptionist's desk. Both take pens. Later that day, the receptionist needs to take an important message. . . but she has a problem. There are no pens left on her desk.[15]

The examples are plausible, but as Julia Driver herself shows, there are – hardly surprisingly – objections. These objections vary in nature and I will not delve further into them but only mention a few. One criticism is based on the premise that omission cannot cause something. Another on the premise that some consequences are unavoidable in a certain situation: if John leaves a room, Lisa will be the shortest person remaining in the room. But has John caused this, and if so, in what sense? There is also a discussion on the order in which the moral blame and causality is assessed: is the cause-effect assessed first and then the moral blame, or does the moral blame come first and then the determination of the cause? It might

---

[13]   Julia Driver, 'Attributions of Causations and Moral Responsibility' in *Moral Psychology Volume 2* (n 10).

[14]   Ibid.

[15]   Joshua Knobe and Ben Frazer, 'Casual Judgment and Moral Judgment: Two Experiments' in *Moral Psychology Volume 2* (n 10).

seem most likely here that there must first be a reason, but there are different views on this.[16] The described problems are not unknown in legal contexts, for example, it may be easy in an action for damages to confuse the duty of care with the standard of proof.[17]

## 3.3  PARALLEL THOUGHT PROCESSES

In modern research, intuition has become increasingly linked to logic and rationality and has experienced a renaissance and gained credence. Some recent research is based on experiments in which people were made aware of a large number of sequential factors which they were given opportunity to carefully study in order to make a decision. When the study method instead involved giving the study participants information on a great deal of facts and then asked them to make spontaneous decisions, it was found that: 'spontaneous judgements and decisions can indeed reflect the total of prior experiences rather than a subset of information'.[18]

The findings further suggest that intuition is an automatic process that is partially or sometimes completely unconscious.[19] This automatic process is fuelled by a reservoir of life experience accumulated over the years. This experience provides a judgement that is not based on the recollection and analysis of each individual factor in a person's memory bank. The foundation of life experience instead produces a feeling of how something should be. Concurrently with the use of the reservoir of life experience, which provides an intuitive feeling of how something should be, the problem can be processed intellectually.[20] It then becomes a matter of parallel thought processes, the one based immediately on intuition, the other containing cognitive processes. Kahneman calls these parallel processes 'step 1' and 'step 2'.[21]

---

[16]  For further discussion, see Driver (n 13).

[17]  Regarding the relationship between duty of care and standard of proof, see Bengt Lindell, *Civilprocessen – rättegång samt skiljeförfarande och medling* (Iustus 2012) 524.

[18]  Tilmann Betsch, 'The Nature of Intuition and its Neglect in Research on Judgment and Decision Making' in Henning Plessner, Cornelia Betsch and Tilmann Betsch (eds) *Judgment and Decision Making* (LEA 2008).

[19]  Ibid., 6, Minna Gräns, *Decisio Juris* (Iustus 2013) 194.

[20]  Daniel Kahneman, *Tänka snabbt och långsamt* (Månpocket/Fakta 2014) 29ff, cf Simon (Ch 2 n 2) 133, who says that intuition is also used by professional chess players, who have stored a great deal of information about chess in their brains – information that is used intuitively.

[21]  Cf (Simon, ibid., 131, who talks about 'Split Brains and the Forms of Thought.'

There is thus some research suggesting that intuition is underrated in the sense that it would provide poorer results than an analysis and empirically confirms the thesis of parallel thought processes.[22] However, Kahneman still regards intuition with a certain degree of distrust due to certain errors in thought people often make, as the example below is intended to illustrate.

> An individual has been described by a neighbour as follows: 'Steve is very shy and withdrawn, invariably helpful but with little interest in people or in the world of reality. A meek and tidy soul, he has a need for order and structure, and a passion for detail.' Is Steve more likely to be a librarian or a farmer?[23]

In this example, most people spontaneously reply that Steve is a librarian. However, what most people fail to consider is that, at least in the US, there are far more farmers than librarians. The statistically probable answer should therefore be 'farmer'. Regardless of statistics, there is also a stereotypical image of librarians that contributes to the oversight. This is just one example of mistakes or distortions people make. Kahneman gives many more examples of this.[24]

When it comes to legal assessments, the situation concerning the use of intuition is different compared to non-inferred moral convictions and automatic processes with spontaneous decisions because a court is always presented with certain facts on which it bases its decision. These facts are often assessed intuitively, but because the intuitive assessment is based on facts, it is inferred. A court must furthermore usually justify its decisions and meet the requirements for foreseeability and non-discrimination. In the judgement, an automatic process therefore must be combined with an analytical process.

Intuitive assessments based on fact and general life experience are often found in balancing of interests and overall assessments. What is distinctive in these situations is that the court has a large number of factors to take into account. Judges and other decision-makers also use heuristics, which will be discussed further below. If MCA is used, it is easier to discover the nature of these, because the decision basis is broken down into smaller parts and each criterion for the ruling is given a score and weight.

---

[22]  Ibid.
[23]  Kahneman (n 20) 14.
[24]  Ibid., 14ff.

## 3.4  HEURISTICS – SHORTCUTS TO DECISIONS

There is a difference between how decisions are actually made and decisions under different normative decision models.[25] Psychological research has shown that decision-makers cannot assimilate more than a handful of factors in their decision-making.[26] Heuristics are simplified and shortened forms of reasoning that contain intuitive elements.[27] In a heuristic decision model, people in decision-making situations often take the easy road by following some rule of thumb that determines the decision. There is no question of a meticulously constructed model for decision-making, but rather heuristics simply describe what to do. The simplification of the decision-making process has, it has sometimes been explained, that people are not always rational. If this is true, then we humans are not intellectually equipped to handle complex decisions. For this reason, researchers have criticized Kahneman and Tversky and others, arguing that on the whole, we can handle even difficult decision-making situations and are largely effective decision-makers.

In this context it should be mentioned that Simon uses the expression bounded rationality to describe how the brain's limited ability to handle large amounts of information leads to approximative methods for handling decision problems, which we are more likely to find 'satisficing' than optimal solutions.[28] I will return to this below and in section 3.6. A brief example of shortened decision paths is given below.[29]

### 3.4.1  The Recognition Heuristic

In this case, it is assumed that a choice must be made between two options. For example, a camera will be purchased and a choice must be made between two brands, one of which is well known and the other is new on the market. The strategy means that the well-known brand is chosen because it is recognized and associated with quality, while the

---

[25]  Heuristics are discussed in detail by Gräns (n 19), where they are connected to legal decision-making.

[26]  Goodwin and Wright (Ch 1 n 2) 13.

[27]  Gräns (n 19) 62, which refers to studies conducted by Kahneman and Tversky in the 1970s.

[28]  Herbert A Simon, *Models of Bounded Rationality. Empirically Grounded Economic Reason* (The MIT Press 1982) 291ff.

[29]  See for the following Gerd Gigerenzer, Peter Todd and the ABC Research Group, *Simple Heuristics That Make Us Smart* (Oxford University Press 1999) 37ff and Goodwin and Wright (Ch 1 n 2) 14ff.

other feels more uncertain, even though it may be just as good as the known brand.

### 3.4.2  The Minimalist Strategy

The decision-maker first tries with recognition, but if none of the options are known, a factor is randomly selected that differentiates between the options, and this discriminating factor becomes decisive for the choice if it represents something positive; for example, the camera with the larger digital zoom will be selected.

### 3.4.3  Take the Last

This is a minimalist strategy. Instead of selecting a random criterion that discriminates between two options, the decision-maker chooses to do what they did the last time they were in a similar situation.

### 3.4.4  The Lexicographic Strategy

Sometimes the decision-maker can rank criteria in order of priority. When buying a car, the purchase price may be absolutely the most important factor. In this case, the least expensive car is chosen. If two cars have the same price, the decision-maker chooses the car that also meets the second most important criterion, and so on. Just like the other strategies, this strategy means that the decision is taken based on very limited data.

### 3.4.5  Elimination by Aspects, EBA

If this strategy is used, certain important criteria are identified at the same time that a limit is decided and options that do not reach this limit are eliminated. Price can, for example, be the most important factor for the purchase of a car: all cars that cost more than SEK 100000 are eliminated. The number of seats in the car may be the next important: two-seater sports cars are eliminated. Engine power may be the third most important: all cars under 1.6 litres are eliminated. The used car must not have too much mileage: cars with a mileage of over 100000 km are eliminated. The car's service history is the fifth most important: cars without service books are eliminated. Continuing in this manner, the list of potential cars can be narrowed down. EBA is easy to apply and explain for others. The strategy is not compensatory. A 1.5-litre car that meets all other criteria may be the best, but will not even be included as a potential option.

### 3.4.6 Sequential Decision-making: Satisficing

In the example above, all options (cars) are available at the same time. A family buying a home, however, often searches for a longer period of time for a house they like and goes to a lot of showings. Also they do not know what houses will be put up for sale in the future. In this case, the family looks until they have found a house they are satisfied with and that meets their needs ('satisficing'). The requirements the family has are thus the deciding factors because the search ends when these requirements have been met. However, the requirements can change during the search process, and may be lowered or raised.

### 3.4.7 Reason-based Choice

This strategy is used if the decision-maker needs to justify his or her decisions to others. A good example of this is courts that must justify their rulings in the reasons for the judgement.

### 3.4.8 Selection of Strategy

Important factors that affect what strategy is selected are:

- the time available to make the decision;
- the effort that a strategy entails;
- the decision-maker's knowledge of the decision situation;
- the weight of making a correct decision;
- whether or not the decision-maker needs to justify his or her decisions to others;
- the desire to minimize a conflict.[30]

As briefly discussed above, according to Simon, bounded rationality ends in something he calls 'The Satisficing Alternative'. Simon explains this concept as follows:

> Faced with a choice situation where it is impossible to optimize, or where the computational cost of doing so seems burdensome, the decision maker may look for a satisfactory, rather than an optimal alternative. Frequently, a course of action satisfying a number of constraints, even a sizeable number, is far easier to discover than a course of action maximizing some function.[31]

---

[30]  Goodwin and Wright (Ch 1 n 2) 21.
[31]  Simon (n 28) 295.

Simon argues that the satisfactory option can be technically converted into a process in which the costs for optimization are included. The problem then becomes that the decision-maker falls once again into a process that takes time and costs money.[32] These problems are not unknown in legal contexts, where they fall under the heading of investigative interest. Rödig speaks in this context of the principle of commensurability. He argues that there are two elements in the legal concept of truth: the true judgement and the costs for reaching this, and that these two elements must be weighed against each other.[33] Such weighting is also done in the legal world, though not according to any calculation but rather through pre-classification, for example abstention from prosecution and summary imposition of fines for less serious crimes because the state's costs for a full investigation and trial would be too high in relation to the value of materially accurate decisions in these minor criminal cases.

## 3.5   INTUITION VERSUS MATHEMATICS

One question that cannot be ignored in this chapter is whether mathematics can be fairly used in a legal context. Of course, it is not necessary to use numerical values in MCA and the simple additive model – a performance matrix can suffice instead. But if numerical values are used, can these really provide better and more reliable results than an intuitive overall assessment or balancing of interests? Is the law not too complex and multifaceted to make this possible? And are factors not always dependent on each other in some way and thus all must be assessed together? Every time it is suggested in jurisprudential literature that mathematical formulas should be used, this discussion arises. When Professor Tribe wrote his famous article 'Trial by Mathematics' in the *Harvard Law Review* in 1971, one of the things he attacked was Finkelstein and Fairley and their 1970 article in the same journal, 'A Baysesian Approach to Identification Evidence'. Part of Tribe's criticism, however, was directed against the use of mathematics in criminal cases in general. Today, several decades later, the arguments are still the same from both sides. Those attacking formalized assessment of evidence argue that the risk for mistakes is too great, that the mathematics are too complicated for judges who are not schooled in mathematics,

---

[32]   Ibid., 296.
[33]   Jürgen Rödig, *Die Theorie des gerichtlichen Erkenntnisverfahren: die Grundlinien des zivil-, straf- und verwaltungsgerichtlichen Prozesses* (Springer 1973) 160.

that it can seem inhumane, that it is not possible to combine established statistical frequencies with 'softer' evidence such as witness statements and that there is therefore a risk of overvaluing technical evidence. Supporters of formalized methods for the evaluation of evidence argue above all that it provides more accurate results. One difference today compared with the 1970s is that technical evidence has become increasingly common as technology has advanced. Consider DNA evidence, as just one example. The need for mathematics in the evaluation of evidence should therefore have increased.[34]

The question on the choice between intuition and mathematics has also been discussed in Swedish evidentiary literature. In 1975, Anders Stening wrote a dissertation entitled *Bevisvärde* (Evidentiary Value). In it, Stening argues that the discursive overall assessment using formulas cannot be more reliable than the intuitive assessed input component values, but that an intuitive combined weighting of the intuitive components yields even more unreliable results.[35] Stening further argues that the results provided by the formulas in the combined weighting itself should take precedence if an intuitive overall assessment gives different results. The reason for this is that the combined weighting is done according to logical rules, which do not require any empirical knowledge.[36] Ekelöf, who previously launched calculation rules and who was Stening's mentor, however, felt that the intuitive assessment of the whole should take precedence in contradictory results.[37]

The evaluation of evidence concerns assessing what has happened or what is likely to happen. How reliable it is depends on our knowledge of the actual situation. In this book, MCA is used in legal matters as decision support. MCA and the simple additive model are tools for making the best decisions possible when there is essentially no uncertainty regarding facts and when there are multiple options and criteria. While evidentiary models, such as the evidentiary value method and the evidentiary theme method, are used to calculate probabilities, SAW does not aim to establish the objective truth, but instead to say what is good and bad, important and unimportant. Consequently, the scoring and weighting that is done with SMARTS and SAW, for example, depend on

---

[34]   Ken Strutin, *Calculating Justice: Mathematics and Criminal Law*, <http://www.llrx.com/features/calculatingjustice.htm> (retrieved 8 July 2016).

[35]   Cf section 2.3.7.1, above.

[36]   Anders Stening, *Bevisvärde* (Acta Universitatis Upsaliensis, Studia Juridica Upsaliensia (1975) 29.

[37]   Per Olof Ekelöf, *Rättegång IV* (4th edn, PA Norstedt & Söners förlag 1977) 32.

the assessor's subjective appraisals, which may not be shared by others and actually need not be shared by others. Evaluation of evidence is, on the other hand, an objective activity in that a legal probability assessment must be approved by others if the ruling is not to be appealed. The MCA method chosen in this book, the simple additive model (SAW) is, I argue, easier to use and understand for a layman than many of the formulas that exist for evaluating evidence. Furthermore, the model's requirement for independence is not as strict as the evidentiary independence requirement.[38]

Thus, MCA does not provide a fixed and objective mathematical value that then automatically forms the basis for a decision. Instead, MCA is seen as a tool for analysis and decision support. Stirling and Meyer have aptly stated that MCA methods should rather be seen as a way to map problems than as methods that deliver a turnkey solution.

> In short, rather than using them to rationalise a particular uniquely 'objective' or otherwise ostensibly definitive position, multi-criteria appraisal methods can instead be used as a way of 'mapping' a risk debate. Here, the explicit separation of the concepts of relatively technical 'scores' and more openly subjective 'weightings' (an ideal common to all multi-criteria approaches) constitutes an especially important feature and establishes a significant precedent for the treatment of other dimensions of appraisal. Factors such as the scope of analysis, the framing of crucial assumptions and the treatment of uncertainties can also be handled in multi-criteria appraisal as a decision 'heuristic' offers a way of establishing the main contours in a risk debate and of clarifying key areas of dissent and convergence between different constituencies. When used in this fashion, a multi-criteria technique may be distinguished from the more conventional 'analytical fix' by referring to it as 'multi-criteria mapping' (MCM) approach.[39]

Even the fact that different MCA methods can provide different results means that the decision-maker must be careful.[40] If an intuitive assessment yields a different result than MCA, this may be due to an important factor being omitted or not described correctly.[41] Another reason could be that there is a dependence between different factors, which could then give a misleading value. There are of course many reasons other than

---

[38]   Cf section 2.3.3, above.
[39]   Sterling and Meyer (Ch 1 n 5) 13.
[40]   Similarly, different theoretical models for the evaluation of evidence can also yield different results.
[41]   See Goodwin and Wright (Ch 1 n 2) 54, which discusses 'conflict between holistic and analytic rankings'.

those listed here for there being a mismatch between the model and intuition, miscalculation for example. The premise, however, is that there should not be a conflict between the analytic model and intuition if the decision-makers have familiarized themselves with the axioms used in MCA.[42] If such conflicts still occur and do not go away, it may be that MCA is not suitable for solving or providing decision support for this particular problem.[43]

## 3.6   SUMMARY AND CONCLUSIONS

The concept of intuition is ancient. What it designates is probably as old as humankind itself. More modern research, most recently Kahneman, argues that intuition is about two parallel thought processes, one rapid as it is based on the person's cumulative life experience, the other slow because it is analytical and problemizing. Satisfactory, but not optimal, solutions ('satisficing') are the result of a sort of compromise between these ways of thinking. The notion of parallel thought processes has, along with empirical studies on how intuition works, given this greater credibility. Not that analytical processes can be replaced with intuition and that intuition would be 'harmless'. On the contrary, Kahneman's studies show that there is good reason to be wary of intuition, but this has been given its own place and upgraded scientifically.

Shortened decision paths or heuristics are not unknown in a legal context, but they express themselves differently. Considering the extensive number of legal decisions that are made every day, there must naturally be a large number of rules that in different ways simplify both administration and decision-making. The decision options may be limited in advance. There may also be in dubio rules of different types. Even the ambiguity rule could be said to be a heuristic, as well as presumptions based on how things usually are. Overall, there are a very many rules for how to manage legal decision-making, including simply excluding possible approaches in advance.

What Simon calls 'satisficing' would seem to be of great importance in making judgments. Over the years, experienced judges have built up a huge bank of knowledge and experience, with which they can quickly identify what issues are relevant and which are not relevant. Through this experience, even important issues in a very big and complex case

---

[42]   Ibid.
[43]   Ibid.

are therefore quickly identified. This process is intuitive precisely because there is so much information stored in the judge's brain. If the judge were to be asked about similar cases, we could not expect that he or she could recall all of the cases and events this intuitive feeling is based on.

The judge is thus an expert and can therefore quickly identify legal problems. If someone who does not have this expert knowledge were forced to delve into these issues, it could take a lot of time. And the cost would be high. One danger of professionalism might be that the cases that deviate from the usual pattern could run the risk of being judged incorrectly. Another risk is that routine decreases vigilance. And then there are the pitfalls that Kahneman described, which are often associated with preconceptions. Moreover, professionalism in the adjudication process does not guarantee optimal or even 'satisfying' decisions in each and every case. The courts handle a lot of cases and matters every day, which means everything is not always correct. The possibility of appeal and review dispensation shows that legislators have anticipated this. If all court rulings were allowed to be appealed to an appellate court, more rulings would be changed, even if no new information or evidence came forward. And if all cases could be appealed and tried by the Supreme Court, even more rulings would be changed. It is not, however, necessary for each individual case to have an optimal resolution. It is enough that they are settled in a satisfactory way.

Whether or not the different formal decision methods can yield different results, which may also be contrary to an intuitive assessment, in the end the question must be asked: Does intuition provide a better result? Intuition does not provide transparency and clarity and can entail significant risks, such as bias. However, at the same time, intuition is important for MCA and the simple additive model, SAW, being able to be used in legal overall assessments and balancing of interests, because numerical scoring and weighting of individual legal facts must usually be intuitive. Because the total combined weighting with SAW is performed according to logical rules and not intuitively, however, intuition will not have a double impact. Here, there is a clear parallel to the previous discussion on Stening's reasoning on intuition and the use of formulas in the evaluation of evidence.

Intuition and formal analysis coexist well together. One might say that, purely practically, intuition and structural analysis work interactively together in the sensitivity analysis, because the decision-maker, with the help of intuition, can change and adjust the values that have been inserted in the model. This does not mean that scoring, weighting and numerical calculation are unnecessary because intuition will always win out. Instead, it means that intuition can be challenged. If an intuitive overall assessment leads to another result than a correctly performed MCA analysis, there is every reason to carefully reflect on why this may be. It may prove to be that the initial intuitive overall assessment or balancing of interests was not reasonable. Or that it was.

# 4. Legal examples of decision-making with SAW

## 4.1 INTRODUCTION

This chapter will first provide an overview of the decision process under RB before the court's ruling in a case. A brief description will then be provided of how process materials are structured under RB to be manageable, and it will be shown how this is part of a rather complicated decision process. The aim is to clarify decision aspects of well-known procedural law concepts and principles and demonstrate how MCA can be adapted into this decision process. MCA and the simple additive model, SAW, will then be applied in three overall assessments. The first example describes a hypothetical procedural situation with respect to the choice between video conferencing and a court hearing. The other, which describes a civil action, concerns the application of 36 AvtL. The third example concerns a decision on penalty in a criminal case: prison or suspended sentence. Examples two and three are based on actual legal cases from the Supreme Court – NJA 1999 p. 408 and NJA 1997 p. 652. The use of these has both advantages and disadvantages. One advantage of course is that these are real cases that show practically how SAW could have been used in practice. One disadvantage could be that the outcome of the assessments is known through the pronounced judgements, which may have affected the assessments that are done in the analyses. Furthermore, this chapter also presents and provides an introduction on fuzzy logic, which is applied along with SAW in NJA 1999 p. 408.

## 4.2 RB AS DECISION PROCESS

RB contains a number of concepts, principles and legal constructions as well as concrete procedural rules, which focus on decision-making. However, it is only the voting rules that immediately address the fact that different members of the court have different opinions about how the case should be determined. Concerning overall assessments, balancing of interests and vague and indeterminate prerequisites, such as 'the best

*Figure 4.1     Court decision process*

interests of the child' or 'unreasonable' under 36 AvtL, it is not possible
to vote specifically on the concrete legal facts that constitute the necessary conditions in question. Under the voting rules, it is deemed to be
too complicated to put them up for separate vote. It is, however, always
possible to vote on different legal alternatives (options). If, for example,
parents disagree on who should have custody of the child – and shared
custody is out of the question – MCA can be used to support the analysis
and as decision support, before any vote is taken on the choice of legal
alternatives (custody to the father or the mother) under the rules for this
in RB. As far as 36 AvtL is concerned, the alternatives are to modify the
agreement clause, to set aside the agreement clause, or to set aside the
entire agreement. Another option, of course, is to disapprove the statement of claim so that the signed and challenged agreement remains intact
and in force.

Figure 4.1 shows a simplified description of the decision process in
court. Material is collected before the process by the parties. This is
adapted to the terms and concepts of procedural law and forms the
basis of the parties' positions and evidence. The outcome is a ruling – an
output – which has been placed outside the box to highlight the results of
the process.

An important objective for the administration of justice is that the decisions should be substantively accurate. A number of fundamental procedural principles exist for achieving this objective, such as the principle of
free evaluation of evidence, the principle of the best evidence, the principle
of immediateness, the principle of oral proceedings and the principle of
a concentrated hearing. These principles are also intended to promote a
fast and effective procedure. They also simplify – more or less – decision-
making. The principle of a concentrated main hearing, for example, makes
it easier to review the process material. RB also contains rules that are not
directly aimed at ensuring a substantively accurate judgment, but rather at
clarifying and structuring the process material. A few important rules and
concepts regarding this are briefly described below.

The judge is entitled to intervene in the case and ask questions with
respect to disputed issues – direction of proceedings – in order to clarify
what is in dispute in the case and what the parties want to allege. In

cases amenable to out-of-court settlement, the requirement for allegation requires even small parts of the course of events to be expressly alleged so that the other party knows what he or she must provide defence against and so that the framework of the proceedings becomes fixed. Furthermore, concrete legal facts must also be proved, if they are contentious. Direction of proceedings may, depending on the circumstances, either extend or limit the court's decision basis. Concessions and admissions in cases amenable to out-of-court settlement make further investigation superfluous and thus limit the investigation.

The plaintiff's claim for relief and the substantive legal facts alleged to support it, which is usually called the foundation of the claim, constitutes a cause of action. On closer examination, the foundation is composed of several different concrete legal facts. This is true in particular with respect to balancing of interests and overall assessments. Furthermore, if the plaintiff claims a sum of money from the defendant, the plaintiff can also have alleged first, that they had entered into an oral agreement, second, that an agreement was concluded by implication and third, that the agreement arose through passivity on behalf of the other party. In this case, three grounds or foundations have been alleged as support for the same claim. Each contains details on the manner in which the agreement was entered. Furthermore, even if the legal facts in the different foundations overlap each other, they belong to three separate legal foundations for the claim. This is basically due to the fact that civil law recognizes these three different ways in which an agreement can be entered. Consequently, the court will examine each legal ground separately. In addition, if the members of the bench have dissenting opinions with respect to which, if any, necessary condition or legal ground is met, separate votes can be taken on each of them. This situation thus differs from the application of the prerequisite 'unreasonable' above, where there is only one prerequisite (legal ground), and separate voting with respect to individual legal facts is not allowed.

The aim of breaking down a disputed general fact into smaller units through the requirement in 17:3 RB, that the judgement may not be based on circumstances other than those alleged by a party as the foundation of the action, is to create a clear structure adapted to the procedural rule system. In general, breaking down a general fact into smaller parts is good and also necessary, if it is disputed. In addition, it is the legislator's view that breakdown rules sometimes are good for decision-making. Smaller parts can then be put together to form something larger. Joinder of claims is a good example of this. Different units – claims – are brought together for joint adjudication if they are connected.

A claim must contain components that either give rise to a legal consequence or establish a legal relationship. As mentioned above, if different claims have a connection with each other, it is generally advantageous to combine them to joint adjudication in the same judicial process. In RB, the related condition may be that it is 'essentially the same ground' that forms the basis for the different claims. Only if there is a common denominator or at least some connection between the foundations for the claims, there is an advantage with joint adjudication. This helps prevent, for example, taking the same testimony or evidence twice. Furthermore, fewer appearances in court will be necessary, and proceedings will be faster and cheaper.

In the joinder of claims, the trial will thus deal with something larger than if the cases were adjudicated separately in two or more judicial processes. Joinder is due to practical considerations. This refers not to the possibility of making well-balanced decisions, which is likely aggravated if the judicial process is extended too much through a joinder of claims. However, cases can be separated again, if the joinder is optional under 14:6 RB. On the other hand, the concentration principle is generally promoted in the event of a joinder. From a decision standpoint, joinders are normally seen as an advantage. Conflicting rulings are then also avoided.

While joinder of claims usually requires the foundations of the claims to be essentially the same, or at least that there is some connection between the different parts, there is no similar requirement for changing the 'matter at issue' in accordance with 13:3 paragraph 3 RB. At least according to Ekelöf's theory on the identity of the disputed matter, the plaintiff may allege a completely new course of events to support the same claim without changing the matter at issue. Thus, the plaintiff can allege a new independent course of events as a ground for the same claim without there being any connection between this course of events and the original. If the plaintiff, on the other hand, presents an additional claim arising from this new course of events, the claims cannot be joined if there is no connection between the courses of events. For a joinder to be possible, pursuant to 13:3 paragraph 1 (3) RB, the plaintiff's new claim must, as mentioned, be based on 'essentially the same ground'. Thus, the legal term claim and disputed matter is central in RB, in particular with respect to res judicata, and should therefore be thoroughly defined. The same applies for the condition(s) that constitute the connecting necessary conditions. If the definitions do not work, neither will the system.

Through an intermediate judgement, the entire claim can be decided. An intermediate judgment refers to an issue of relevance for the rest of the case. For example, the plaintiff alleges in the first place that no contract has been entered between him and the opposing party, and second, that the contract, if deemed to be entered, is not valid because of fraud. In this situation, the court can render a judgment on either of these legal facts in accordance with 17:5 RB, if it believes that the case thereby will finally be settled. This involves a prognostic assessment that is often difficult to make; will an intermediate judgement resolve the case or will it be appealed and cause delay. Furthermore, a declaratory judgement refers to something bigger than a performance judgement, but a judgement can, on the other hand, refer to something small. In arbitration, for example, it is possible to pick out a single piece of evidence or a single legal fact and be awarded arbitration based on this fact, which is convenient if this resolves the entire dispute. However, this fact may, after the award, need to be considered by the court in a new legal context. In this latter case, it may prove that the result was not at all what the party had in mind.

The question of whether the quality of the judgement will be better or worse from a substantive standpoint if the process is entertained in one way or the other is not empirically investigated. One difficulty in this context is defining in a meaningful way what is 'better' and what is 'worse' from a substantive point of view. What can be said, however, is that the rules of judicial procedure are carefully thought out and have advantages. They are also tried and tested for a long period of time. It should also be mentioned that different modern rules of judicial procedure are rather similar in an international context. That there are differences between countries, for example regarding the use of written procedure can, of course, be a rather significant difference, but does not change the common fundamental features.

According to this brief summary of RB's structure, it could be said from a decision theory perspective that RB works with multiple aims and multiple building blocks, of which the quality of the judgement is an important aspect. It was previously shown in this book that MCA does not conflict with RB on overall assessments and balancing of interests if multiple different concrete legal facts together constitute a prerequisite, such as 'unreasonable' in 36 AvtL. MCA can therefore in these situations be easily fit into RB's system for decision-making. Voting may, as noted above, nevertheless in other situations need to be done if several legal foundations or grounds have been alleged to support a claim. In such a situation, the different legal grounds can, in accordance with MCA, be regarded as alternatives. It can be used for analysis before an eventual voting is performed.

### 4.2.1   Voting

As mentioned above, disagreement among the members of the court as a pure decision problem is addressed only in the voting rules. However, voting is rare. Yet, this does not mean that the members of the court are always in agreement. Disagreements are instead usually handled through a sort of negotiation between the members of the court during deliberation, in which different opinions are brought together in a compromise on what should be included in the judgement.

Voting is thus used when opinions differ among the members of the court on what the outcome of the case should be and they cannot agree through a compromise. The following is confined to voting rules in civil disputes, which is included in 16 RB, but the basic principles for voting are essentially the same in criminal cases. One such basic principle is that a member of the bench who has been outvoted on one issue is obligated to participate in subsequent votes. The reason why members of the bench must take a stand on all issues is that the court's collective capacity can then be utilized as far as possible. This means, for example, that if A wants to sustain a claim for payment, B wants to disapprove the claim because of no loan agreement and C because of fraud, a vote must first be taken to determine if an agreement was entered. A and C will then outvote B. Additional voting will then be conducted to determine if the agreement is invalid due to fraud. If B also supports the opinion that the agreement is invalid due to fraud, the claim should be approved, even though two out of three judges wanted to dismiss the claim on the merits.[1]

As discussed above, in the use of MCA, the axiom of transitivity applies.[2] If option a is preferred over b and b is preferred over c, then a is preferred over c. Suppose that three judges will evaluate three different options: a, b and c. Judge A thinks that a is better than b and b is better than c. Judge B thinks that b is better than c and c is better than a. Judge C thinks that c is better than a and a is better than b. If they vote, the outcome will be 2:1 for a being better than b and a 2:1 majority will determine that b is better than c. The principle of transitivity, however, says that a is better than c, while voting determines that c is better than a. It is thus not possible to express or replace the results of the vote with value functions. MCA is therefore not suitable to use if voting is conducted under the rules of RB because it is not based on the principle of transitivity. MCA can, on the other hand and as mentioned above, be used for analysis before any voting is undertaken. Voting may then prove to be unnecessary. Or it may be confirmed that voting is required.

---

[1]  This example is taken from Per Olof Ekelöf, Torleif Bylund and Robert Boman, *Rättegång III* (6:e uppl Norstedts Juridik 1994) 89. Also, see Bengt Lindell, 'Sweden', in Piet Talman (ed.) *International Encyclopaedia of Laws: Civil Procedure* (Kluwer Law International 2013) para. 392.

[2]  See section 2.1, above.

## 4.3   VIDEO CONFERENCE OR COURT SESSION?

RB contains a general provision on video conferencing that was introduced through the reform 'En modernare rättegång – reformering av
processen i allmän domstol' ('More modern court proceedings – a reform
of proceedings in the general courts').[3] Parties, people to be examined for
evidence purposes and others participating in a court session could take
part through video conferencing. The general rule is still, however, that
persons participating in a session should appear in the courtroom where
the session is held.

When the courts decide on whether there is reason for a person to participate in a court session through video conferencing, special consideration should be given to the costs or inconvenience that would otherwise
arise and if anyone concerned has a palpable fear of being present in the
courtroom. Participation through video conferencing is not permitted if it
is inappropriate with respect to the purpose of the person's appearance in
court and other circumstances. An important purpose of enabling the use
of video conferencing is, however, the rationale that the individual could
participate in the session without this being too burdensome.

A party's or a witness's appearance in the courtroom can in many cases
be associated with costs or inconvenience.[4] One example is when such an
appearance requires a long journey from the person's home to the court.
The possibility of participating through video conferencing in such a situation could mean both financial and time gains. In conformity with SOU,
the government deemed that one reason for participation in a session
through video conferencing should be to avoid or limit costs or inconvenience that would otherwise arise with a courtroom appearance. This may
concern costs or inconvenience for the person in question or for others.
Fear can also be a reason for being permitted to participate in a session
through video conferencing. The justification for this applies not least
to witnesses and victims in criminal cases for the indictment of persons
suspected of being linked to organized crime.[5]

What should be ultimately decisive in assessing whether video conferencing is inappropriate in a particular case is whether it is possible to
conduct the session without impairing the quality of the legal process or

---

[3]   SOU 2001:103, Government Bill 2004/ 05:131. The reform entered into
force in November 2008. The provision on video conferencing is laid down in 5:10
RB.
[4]   Government Bill 2004/05:131, 93.
[5]   Ibid., 95.

otherwise compromising law and order.[6] What is of particular importance for the court's assessment in a particular case will, according to the preparatory work, vary depending on who is to appear and why. Consideration must be given to the nature of the case, the type of session in question, the role the person has and what will be discussed at the session. This may, for example, concern the court's opportunity to evaluate evidence, the importance of young defendants being present in the courtroom during the examination of charges against them, or the need for personal presence to bring about settlement negotiations. When the question of participating through video conferencing arises, the court should thus take into account the aim of the person's appearance and other circumstances and determine if video conference participation is inappropriate or not. The rule in question is mandatory, but great consideration should be given to the opinions of the parties.[7] Although only in exceptional cases should a party be called to participate in video conferencing against their will, there is scope for the courts to decide on such participation.

In its position on whether video conferencing should be used in a court session, the court should make an overall assessment.[8] In Figure 4.2 below, the decision tree looks like this:

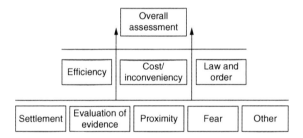

*Figure 4.2     Decision tree, video conference or court session*

The objectives of video conferencing can be summed up as being to avoid costs and inconvenience for the individual while maintaining quality in the administration of justice. These are objectives which are weighted together in the overall assessment for the final position on whether video conferencing is inappropriate or not.

The criteria that will be used are, as shown in the above figure, the following:

---

[6]  Ibid.
[7]  Ibid.
[8]  Ibid.

- settlement
- evaluation of evidence
- distance
- fear
- other.

These criteria can be broken down into more precise criteria, but this is not necessary for schematically showing how SAW or the simple additive model can be used. It is not specified in Figure 4.2 what criteria are linked to each objective. Settlement, however, influences efficiency and costs. Evaluation of evidence is linked to law and order, distance with time and travel costs, and fear with all three objectives. 'Other' can be circumstances that appear from the concrete data. Figure 4.2 captures the most important aspects according to what is stated in the preparatory work, but it is not necessarily exhaustive.

The background of the example is that it is a process amenable to out-of-court settlement, the question is if one of the parties, who will be examined for evidence purposes, can participate in the session through video conferencing. The object for assessment is thus what value each option – court session or video conference – has for the selected criteria, and what the outcome of an overall assessment would be for the set goals. The options court session or video conference should thus first be scored for each criterion. What is really being rated is, as previously mentioned, what the consequences of an option will be as concerns a specific criterion. We begin by going back to the relative scale, Figure 4.3. Preferences for the options are rated on a scale of 0 to 100, where 100 is the best option and 0 the worst option with regard to the given criteria. [9]

For scoring the options on the criteria, the following assumptions are made: there are certain evidentiary questions, though these are not central and conclusive; settlement is not ruled out; the case is large; and the travel for the party, who has expressed a fear of appearing in person, is not insignificant. Scoring will be primarily based on what advantages and what disadvantages are normally and typically associated with video conferencing

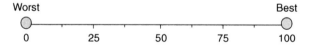

*Figure 4.3    Interval scale*

---

[9]    See section 2.3.4.1, above.

and court session in a situation like the one at hand. Because the decision tree in the example is small, the assessment can be made directly for all the criteria set out in the decision tree.

Concerning weighting, the decision-maker – in this case the judge – must ask which criterion he thinks is most important. The weight given to a criterion reflects both the difference in scores between the alternatives and the importance this difference has.[10] Weighting is then done with regard to the specifics of this case. Even if meeting face-to-face offers the best chances of settlement, in this specific case, it is deemed that there is little prospect of settlement. If there are three judges scoring and weighting, some differences can be expected. For example, the meaning of 'cost/inconvenience' in relation to fear might be assessed differently by the judges in this specific case. And the relative importance of the possibility of settlement may be deemed by all judges to have a greater relative importance than evaluation of evidence if it is a large case that could then be crossed off the court's agenda. The outcome thus depends on how different judges value the objectives, particularly the objectives of efficiency and process economy. One advantage of MCA is, as discussed previously, that it forces decision-makers to take clear positions on the matter and thus provides transparency.

Because the judge does not know exactly what the chances of settlement are or what difficulties the evaluation of evidence may entail, it could be said that this requires a prognosis, that is, a probability estimate. As been explained above, SAW does not handle uncertainty, which, however, is difficult to completely eliminate.[11] In this case, the starting point is that a court session provides the opportunity for direct settlement discussions between the parties under the direction of the judge, which video conferencing does not do (or at least makes it much more difficult to do). The same sort of reasoning can be applied to the evaluation of evidence; it may prove possible to carry out even a relatively complex evaluation of evidence through a video recording. However, it seems clear that a court session would usually provide better conditions for evaluating evidence in complex situations than a video conference.

Scoring in this example, where 'other' circumstances are omitted, has been deliberately simplified to more easily show the basic elements of SAW. For scoring, 100 points has thus been given to a criterion for one option if it is clearly better than the competing option. Consequently, the possibility of settlement in a court session has been given 100 points and 0

---

[10]   Dodgson and others (Ch 1 n 2) 63.
[11]   See section 5.2, below.

*Table 4.1  Video conference or court session*

| | Video conference or court session | | | | Total |
|---|---|---|---|---|---|
| | Settlement | Evaluation of evidence | Cost/ inconvenience | Fear | |
| Court session | 100 | 100 | 0 | 50 | 75 |
| Video conference | 0 | 80 | 100 | 100 | 54 |

points for the video conferencing option. The possibilities for evaluation of evidence are, as shown in Table 4.1 above, 20 per cent lower for video conferencing than for a court session. And video conferencing is twice as good as a court session for the criterion fear. As appears from the table it is not deemed to be impossible to tackle fear in a court session. For example, the frightened party could most of the time sit in another room and follow the proceedings through a loudspeaker.

The weights in the matrix have been allocated a total of 100 points. Settlement has been given a weight of 40, evaluation of evidence 30, cost/ inconvenience 20 and fear 10. Settlement is thus judged to be four times as important as fear and double as important as cost/inconvenience, while evaluation of evidence is three-quarters as important as settlement. The final outcome after aggregation is 75 points to court session and 54 points to video conferencing. As shown in Chapter 2, the outcome for an option is obtained by multiplying the points for this option with the weight for each criterion and then adding together all of the totals.[12] It is of course easier to use the model in a real situation with complete information on various circumstances. One can then, to check one's own intuitive assessment, try to do a scoring and a weighting to more precisely clarify what is important and less important in that particular situation.

SAW is thus used in the example above. For the location of a new main office in Chapter 2, SMARTS was used, which is also additive. Under both, 100 points can be the total weight points to be allocated, or 100 points can be used for each criterion and option, which is done above in the office location example. Giving each criterion 100 points enables more precise ratings. In this example, however, a simpler variant is used because there are so few criteria.

Even if SAW and SMARTS are both additive, they do differ somewhat. In the office location example above using SMARTS, the options were

---

[12]  Section 2.3.7.1, above.

scored and ranked from best to worst. In this example, using SAW, the
options are scored with regard to the criteria and then weighted. MCA was
also carried out in this way in the car purchase example.[13] Then the best
and the worst options are decided. The table shows that the options court
session and video conference are not ranked in the manner they would be
in using SMARTS, but rather the ranking in a clearer way will be a result
of the overall assessment. In a legal context, it would appear to be better
to do it this way than first ranking the options, which perhaps could be
deemed as pre-assessing the legal alternatives. However, SMARTS certainly could have been used. It is very much a matter of discretion which
model the decision-maker prefers to use.

If the totals in the columns are added together before weighting is done,
there will be a score of 250 for court session and 280 for video conferencing. That the court session still wins is due to the relative importance of
the criteria, for example, video conferencing has 100 points for fear, but
because the relative importance of fear is deemed to be small, it does not
have a great impact in a combined weighting. As the table shows, court
session has been deemed to be somewhat better than video conferencing
when it comes to the evaluation of evidence. However, the difference is not
particularly large as it is only 20 units. If fear is expressed, video conferencing is of course best. However, because it is uncertain how strong the fear
is, a court session is not ruled out; video conferencing is just deemed to be
twice as good.

The weighting is the most important and difficult element in the use of
MCA. As mentioned above, in a situation that is difficult to assess, a sensitivity analysis can be used to test different scores and weights. It is then
important to consider what the weights signify: is criterion A really twice
as important as criterion B? Even if MCA does not provide an 'absolute
truth', it is a valuable tool that enables structured overall assessments.

## 4.4    SECTION 36, THE CONTRACTS ACT

This provision was presented in Chapter 1. The legal text is reproduced
here in full.

A contract term or condition may be modified or set aside if such term or condition is unconscionable having regard to the contents of the agreement, the circumstances prevailing at the time the agreement was entered into, subsequent

---

[13]    See section 2.3.7, above.

circumstances, and circumstances in general. Where a term is of such significance for the agreement that it would be unreasonable to demand the continued
enforceability of the remainder of the agreement with its terms unchanged, the
agreement may be modified in other respects, or may be set aside in its entirety.

Upon determination of the applicability of the provisions of the first paragraph, particular attention shall be paid to the need to protect those parties
who, in their capacity as consumers or otherwise, hold an inferior bargaining
position in the contractual relationship.

The provisions of the first and second paragraphs shall apply mutatis mutan-
dis to questions relating to the terms of legal acts other than contracts.

The fact that 36 AvtL is a general clause with unclear objectives makes
it difficult to apply. The use of multi-criteria analysis does not overcome
these inherent difficulties; these come along in the problem structuring and
analysis. The precedent on which this analysis is based (NJA 1999 p. 408)
is described in detail in accordance with the abstract from the case, which
is necessary in order to provide an account of all relevant circumstances.

### 4.4.1  MCA Analysis of NJA 1999 p. 408

A company had signed a guarantee for a construction loan agreement.
A partner, L.S. and his spouse, A-C.S., jointly owned the company
Kulsprutan, which conducted real estate activities and sold single-family
houses. To expand activities to also include property management, the
company Träslott was formed as a wholly owned subsidiary of Kulsprutan.
For a new construction, which would be carried out by Ettan, the company
took out a bank loan of approximately SEK 7.5 million. A guarantee was
provided by Kulsprutan as collateral for the loan. When the loan was
taken out, L.S. had to sign a 'DECLARATION' concerning the personal
guarantee for Ettan's 'current and future obligations' (general guarantee).
When the construction was completed, interest rates had begun to rise as
a result of the 'financial crisis' and it turned out that the construction loan
agreement – apart from the government loan part in the amount of SEK
1923000 – could not be placed in any first mortgage loan institute. By
this time, mortgage deeds in the newly developed properties had also been
offered as collateral for the loan. After consultation between the bank and
L.S., the loan was converted to a foreign loan, which carried lower interest
rates. Due to exchange losses, the foreign loan was terminated and in 1993,
converted to a regular bank loan of just under SEK 8.7 million for Ettan,
which had changed its name to Träslott. Before that, the bank had transferred the loan to Retriva Kredit Aktiebolag (Retriva), which demanded
under the guarantees that the guarantors pay the residual debt, which after
realization of the collateral totalled SEK 4297636, including interest.

## 4.4.2 Statement of Facts

As grounds for the claim, Retriva referred to guarantee commitments.

L.S. and A-C.S. alleged: when the construction loan agreement was granted, L.S. signed the guarantee for the loan agreement on behalf of Kulsprutan. In connection to this – or possibly shortly afterwards – the bank explained that a private guarantee from L.S. and A-C.S. was also requested for the loan. When L.S. questioned this, the bank explained that the private guarantee was only required during the construction period and until mortgages – after final inspection of the construction – could be taken out on the property and the loan placed in accordance with the agreed financing plan. When L.S., after reviewing the wording of the personal guarantee, wondered why it was general he was referred by the bank to look at the personal guarantee for Kulsprutan, which showed that the collateral only applied to the construction loan agreement. The document that the bank referred to was the 'guarantee declaration'. With this information, L.S. assumed that the bank – in accordance with normal procedures – undertook to, after final inspection, place the construction loan agreement with a first mortgage loan institute, and he agreed to sign the guarantee agreement. When asked by A-C.S., he explained that the guarantee agreement only applied to the construction loan agreement and that the commitment carried no risk, apart from the risk of potential loss during the construction period, a risk which, however, he deemed non-existent because production was insured by Skandia. A-C.S. then also signed the personal guarantee. There was no contract between her and the bank. When it then turned out that the construction loan agreement – apart from the government loan part – could not be placed in the intended manner, it was decided that the remaining portion of the loan would be placed as a foreign loan, mainly in German Deutschmarks. L.S. assumed then that the personal guarantee had been terminated because there was a new loan. When the Deutschmark fell, the bank unilaterally decided – despite L.S.'s protests – that the foreign loan must be settled and replaced with a new loan (which was posted in June 1992) in the amount of SEK 8 667 863. Exchange loss amounted to about SEK 3 140 000.

As grounds for the contestation, L.S. and A-C.S. alleged first that an oral agreement had been made between the bank and L.S. – primarily through the bank's referral to the 'guarantee' to the effect that the guarantee commitment only applied to the construction loan agreement and would be discarded when this was placed after the final inspection of the construction. L.S. and A-C.S. argued that, in any case, the statements from the bank in a decisive way influenced their decision to enter into the guarantee agreements. Second, and in the event that the District Court should not find the guarantee commitments to be restricted through agreements to apply to the construction loan agreement, it was asserted that this restriction was in any case a material assumption in the defendant's decision to sign the guarantee and that this factor was obvious – or at least should have been obvious – to the bank.

Third, it was argued that the guarantee agreements, in accordance with the provisions of 36 AvtL, should be modified or set aside because they were unreasonable with regard to the circumstances in which the commitments were entered into, to subsequent events, and to the circumstances in general. Regarding the first, it was in particular alleged that, apart from grounds for contestation 1 and 2 (above), the bank's demand for personal and general guarantee without monetary limit was not in accordance with good banking ethics and with Swedish financial supervisory authority (Finansinspektionen's) general guidelines for guarantee agreements, all considered against the backdrop of the guarantors' financial and personal circumstances, and the purpose and amount of the loan. The bank had therefore failed to do a proper credit check of the guarantors and to inform them of the implications of the guarantee commitments. Regarding subsequent circumstances, it was alleged that the bank, when the loan was converted to a foreign loan, should have informed the defendants of the significant increase in risk that this new loan carried, and that the guarantee agreements also applied to the foreign loan.

With respect to additional circumstances, which included reasons for at least modification of the guarantee commitments, allegations were made of the unforeseen developments on the credit market, currency changes and the bank's unilateral decision to realize the credit loss. As yet another reason for modification, it was referred to that the bank, as a consequence of government bank assistance, acquired its claim at a lower amount than the original debt, which should correspond to a reduction of SEK 1 684 000. The defendants further argued that there was greater reason for modification regarding A-C.S. with respect to her subordinate position in and little actual influence over the management of the companies involved, her lack of training and experience and that she was not given any personal information by the bank regarding the implications of the personal guarantee.

For the 1990 tax year, L.S. declared a taxable income – after tax loss carry-forwards – of SEK 0 and a net wealth of SEK 0, and for tax year 1991 a taxable income of SEK 149 500 and a net wealth of about SEK 385 000. Of this last amount, however, SEK 320 500 comprised a property that he bought in 1991 but did not pay in full until 1992. The property was later sold for an amount equivalent to the borrowing. The net wealth also included a property in Vejbystrand, of which L.S. owned half and A-C.S.

owned the other half. This property was sold in 1995 for SEK 1 250 000, which was equivalent to the loan on the property. Finally, L.S. also had a time share in a house in Sälen. This was nominally appraised at SEK 5759, but had no real market value. For tax year 1990, A-C.S. declared a taxable income of about SEK 60 000 and a net wealth of about SEK 62 000, of which 50 000 consisted of shares in Kulsprutan. For 1991, A-C.S. declared a taxable income of about SEK 178 000 and a net wealth of SEK 33 000.

Concerning Finansinspektionen's general guidelines for guarantee agreements, particular reference was made to the following section of FFFS 1991:7 (translation mine):

> As concerns credit for purposes other than the consumer's own use, it happens that the creditor requires so-called ownership or management guarantees of a natural person who has a significant influence over the borrower's business activities due to part-ownership in this. Such a guarantee agreement should be accepted only if a credit check of the guarantor indicates that the guarantee commitment is not unreasonable with regard to the guarantor's ability to pay.

Retriva replied with the following: it was disputed that any verbal agreement was made on limiting the guarantee agreements to a certain time period or to a certain type of credit or that the bank had made any statement on this. That the 'guarantee declaration' the bank was alleged to have referred to stated 'construction loan agreement' had no independent significance; only the personal guarantee was relevant. The purpose of the 'guarantee declaration' was to 'put the guarantee company in bad faith' concerning the restrictions provided in Chapter 12, Section 7 of the Companies Act for a limited company to, among other things, sign guarantees. Against the defendant's first and second pleas, a general objection was lodged that a Swedish bank was never able to guarantee that credit could be transferred to another credit institution. If a general guarantee agreement was limited to apply only to a certain type of credit, this must be expressly stated in the agreement. As regards the second plea, it was alleged that the factor was neither significant, evident to the bank nor relevant.

Finally, Retriva disputed that there was any basis under 36 AvtL for discarding or modifying the payment obligation. Both the original credit and the guarantee commitments were quite normal at the time they were undertaken and the bank's credit check, of both the debtor and the guarantor, was conducted in accordance with good banking ethics and the Finansinspektionen's general guidelines. This last does not mean that the bank must assure itself that each guarantor has the assets or financial position in general to cover a debt. The couple's financial position was, when the original debt was incurred, sufficient for the credit check of them to have been considered acceptable. Even if it were accepted that the general guidelines of FFFS 1993:22 had retroactive effect, the bank had met the requirements of these guidelines. Considering the guarantors' insight into the company's (Ettan's) economic conditions, the bank had not breached any obligation to provide information concerning the subsequent changes in the company's financial position. The consequences of the so-called financial crisis affected both credit institutions as well as a large number of debtors and could not constitute grounds for modification of the guarantee commitments. The extent of these was furthermore not affected by the government bank assistance the bank received, because the bank assistance did not have any legal bearing on the relationship between the creditor and the debtor.

### 4.4.3  Summary of Parties' Positions

The defendants thus pleaded first, that a verbal agreement had been made to limit the guarantee commitment and second, the doctrine of assumptions. These grounds for contestation were also invoked to support the guarantees being modified or set aside under 36 AvtL because they were unreasonable. This objection means that the defendants wanted the concrete legal facts invoked to support the first and second objections to be considered in the application of the assessment of unreasonableness under 36 AvtL, if they should not be successful as first and second pleas for contestation. Applying 36 AvtL, we therefore get the following legal facts for assessment:

A    agreement on limited guarantee;
B    oral agreement on limited guarantee;
C    limitation was material assumption;
D    banking ethics;
E    the bank should have provided information;
F    unforeseen developments;
G    currency fluctuations;
H    unilateral decision to realize the credit loss;
I    bank assistance;
J    personal circumstances;
K    Finansinspektionen's general guidelines.

This outline below is based on 36 AvtL and what the defendants have asserted. It is preliminary because it needs to be further analysed. Based on this initial outline, it is possible to sketch out the decision tree in Figure 4.4.

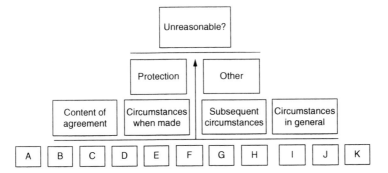

*Figure 4.4    Decision tree, unreasonable*

A–K are thus criteria or legal facts. These are at the bottom of the decision tree. The higher or more general categories are taken from the wording in 36 AvtL. A–K can be sorted into these boxes to create clarity.

### 4.4.4    Decision Tree and Structuring

The decision tree is constructed from the bottom up, because it is based on the circumstances that the defendants have alleged (and the plaintiff contested). The criteria on the bottom level will make it possible to take a well-grounded position on the question of whether the guarantee commitment should be modified or set aside; they will have a legal value for the assessment of this question. At the highest level, the objective is in this case the desire from the legislator to counteract unreasonable agreements. In Figure 4.4, 'need for protection' has been given as a specific objective because, in accordance with 36 AvtL, special consideration must be given to the need to protect consumers or others who have an inferior position in the contractual relationship. The provision should thus counteract a stronger party from utilizing its position against a weaker party and be a tool for smoothing out such power imbalances, which often find expression in an agreement strongly favouring one party. It is otherwise unclear what the purpose of the provision is. The overall purpose of the provision would seem to be to safeguard a well-functioning market.

Unclear purposes make it of course more difficult to value the circumstances that the parties are asserting because the judge must set the factors at the bottom of the decision tree in relation to the prerequisite 'unreasonable' without any clear guidance. On the other hand, the preparatory work for the law is extensive, with many examples of situations in which a clause can be considered 'unreasonable'.

In the decision tree, the stated purpose is to determine if the guarantee commitment is 'unreasonable'. An alternative would have been to try to find overriding interests which the administration of justice should promote, such as that the judgement must stand out as 'fair', and that it must meet the market's needs or promote behaviour modification or conflict-resolving. Given that objectives of this kind have an elusive content, this alternative has not even been considered. The objective for the court is instead to render a judgment on the matter of whether the guarantee commitment in this case should be modified or set aside because it appears to be 'unreasonable' or if the plaintiff's claim should be approved. From this starting point, the assessment is made, as discussed above, from bottom up with the allegations of the parties, which appear to be reasonable and consistent in a party-controlled civil procedure amenable to out-of-court settlement. The other starting point, which is a kind of top-down process, is better suited to a civil procedure that is not amenable to out-of-court settlement. The purport of applicable legislative rule is of course significant to what invoked legal facts are relevant. It will thus be a matter of interplay between norms and facts that will determine the final decision basis.

Thus, in the application of 36 AvtL, the purpose will quite simply be to determine if the guarantee commitment should be set aside or modified because it is 'unreasonable'. The provision's objectives, the interpretation and application of the provision as well as overriding interests of different sorts are included in the decision context. Different decision-maker's opinions on the importance of, for example, 'fairness' or the market's needs and interests will thus have an impact in the scoring and weighting of concrete legal facts with regard to the options.[14]

Regarding overall assessments in accordance with 36 AvtL, the Government Bill provides for example the following:

> As already stated, the application of the general clause must be grounded in an overall assessment, *in which all circumstances of the particular case are taken into account* [. . .] The above-stated does not prevent that the courts should be able to label a certain condition as unreasonable in itself.[15] (author's translation, author's emphasis)

Ramberg and Hultmark argue that the provision expresses a new technique for resolving contractual problems, stating:

---

[14]    See also section 2.3.7.1, above.
[15]    Government Bill 1975/76:81, 111.

We find no focus on the contracting parties' wills, declarations of intention and reliance – the traditional building blocks of the Contracts Act – but rather a general reference to all circumstances and relationships whether they occurred before, during or after the agreement was entered. The judge does not need to make his way through a thicket of difficult-to-apply necessary conditions, but rather has full freedom to arrive at the outcome *taking into account all asserted circumstances that he finds significant.*[16] (author's translation, author's emphasis)

The overall assessment thus means that all circumstances in the specific case that are of legal significance should be taken into account. This begs the questions of what type of account should be taken and what is meant by 'of significance'.

### 4.4.5 The Concept of Legal Value

As discussed previously, this book uses the term legal value.[17] It is reasonable here to stop for a moment to contemplate this term. One important reason for this is that the reasons for the judgement in this legal case indicate a manner of assessment that is not consistent with MCA, or with how overall assessments should be made in accordance with the cited preparatory work statement and doctrine.

A legal value denotes the degree of legal significance attached to a concrete legal fact. The legal value can be low or high. If the circumstance is not legally relevant, the legal value is 0. It is important to distinguish between the existence of a concrete legal fact and the legal value of this. Concrete legal facts in a dispositive case must be proven, if they are disputed and not notorious. If an overall assessment is made – whether or not MCA is used – significance can be attached to a proven legal fact to a certain extent. It is thus not so that the legal value of a concrete legal fact is 1 or 0 or must reach a certain legal value threshold to be relevant, at least not when an overall assessment (or balancing of interests) will be done. However, the existence of the legal fact must be proven according to applicable standards of proof. If it thus is asserted, as one of several reasons why a clause in a contract should be modified or set aside, that the other party was 'aggressive' and used 'threats' when the terms of the contract were negotiated, this statement must be proven if it is denied. Applicable burden of proof rules and standards of proof will then apply. As concerns then the legal value of these circumstances, if proven, for the assessment

---

[16]  Ramberg and Hultmark (Ch 1 n 57) 190.
[17]  Section 1.1, above.

of whether the clause should be modified or set aside, this depends among other things on how serious the aggression was and how the threat was expressed.[18]

Virtually all legal facts are non-contentious in this legal case. If in an overall assessment there are, for example, seven non-contentious or concrete legal facts proven with the sufficient degree of probability, and they only in combination and after an overall assessment could result in the determination that an agreement clause should be modified, the combined legal value can be calculated with the simple additive model, SAW. It may then be so that one legal fact has a considerably higher legal value than the others, yet still not be sufficient to determine the case. One question then is whether the legal value of other legal facts can strengthen the strongest circumstance's legal value so that it becomes sufficiently strong. This method of reasoning makes one consider the effect that auxiliary facts can have in the evaluation of evidence. Auxiliary facts are considered to have the power to strengthen or weaken the evidentiary value of an evidentiary fact for the evidentiary theme. Can MCA provide a similar effect? No, if concrete legal facts are mutually independent, MCA, and in this case the simple additive model, means that scores and weights are multiplied for all legal facts in the manner previously described.[19] Each concrete legal fact thus has its own impact and thereby gives its contribution to the overall assessment. If there should be a dependent relationship between two (or more) concrete legal facts, however, the dependent concrete legal fact does not have any independent significance, but rather provides a strengthening or weakening effect on the concrete controlling (mothering) legal fact. Only in this respect can a certain similarity arise with positive or negative auxiliary facts in evidence. There is no term for dependent concrete legal facts that strengthen the legal value of other independent controlling legal facts, but we could call them non-independent concrete legal facts.[20]

---

[18]  For how these vague evidentiary themes can be proven, see sections 4.6 and 6.5 on fuzzy logic.

[19]  Section 2.3.7.1, above.

[20]  The defendants have collected certain circumstances in a cluster by invoking the Finansinspektionen's general guidelines against the backdrop of the guarantors' financial and personal circumstances, the purpose of the loan and the amount of the loan. The bank has therefore, according to the defendants, failed to do a proper credit check and to inform the guarantors of the implications of the guarantee commitment.

### 4.4.6   The Courts' 'Overall Assessment'

One possible way to move forward in this book could have been to say something about how the courts ruled on this case. One advantage of doing this would have been that the reader, unaffected by the outcome of the case, could have more easily assessed the merits (and drawbacks) of using MCA. However, in light of what was said above about the courts' positions and how they carried out the overall assessment, it is important to carefully report how they reasoned. The relevant parts of the reasons for the judgements of both the District Court and the Court of Appeals will be recounted below.

> The District Court is initially unable to find that the defendants have succeeded in substantiating their claim of a verbal agreement deviating from the personal guarantee. As concerns the defendants' objection with reference to the so-called doctrine of assumptions, this certainly does provide support for the assumption that both the bank and the defendants when the original loan was granted to Ettan assumed that the loan – a so-called construction loan agreement – could be transferred in the usual way and against only mortgage security be placed in a first mortgage loan institute after the final inspection of the construction. As Retriva stressed, however, a bank cannot provide any guarantee for a transfer or for when this might take place. The District Court likewise cannot find it reasonable that the creditor in such a situation as this case shall bear the risk that a presumed transfer will not come about. Nor can this objection from the defendants prompt the dismissal on the merits of the plaintiff's claim. (author's translation)

The District Court then goes directly into the question of whether the bank's acceptance of an unlimited and general guarantee from each of the defendants for an amount of roughly SEK 7.5 million was in accordance with good banking ethics and the Finansinspektionen's general guidelines and finds that these circumstances should prompt modification. That one circumstance is given dominance in this way is not unusual, but at the same time begs the question of the significance of other grounds for contestation.

The District Court then moves on to other objections and states:

> The defendants have further argued that the guarantee commitments should be set aside or modified on the grounds that the bank in various respects has failed in its obligation to provide information to them. Through the printed text of the guarantee commitments and in the annexed general terms and conditions of these, the guarantors must be deemed to have received sufficient information on the implications of the guarantee commitment. Nor can the bank otherwise – the District Court notes in particular that the so-called foreign loan came about at the request of L.S. – be deemed to have neglected its obligation to

provide information. The District Court can furthermore not find that the government bank assistance that Göta bank received is such a circumstance that should prompt modification of the payment obligation under the guarantee commitments. (author's translation)

The Court of Appeals makes the same assessment made by the District Court regarding the defendants' grounds for contestation 1 and 2 and states:

As then concerns the matter whether the guarantee liabilities should be set aside or modified under the provisions of Section 36 of the Contracts Act, L.S. and A-C.S. have in the Court of Appeals presented the following clarification. They assumed that the guarantee commitment did not cover anything other than the construction loan agreement, which would be solved by placing the loan. If the bank intended for the guarantee to possibly cover other loans, there is discrepancy in the original conditions. In any event, the guarantee commitment was undertaken on condition that the construction loan agreement would actually be placed in first mortgages. Demanding fulfilment of an extensive guarantee commitment, which for both parties was obviously entered on this condition, appears for them to be clearly unreasonable. L.S. and A-C.S. have also, as reason for modification, argued that the guarantee commitment was a formal matter in order to secure the completion of the construction project. (author's translation)

The Court of Appeals then stated:

The circumstances that L.S. and A-C.S have thus asserted as grounds for modification coincide or are closely connected with their first objection, which is based on the allegation of a contractual limitation of the guarantee commitment and on false assumptions, and which has not won support of the Court of Appeals. The Court of Appeals, which takes into account that the guarantee commitments have been part of a business activity, is not of the opinion that the circumstances in question warrant modification of any part of the guarantee commitments under Section 36 of the Contracts Act.

L.S. and A-C.S. have furthermore as reason for modification alleged that the bank has in various respects failed in its obligation to provide information to the guarantors, that the bank unilaterally decided to realize the incurred exchange loss, that Göta bank received government bank assistance and that unforeseen events occurred on the credit and currency markets.

The Court of Appeals finds, like the District Court, that neither of these circumstances should lead to modification of the guarantee liability. (author's translation)

As the Court of Appeals points out, the defendants have alleged their primary objections also as support for modification. It was said above that this was not about evidentiary issues, but rather about how the defendants understood the bank's reference to the 'personal guarantee'. L.S.

perceived this as that an oral agreement was made to the effect that the guarantee commitment only applied to the construction loan agreement, while Retriva claimed that the 'guarantee declaration' that the bank was alleged to have referred to, which cited 'construction loan agreement', did not have independent significance, that only the personal guarantee itself was relevant and that the purpose of the guarantee declaration was to put the guarantee company in bad faith regarding the restrictions stipulated in Chapter 12, Section 7 of the Companies Act for limited companies to sign guarantees.

The District Court and the Court of Appeals found that the primary and secondary objections did not warrant modification and then moved on in their examination. Thus, these legal facts were not given any significance at all. The same approach has been taken with respect to other circumstances that were referred to in support of modification. In any case, the District Court addressed the failing obligation to provide information and the government bank assistance separately and because the Court of Appeals shared the District Court's assessment, it may well be assumed that the Court of Appeals also considered the circumstances referred to in support of modification separately. For each circumstance, the question has been asked: Does this warrant modification? When the answer was negative, the next circumstance was assessed, and so on.

Judging by the abstract of the ruling, neither the District Court nor the Court of Appeals thus examined all criteria (legal facts) together, but instead examined them each individually or in small groups. The examination therefore appears to have been made successively: legal facts have been examined and disapproved one by one. Consequently, they have not been included in an overall assessment. However, the fact that a concrete legal fact is eliminated in this way can hardly mean that it completely lacks legal value. This can at least not reasonably apply to all legal facts that are eliminated or extinguished. If the legal value has not reached a qualified point, however, it seems to have been completely ignored by the courts, although according to the preparatory work and doctrine everything of significance should be taken into account in the overall assessment.[21] It can certainly not be ruled out that the courts considered these circumstances to be entirely without legal value, but that does not seem likely. Another possibility is that courts immediately saw which circumstance had dominance and could be successful and therefore ignored the others, which actually seems rational. The approach to the examination described

---

[21]    There is thus no legal value point (compare the term evidentiary value point) for a legal fact's legal value.

in the reasons for the judgement, however, would seem to indicate otherwise. The principle of successive relevance, which the courts seem to have applied, is applicable only with respect to independent legal grounds such as 'purchase' or 'limitation', which are each linked to a legal consequence. It should therefore not be considered applicable if several concrete legal facts in an overall assessment only together can give rise to a legal consequence.[22]

### 4.4.7   Technical Issues and the Independence Requirement

MCA is used to assess how the options work or perform for the relevant criteria, which in a legal context means assessing the legal value of the legal facts. In this example, there is no explicit legal theme for the alleged legal facts and invoked legal facts appear as disparate, but they of course have a relation to unreasonableness, at least in the opinion of the defendants. It is already at a quick glance clear that all invoked legal facts do not have the same legal value; some are more significant than others. This difference is expressed when using MCA in scoring and weighting. Personal circumstances (including a person's financial position) have a legal value in relation to the need for protection, while at the same time the objective of upholding the principle that entered agreements must be kept (pacta sunt servanda) is obvious. There is thus a conflict between objectives. As grounds for his action, the plaintiff has referred only to personal guarantee (A), that is, the agreement on this that was indisputably entered. The personal guarantee is obviously essential because agreements must be kept, something that the Supreme Court also refers to in this case.

In the MCA analysis that will be made, the defendants' grounds for contestation regarding agreements on limited guarantee and the doctrine of assumptions will not be included because they concern independent grounds for contestation. As mentioned previously, MCA is only used in this book for overall assessments concerning a situation where several legal facts together constitute a prerequisite, in this case the necessary condition of unreasonableness in 36 AvtL. This limitation is made partly with respect to scope of application of the voting rules.[23] However, in this case the defendants have also alleged that these grounds for contestation together with the other legal facts should lead to modification. Because of

---

[22]   For further discussion on the principle of gradual verification and gradual relevance, see Karl Olivecrona, *Rätt och dom* (Norstedt 1966) 219.

[23]   Section 4.2.1 above.

this, they are therefore included in the MCA analysis, but not as independent legal grounds for modification.

An additional technical question is the following. The option of approving the plaintiff's claim is negative for the defendants and positive for the plaintiff. Can these options be compared on a single scale or are two needed? When using MCA, all criteria are usually on the same scale. If, for example, a car buyer wants to buy a car with low fuel consumption, very high fuel consumption is something negative. However, a separate scale is not made for this. Instead, the car model with very high fuel consumption is given a value of 0 or at least a low value for the criteria in question. In an overall assessment, it is rather a question of more or less of something, like fuel consumption. Very high fuel consumption would maybe not completely exclude a car model. This approach is integrated in the structure of the model.[24]

The use of MCA and in this case the simple additive model (SAW) means that if, for example, the modification option is given 40 points after an overall assessment, the plaintiff's action must be approved because 40 points for the defendants implies 60 points for the plaintiff. The forthcoming analysis will comprise the options to (1) set aside the clause or (2) modify the clause. If either of these options has a combined weight of over 50 points when weighted together, the plaintiff's petition should not be fully approved. It should probably be pointed out that the combined value for both options should of course not be combined because the options are independent. Due to the fact that an agreement has been entered and to the principle pacta sunt servanda, the status from the start is 100 points in favour of fully approving the plaintiff's claim.[25] A combined excess score weight must thus be found (more than 50 points) for either modification or setting aside in order for the agreement to not apply in full. If an excess weight is determined in the combined weighting, that is, more than 50 points for one or the other option, these points are subtracted from the initial 100 points for full approval. This deduction means that the agreement will not apply in full. MCA is thus useful even if the question only applies to modification. There are then two options – modification or approving the plaintiff's petition. In this legal case, only the question of modification was up for consideration in the Supreme Court since the defendants had abandoned their claim to set aside the

---

[24]  See literature referred to in Chapter 1 footnote 2.
[25]  Note that I am here not referring to the contract, but to how the defendants understood or interpreted the bank's reference to the 'personal guarantee', which they understood as an oral agreement.

guarantee commitment. However, as mentioned above, the analysis will also contain the option to set aside the clause. This provides a richer demonstration of the model.

What about the independence requirement? Has this been met? If it is not possible to score the preferences for an option with respect to a concrete legal fact without taking into account another concrete legal fact, the requirement for independence is not met. The two grounds for contestation, verbal agreement and that a limitation was a material assumption, are mutually independent according to the test in question. The grounds for contestation are also legally independent in the sense that they constitute two independent grounds for the contestation. When the grounds for contestation in question are considered in the application of 36 AvtL and not as independent grounds for contestation, they are moved to another context. Even if the concrete legal facts behind these are not sufficient for dismissal of the plaintiff's claim on the merits, they may have significance for the question of whether the guarantee commitment should be set aside or modified.

Regarding the other circumstances, the following has been considered. The Finansinspektionen's general guidelines and the defendants' financial situation have been assessed as one criterion. According to the general guidelines, the bank must take into account the ability to pay, which is why it is difficult to assess the defendants' ability to pay and the general guidelines as two independent criteria. Bank ethics is a broader concept than the general guidelines, which are regulations, in this case with a clear purport. But bank ethics could possibly be seen as a 'parent' criterion, with the Finansinspektionen's general guidelines as a 'child' criterion. It has been decided here, however, to connect bank ethics with the bank's obligation to provide information about increased risk and foreign loans because it was alleged that the bank should have provided information on this. Another reason for the merging is that Finansinspektionen's general guidelines and bank ethics are rules and not circumstances in the case. Thus, through merging the risk for double counting is avoided. The unforeseen developments on the credit market should likewise have been combined with the currency changes, although the drop in the exchange rate with all probability was due to the so-called financial crisis. This aggregation is doubtful, however, because the cause–effect relationship is not tantamount to a dependence relationship. On the other hand, this constitutes conciliation because dividing two criteria with lower legal values would not significantly affect the results. A unilateral decision to realize the credit loss and bank assistance seem obviously mutually independent from each other and are also considered to be independent from banking ethics. Even if these factors were connected to the financial crisis, a bank can, regardless of the economic situation in the country or in the world, make a unilateral decision to realize a credit loss, and bank assistance is in itself legally independent of actual events.

The independence requirement can be difficult to take a position on and there are no strict rules for how this should be assessed. As discussed in Chapter 2, it is the decision-maker who must decide if he or she thinks that a criterion can be assessed independently of another or not. Verification of this requirement, as well as scoring and weighting, is thus subjective unless there are no objective standards or values that can be used. One starting point in a legal case analysis is to use the parties' and the court's opinion on what a legal fact is. Problem structuring based on the independence requirement is, even if it can be difficult, a useful and valuable review of the decision basis because it problematizes the significance of individual legal facts. It makes it possible to remove those that do not seem relevant and avoid examining the same circumstances several times because they occur under different designations. The courts might not always carefully consider whether legal facts overlap from a more strict perspective, and this could lead to overestimation or underestimation. In this case, I have therefore taken the liberty of doing some aggregations, which appear to be justified. It should be emphasized that the fact alone that MCA forces the legal decision-maker to take a stand on the independence requirement is a valuable feature of the model.

### 4.4.8 Scoring and Weighting, End Result

What remains is the following outline, which should be compared with the preliminary outline that was shown above.

A  An oral agreement on the limited guarantee;
B  limitation was material assumption;
C  Finansinspektionen's general guidelines (and personal financial situation compared with size of loan);
D  unforeseen developments, currency changes;
E  unilateral decision to realize the credit loss;
F  bank assistance;
G  banking ethics (and the bank should have provided information on increased risk and foreign loans).

Scoring means that the relative strength of one option is expressed as a number that represents the consequences of the option with respect to a criterion. Translated to a legal context, this means that the current legal alternatives (options), the guarantee commitment is set aside or modified or the plaintiff's petition is approved will be scored with regard to each of the alleged legal facts A–G. The legal fact that has the greatest significance for each option is given the value of 100, and the one that has the least is given the value 0. To simplify the assessment, one can rate on a scale with 0 and 100 as minimum and maximum values and then put the value of 50 at the middle of the scale. The values 25 and 75 can then be inserted on the scale. This provides clearer references for scoring.

Considering that the options are few and the difference between modifying and setting aside the guarantee commitment is small, the alleged legal facts will be scored according to the following for modifying or setting aside the payment obligation.

C = 100/90
B = 75/60
D = 50/40
G = 30/25
F = 20/20
E = 15/10
A = 0/0

Criterion C, that is, the Finansinspektionen's general guidelines, is thus given 100 points for modification and 90 points for annulling the guarantee commitment. Other criteria are then read in the same way; the first number refers to modification, the second to annulling the guarantee. According to the preparatory works, modifying should be the first-hand option. Setting aside is thus a slightly more severe measure. For each criterion, completely setting aside the guarantee commitment is therefore given slightly lower scores. It should be emphasized that the values are not set according to a thorough and extensive substantive review. The primary intention is, like in the other examples, to demonstrate the method.

The scoring that has been done means that the Finansinspektionen's general guidelines and personal situation, C, has the greatest importance for the alternatives modification and setting the clause aside. On the other end is A with no score at all. The scoring that emerges is prima facie. It is based on a transparent assessment of the case in question with respect to criteria A–G. Weighting, however, is done with regard to the circumstances in the specific case and is therefore often decisive.

As shown in Table 4.2, 100 weight points have been allocated on the criteria. The values are given in a frequency distribution, that is, the value 50 is the same as 50 per cent of the value 100, and so on.[26] The

---

[26]   Above section 2.3.5 and Dodgson and others (Ch 1 n 2) 64.

*Table 4.2    Overall assessment 36 AvtL*

| Overall assessment 36 AvtL | | | | | | | | |
|---|---|---|---|---|---|---|---|---|
| | A | B | C | D | E | F | G | Total |
| Op. 1 | 0 | 75 | 100 | 50 | 15 | 20 | 30 | 57 |
| Op. 2 | 0 | 60 | 90 | 40 | 10 | 10 | 25 | 47.5 |
| Weight | 0 | 20 | 25 | 15 | 10 | 10 | 20 | |

Finansinspektionen's general guidelines and personal situation have been given the highest weight points, then comes the doctrine of assumptions and then banking ethics and that the bank should have provided information. According to the weighting, the doctrine of assumptions is 80 per cent as important as the Finansinspektionen's general guidelines, unforeseen developments about half as important as this, and so on. It is important to keep in mind when weighting that if, for example, two circumstances have a lot of weight but do not dominate, and thereby become decisive, the impact of other circumstances will increase. The third most important circumstance should therefore have a relatively high weight, and so on. In this example, weighting may also be affected by how the guarantee commitment otherwise affects the agreement, which may lead to a circumstance that in itself does not appear particularly important to be given a higher weight.

Different judges may have different opinions on both scoring and weighting, particularly concerning the importance of legal facts vis-à-vis such a vague necessary condition 'unreasonable'. MCA represents a completely different way of doing the assessment than that shown in the ruling. This is because legal facts are given legal value and no legal fact has been thrown out, except for A. It should finally be mentioned that in the work with scoring and weighting in this case, it was shown that a sympathetic attitude to modification is required for the plaintiff's claim to not be completely approved.

## 4.5    SENTENCING

### 4.5.1    Introduction

In NJA 1997 p. 652 the question arose of what sentence would be given for an embezzlement crime: imprisonment or suspended sentence. The

Court of Appeals sentenced L.E. to imprisonment for ten months. In the Supreme Court, the majority (two Justices, including the Chief Justice) decided on a sentence of imprisonment for ten months. Two members dissented and wanted to impose a suspended sentence. One Justice had dissenting reasons, but agreed with the sentence of imprisonment for ten months. The reasons given in the Supreme Court are given below. The Justice who decided the outcome stated the following:

> When deciding on sentencing, the court shall under Chapter 30, Section 4 of the Penal Code pay particular attention to circumstances advocating a milder sentence than imprisonment. As grounds for imprisonment, on the other hand, the penal value and nature of the crime shall be considered, as well as whether the accused has a criminal record.
>
> L.E. has no previous criminal record. The nature of the crime is not such that it, regardless of penal value, should lead to imprisonment. The question is if the penal value is so high that prison shall be imposed.
>
> The crimes, which together involve a significant amount of money and included abuse of a position of trust, already have a high penal value with regard to the given conditions. Moreover, in this case L.E. used misleading accounting and, regarding count 1, also produced false invoices. The Supreme Court shares the Court of Appeals' opinion that the penal value of the crimes is clearly over one year.
>
> Based on this assessment, there must be some special reason for L.E. not to be imposed a sentence involving the deprivation of liberty. The question is thus if there is any circumstance in connection with L.E.'s person that justifies another choice of sentence than imprisonment (Chapter 29, Section 5, Penal Code).
>
> L.E. has with reference to the cited section of law, alleged that the damages have now been paid in full, that a prison sentence will mean the loss of his current employment as assistant in a municipal business, and that there has been a notable delay in the criminal investigation.
>
> That L.E. has paid the damages imposed on him is not in itself included in any reason provided by Chapter 29, Section 5 of the Penal Code (Brottsbalken III, 4 ed, 1994 p 222 f and 227 f). Nor can this payment be afforded any significance in sentencing. In view of this and regarding that L.E., who on his own admission left employment with the company and Värmeforsk in 1992 due to cooperation difficulties, there is otherwise no circumstance that raises the question of changed choice of sentencing, imprisonment shall be imposed.
>
> As for the length of the imprisonment, there is no reason to deviate from the Court of Appeals' ruling.

One Justice dissented regarding the justification and stated:

> There is no reason to deviate from the Court of Appeals' assessment that the penal value is clearly imprisonment for one year. There is thus a presumption that a sentence of imprisonment must be imposed. In favour of a suspended sentence, on the other hand, L.E. is living in orderly conditions and there is no reason to fear that he would commit further crime. In choosing the penalty, it

should also be considered that L.E. has paid the damages he was ordered to pay in the case. The circumstances in favour of suspended sentence, however, cannot be deemed strong enough that there is reason to deviate from the presumption that the penalty with regard to the penal value should be imprisonment.

As for the length of the imprisonment, there is no reason to deviate from the Court of Appeals' ruling.

## Two Justices dissented and stated:

When deciding on sentencing, the court shall under Chapter 30, Section 4 of the Penal Code pay particular attention to circumstances advocating a milder sentence than imprisonment. As grounds for imprisonment, on the other hand, the penal value and nature of the crime shall be considered, as well as whether the accused has a criminal record.

L.E. has no previous criminal record. The nature of the crime is not such that it, regardless of penal value, should lead to imprisonment. The question is if the penal value is so high that prison shall be imposed.

L.E. committed the embezzlement now under review for several years using his position of trust as bookkeeper and financial manager. The total amount is approximately SEK 189 000.

In recent precedents, crime against property, which is considered a serious crime but not of a particularly serious nature, has led to suspended sentences (see NJA 1989, p. 810 and 1992 p. 190 and 470). However, the penal value of the crime has, at least in one instance, been deemed to ten months' imprisonment (NJA 1992 p. 470).

When the penal value for a crime is imprisonment for one year or more, a presumption is deemed to exist for the sentence of imprisonment. This should, however, not preclude the penalty for a crime against property, in agreement on principle with the opinion expressed in legal case NJA 1992, p. 470, to be decided as a suspended sentence even when the penal value is around one year's imprisonment where there are no other obstacles to such a penalty.

The crime of which L.E. is guilty is fairly typical of embezzlement in instances when a position of trust has been exploited. L.E. has indeed in one instance used false invoices and otherwise misleading bookkeeping. However, the deeds are not characterized by cunning or particular ruthlessness beyond that which lies in the actual utilization of the funds. L.E. has paid the damages that he was obligated to pay. The penal value for his crime may be deemed to be approximately one year.

In light of the above, there should be no obstacle to a suspended sentence for L.E. owing to the penal value of the crime.

## The Justices who decided the outcome stated the following:

This case raises the question of what significance there can be in the choice between imprisonment and a non-custodial sentence of which L.E. has now paid the damages plus interest that was imposed upon him by the District Court and the Court of Appeals. L.E. did not appeal the District Court's ruling whereby he was ordered in connection with count 1 to pay damages in the amount of SEK 62 000 plus interest. In the main hearing in the Court of Appeals, he stated that he had paid the damages including accrued interest. L.E. further did not appeal the Court of Appeals' ruling in the matter of damages plus interest that the Court of Appeals ordered him to pay in connection with counts 2 and 3. These latter damages, including accrued interest, L.E. has paid during proceedings in the Supreme Court.

What has thus transpired means that L.E. has paid in accordance with the binding judgment. This cannot be considered to comprise a special circumstance referred to in Chapter 29, Chapter 5, Section 6, first paragraph, second sentence of the Penal Code, cf. NJA 1988 p.187 and Justices Jermsten's and Danelius' dissenting opinions in NJA 1990 p.84 II. In the aforementioned legal case, however, the Supreme Court expressed a majority, that the circumstance that the accused paid the ordered damages after the District Court's judgement and that he showed sincere remorse over what had occurred (an assault), could not afford any independent significance for the choice of penalty, yet could to some extent be taken into account in the context of an overall assessment, which must always be made as a basis for the sentencing in a criminal case. This statement should apparently be understood as that this was indeed not the sort of situation referred to in Chapter 29, section 1, paragraph 2 of the Penal Code, but that the reported circumstances could nonetheless be considered to some degree in favour of the accused in the sentencing.

As I see it, it must in principle be irrelevant in the choice between imprisonment and a non-custodial sentence that an accused, who has the financial capacity to do so, chooses to pay according to a binding judgment and thereby avoid execution. The matter at issue may, under special circumstances, come into a new light. The accused may, for example, show deep remorse while taking special effort to make amends.

In this instance, L.E. has chosen to sell some assets and borrow from relatives to pay the damages. Asked about the reason for his criminal behaviour, he has merely stated that he cannot explain what happened, stating that he had a higher income before he became employed by Vämeforsk and with the company. Under such circumstances, the payment of the damages cannot be counted in favour of L.E. in sentencing.

(author's translation)

The following circumstances are thus significant according to the judgment:

1  L.E. has no previous criminal record;
2  the crimes, which together involve a significant amount of money, entailed the abuse of a position of trust;
3  L.E. used misleading accounting and also produced false invoices;
4  L.E. lives under orderly conditions;
5  there is no reason to fear that he would commit further crime;
6  L.E. has paid the damages that were imposed in the case;
7  the deeds are not characterized by cunning or particular ruthlessness beyond that which lies in the actual utilization of the funds.

Decisions on sentencing can sometimes be difficult to make, as is clearly illustrated by the legal case in question. As mentioned in the above abstract, an overall assessment of all factors must be made. According to the outline above, this will comprise seven factors. In this instance, as in established practice in general, it is not specified how the overall assessment has been performed. For reasons that will become clear below, item seven in the outline will be addressed in a special manner in the analysis.

### 4.5.2   Has the Requirement for Independence been Met?

As previously discussed, the requirement for independence is not met if the decision-maker does not feel that he or she can assess the preference score for a criterion without taking into account the score for another criterion for the option in question. To take a simple example from this legal case: The decision-maker – the judge – must ask whether (1) L.E. has no previous criminal record and (2) the crimes involve a significant amount of money and involve abuse of a position of trust, are mutually independent with regard to the sentence of imprisonment. The requirement for independence presupposes that the judge can assess the preference for the option imprisonment with respect to criterion 1 without this affecting his assessment of criterion 2 and its significance for the option in question. There would seem in this instance to be no doubt as to whether the requirement for independence has been met.

A judge may deem that there is a dependence between different factors and might, for example, believe that a circumstance should be viewed 'in light of other factors' or that factors 'must be viewed in context'. An even clearer indication that the requirement for independence can be problematic is if the judge says that 'this depends on. . .' or in another way lays down conditions for the assessment of a criterion.[27] There can be several reasons for such an approach. One reason can of course be that the judge not only has a vague intuitive sense of a connection, but also believes that there is actually a dependence between at least some factors. Because the question of whether the independence requirement is met must be determined by the judge himself, his or her own assessment becomes conclusive. The judge must then consider whether it is possible to remedy this dependence, such as by combining two criteria into one or by redefining. This latter is the primary option and often works. In the manner given, the requirement for independence should be checked for all factors with respect to the options. Another reason to believe that a circumstance must

---

[27]   Cf Goodwin and Wright (Ch 1 n 2) 53.

be assessed 'in light of other circumstances' or the like may be that a structured analysis is more arduous than an intuitive assessment or that MCA forces the decision-maker to make assessments for each circumstance, in which sensitive appraisals sometimes become evident, which can be uncomfortable. This, however, provides transparency and can yield more well-considered decisions.

In this legal case, there are some legal facts that may raise the question of whether the requirement for independence has been met. Legal facts 4 and 5 could be seen to be related to each other. It is clear that legal fact 4 can be assessed independently of legal fact 5, but the fact that L.E. lives under orderly conditions also means that there is less risk of him committing a new crime. The same can be said for criterion 1; that L.E. has no previous criminal record implies that he will not continue to commit crimes. Legal fact 1 would not seem, however, to be a prognostic fact for 5, but is probably addressed because it shows that imprisonment is not needed for a correction. The addressing of criterion 4 is likely to have the same purpose. The fact that 1 and 4 also have evidential significance for the assessment of criterion 5 does not, in my view, make the factors interdependent. Criterion 7 deals with how the crime was committed. The crime itself as such has a relatively high penal value, while the approach may – if it is characterized by cunning – affect which penalty is chosen. I therefore believe that there is a dependence between factor 2 and 7, which is why both are assessed under criterion 2. There will thus be six criteria in total in the combined weighting below.

In my assessment, the requirement for independence has been met in this case, with the reservations given. Of significance here is further that the court seems to have explicitly considered the factors mutually independent because they have listed them separately. It should in this context be noted that 'misleading accounting' and 'false invoices' are brought together by the Supreme Court under one point (point 2). The reason for this could have been that they were viewed in one context because false accounting is misleading.

### 4.5.3   Analysis and Results

There are two decision options – imprisonment or suspended sentence – and six legal facts. When deciding on sentencing, the court shall pursuant to 30:4 BrB pay particular attention to circumstances advocating a milder sentence than imprisonment. On the other hand, the choice can be made based on the penal value, which is addressed in points 2 and 3 of the outline. The presumption is, as can be seen in the reasons for the judgment, imprisonment, but this presumption can in this case be rebutted

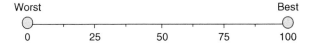

*Figure 4.5    Interval scale*

if there are special reasons. Circumstances 4–6 refer to L.E.'s person and circumstances after the crime. From the judgment it is apparent that this is a case that is balancing between imprisonment and suspended sentence, which makes it more important how the overall assessment is done. The judgment refers to certain preparatory work and judgments and what was said in these. These are interpretative facts which, as discussed above, are not explicitly included in MCA but which influence the scoring and weighting of the individual criteria.

Given that in this case there are relatively few factors included in the overall assessment, the use of multi-criteria analysis may seem unnecessary. On the other hand, this case obviously represents a difficult overall assessment. The use of MCA and SAW in this case makes it easier to see if a certain outcome is reasonable.

The above scale, Figure 4.5, which is used to score criteria with respect to the various options, was introduced in Chapter 2.

As for the question of how significant criteria of this type are in general in assessing if the penalty should be imprisonment or suspended sentence, the preparatory work, precedents and doctrine provide guidelines which should be used in scoring. However, the assessment will also be imprecise because sentencing is not an exact science. Others may therefore have differing opinions on scores and weighting than those presented here. Figures 4.6 and 4.7 below show the assessment has been divided up on to two axes, one for imprisonment and one for suspended sentence. The criteria 'significant amount of money' and 'misleading accounting' have been placed in Figure 4.6 and been given 100 and 60 points, respectively. Misleading accounting has thus been given a lower score. The crime is already serious in view of the amount, which is why 'misleading accounting' is given a lower score.

To make the comparison clearer and thus easier to understand, two axes have thus been drawn – one for imprisonment and one for suspended sentence. In the matrix with the calculations (Table 4.3 below), scores have been addressed as follows: the factors in favour of suspended sentence have, in the assessment of the imprisonment option, been given 0 points. Conversely, the factors in favour of imprisonment have been given 0 points in the assessment of the suspended sentence option.

In the weighting, a total of 100 weight points also in this example will

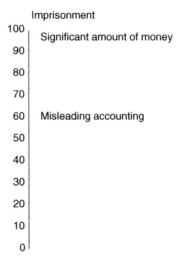

*Figure 4.6    Assessment on two axes*

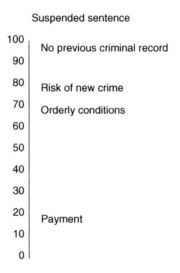

*Figure 4.7    Assessment on two axes*

be allocated for both options for all criteria. This allows the relative importance of legal facts for each penalty in this specific case to be clearly and simply weighed against each other. The significant amount of money has been given a weight of 30, and misleading accounting a weight of 20.

*Table 4.3  Calculation for penalty*

| Penalty | | | | | | | |
|---|---|---|---|---|---|---|---|
| | 1 | 2 | 3 | 4 | 5 | 6 | Total |
| Imprison-ment | 0 | 100 | 60 | 0 | 0 | 0 | 42 |
| Suspended sentence | 100 | 0 | 0 | 80 | 70 | 20 | 36 |
| Weight | 15 | 30 | 20 | 15 | 10 | 10 | |

This latter weight may seem low, but considering that the gravity of the crime is to a large degree addressed in the first criterion, it seems reasonable to give the latter legal fact two-thirds as much weight as significant amount of money. No previous criminal record has been given 15 weight points. It has thus been deemed to be half as important as criterion 1 and three-quarters as important as criterion 2. The same applies for criteria 4 and 5. Finally, the payment has been given a weight of 10, meaning that its relative weight is three times less than criterion 1 and half of criterion 2.

As concerns the results, it can be noted that despite a rather generous assessment of the criteria for suspended sentence, this option differs quite a bit from the imprisonment option. The only reasonable way that the suspended sentence can be relevant is if the assessment of the crime is given a lower score or weight. Other scores and criteria for suspended sentence do not appear to be under-evaluated. This is also how the dissenting judges seem to have reasoned by adding the seventh criterion, which tones down the gravity of the crime, though of course without being an extenuating circumstance. If, for example, criterion 3 is given a score of 30 instead of 60, the total with the same weight (20) will be 36, which means that it would be a tie between imprisonment and suspended sentence. If the scores are lowered even further, suspended sentence will win out. Following this approach, one could try changing the values in the calculation to see what happens, and continue in this way until the assessment seems reasonable and well balanced. In this way, MCA is, as previously discussed, an interactive tool in decision-making. Another legal fact that could be decisive in the case is the voluntary payment, which would seem to be the reason that it was given considerable attention in the reasons for the judgement. How the voluntary payment should be assessed can be discussed. Financial capacity should, however, not provide an opportunity to buy oneself free; it should instead be a matter of a payment made in sacrifice in combination with genuine remorse. However, voluntary payment should in my opinion still be given a value in this case, even if it is low.

Finally, it again should be emphasized that the values of course cannot be precise. They instead fluctuate within specific ranges. Making the assessment of the different criteria within ranges provides minimum and maximum values for them. To simplify comparison, the average values can then be used. Another alternative is to use fuzzy logic, which will be described in the following section.

## 4.6 FUZZY LOGIC

### 4.6.1 Introduction

It was stated above that the simple additive model can be used in combination with fuzzy logic. The following will briefly describe the grounds for fuzzy logic. Fuzzy logic will then be applied along with the simple additive model on the agreement example above in section 4.4. In Chapter 6, fuzzy logic will be applied on evidentiary statements.[28]

In 1965, Lofti A Zadeh published the essay 'Fuzzy Sets' in which he developed the basic concepts and mathematical tools that are now used in fuzzy logic. He was strongly criticized at first by representatives for classical logic, but fuzzy logic has become gradually more accepted and today holds a strong position. Fuzzy logic is used for things like programming machines, such as common household appliances, for electronics in cars and for programming computer games. Fuzzy logic makes it possible to handle vague words like 'tall', 'short', 'early', 'late', 'hot', 'cold' and 'lukewarm', which are not contained in traditional propositional and predicate logic, where statements are either true or false. Fuzzy logic has hardly been noticed yet in legal literature, either in Sweden or in other countries. It has, however, according to Huber, been used on Degree of Beliefs, which has been written about by Dempster and Shafer, among others.[29]

Fuzzy logic thus addresses the uncertainty that arises from vagueness.

---

[28] For an introduction to fuzzy logic, the author recommends Masao Mukaidono, *Fuzzy Logic for Beginners* (World Scientific Publishing Co Pte Ltd 2004), Kazuo Tanaka, *An Introduction to Fuzzy Logic For Practical Applications* (Springer 1997), Hung T Nguyen and Elbert A Walker, *A First Course in Fuzzy Logic* (3rd edn Chapman & Hall/CRC/Taylor & Francis Group 2006) and Daniel McNeill and Paul Freiberger, *Fuzzy Logic. The Revolutionary Computer Technology That Is Changing Our World* (Touchstone & Schuster 1993). In addition, Anders Løvlie, *Rettslige faktabegreper* (Gyldendal Juridisk 2014) 80ff outlines the fundamental features of fuzzy logic in this law book.
[29] Franz Huber, 'Belief and Degrees of Beliefs' in Franz Huber and Christoph Schmidt-Petri (eds) *Degrees of Belief* (Springer 2009).

A witness, for example, says that: 'It was quite far away, but it was a short person, rather heavyset, with dark hair.' This is our natural way of speaking and it is vague. But we understand it, just as we understand what someone means when they way it was a 'hot' summer day or that the job would take a 'long' time or that things seemed 'tense' between the parties. Sometimes, like in trials, more exactitude may be required and in some cases it is possible to clarify more precisely. However, it is not possible in common parlance to specify when 'cold' becomes 'hot' or where the exact line is between 'tall' and 'short' because these are vague expressions, that is, the semantic range of the words is unclear.

Vagueness as a scientific problem has coined many expressions:

'Precision is not truth' (Henri Matisse).
'Sometimes the more measurable drives out the most important' (Réne Dubois).
'Vagueness is no more to be done with in the world of logic than friction in mechanics' (Charles Sander Peirce).
'I believe that nothing is unconditionally true, and hence I am opposed to every statement of positive truth and every man who makes it' (HL Mencken).
'So far as the laws of mathematics refer to reality, they are not certain. And so far they are certain, they do not refer to reality' (Albert Einstein).
'As complexity rises, precise statements lose meaning and meaningful statements lose precision' (Lofti Zadeh).[30]

From these statements, one might get the impression that vagueness is good, and maybe it is. In scientific contexts, it would of course be good if every word exactly reproduced what was observed, but in everyday use, vagueness is rather good. Vagueness would also seem to be necessary for us to be able to quickly communicate the essentials according to the language codes that we generally agree on. How complicated it would be to communicate if there were words for every little detail and we were forbidden to use words with a vague meaning. In any case, there is vagueness in law. Necessary conditions in law are sometimes indefinite, as are the descriptions given by the participants in litigation. Fuzzy logic also seems to be well suited to the appraisal of oral statements in a trial, but can probably also be used for interpretation in general as a tool to describe the scope of application for a rule of law. The premises for fuzzy logic are briefly presented below.

---

[30]   J-S Roger Jang and Ned Gulley, *Matlab, Fuzzy Logic Toolbox, User's guide, Version 1*, <http://andrei.clubcisco.ro/cursuri/5master/ciblf/Artificial_Intelligence_Fuzzy_Logic_Matlab.pdfIntroduction> (retrieved 11 July 2016).

*Table 4.4    Truth table – nonfuzzy sets*

| Truth table - nonfuzzy sets | | |
|---|---|---|
| Statement | Height | Truth value |
| John is tall | 198 cm | True |
| James is tall | 186 cm | True |
| Tom is tall | 180 cm | True |
| Bob is tall | 179 cm | False |
| Nick is tall | 165 cm | False |

### 4.6.2   Linguistic Variables, Fuzzy Sets and Membership Distribution

Fuzzy logic is based on four premises: linguistic variables, membership distribution, fuzzy sets and fuzzy if-then rules.[31] These elements will be briefly described below, except for fuzzy if-then rules, which are not needed to understand the basic ideas behind fuzzy logic.[32]

'Tall' and 'short' are vague expressions. An adult man with a height of 200 cm is indisputably 'tall' and an adult man of 130 cm is indisputably 'short'. Someone who is 175 cm is of 'average height'. In fuzzy logic, real numbers from 0 to 1 are often used to represent what is indisputably false or indisputably true.

In classical logic, the statement that Per is 200 cm tall is a variable (Per) and a value (200 cm). In fuzzy logic, the statement 'Per is tall' contains the variable Per and the value 'tall', but what belongs to 'tall' is in fuzzy logic relative and only true by degrees.

Membership functions can be expressed graphically. The simplest membership function is the triangle.[33] In Figure 4.8 below, we can assume that a set is 'tall men'. If 'tall men' are men between 180 cm and 200 cm, the exterior points of this set are 180 and 200 cm. The peak then represents men who are 190 cm tall. The figure could be supplemented with another triangle – 'very tall men' – that is, men who are over 200 cm tall. Men

---

[31]   Nguyen and Walker (n 28).
[32]   For further discussion on if-then rules, see ibid., 59ff.
[33]   There are a number of graphical expressions for membership functions. The trapezoidal also is a rather simple membership function.

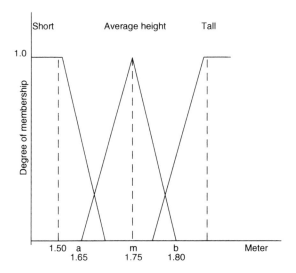

*Figure 4.8    Membership function sets*

who are of 'average height' is a different set for men, which according to Figure 4.8 are between 165 cm (a) and 180 cm tall (b).[34]

Fuzzy logic thus uses degrees of membership and fuzzy sets instead of fixed sets in which statements of membership are either true or false. In a nonfuzzy set, a person over 180 cm can be defined as 'tall'. According to classical logic, the membership value is either 1 or 0. If the definition of a 'tall man' is that he is 180 cm or taller, then Tom, who is 180 cm tall, is 'tall', while Bob, who is 179 cm, is 'short', see Table 4.5 below. As there is only a 1 cm difference between Tom and Bob, this effect is rather drastic, whereas fuzzy logic, which is quite consistent with common parlance, is much better at distinguishing between the options and provides better information.[35] Fuzzy logic thus includes fixed sets, but these will be different. Fuzzy logic makes it possible to make conclusions from information that is vague and imprecise.

The degree of membership µ can have values between 0 and 1. The expression $\mu(x) = 0$ means that x is not in the set and $\mu(X) = 1$ means that x is completely within the set. The distribution curve for a triangular function is calculated as follows:

---

[34]   Cf the examples in Mukaidono (n 28) 31ff.
[35]   McNeill and Freiberger (n 28) 34; Tanaka (n 28) 13.

$$\mu_A(X) = \begin{cases} 0, & x \le a \\ \dfrac{x - a}{m - a}, & a < x \le m \\ \dfrac{b - x}{b - m}, & m < x < b \\ 0, & x \ge b \end{cases}$$ (4.1)

Just as in classical logic, fuzzy logic thus uses sets, which are illustrated in Figure 4.9 by Cantor's Sets.[36]

*Table 4.5    Truth table with fuzzy and nonfuzzy sets*

| Truth table with fuzzy sets | | | Truth table with nonfuzzy sets | | |
|---|---|---|---|---|---|
| Statement | Height | Truth value | Statement | Height | Truth value |
| John is tall | 198 cm | 0,95 | John is tall | 198 cm | True |
| James is tall | 186 cm | 0,8 | James is tall | 186 cm | True |
| Tom is tall | 180 cm | 0,6 | Tom is tall | 180 cm | True |
| Bob is tall | 179 cm | 0,4 | Bob is tall | 179 cm | False |
| Nick is tall | 165 cm | 0,2 | Nick is tall | 165 cm | False |

What belongs to what? A set can contain another set if it includes members of the other set. The smaller set is then called the subset. The set of large lakes, for example, contains all large lakes in Sweden, which is a subset of large lakes, which is in turn a subset of lakes. In this way, a hierarchy of many sets can be created. What belongs to both sets? When two roads meet, they create a square (if they are of equal width): an intersection, which is part of both roads. The intersection is the area in which both sets overlap. The intersection equalizes and excludes. It only accepts members of both sets. Similarly, sets can cross each other.

---

[36]  Cf McNeill and Freiberger (n 28) 25. Georg Cantor (1845–1918) was a German mathematician.

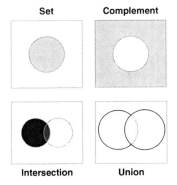

*Figure 4.9    Cantor's sets*

    Set: All golfers
    Set: All swimmers
    Intersection: All golfers and swimmers

What lands outside? The complement to a set is its opposite:

    Set: Long rivers
    Complement: Rivers that are not long

What belongs to one or the other set? The union brings together sets without filters. It is open because it includes every object that falls within one or the other set:

    Set: All golfers
    Set: All swimmers
    Union: All golfers or swimmers (or both).[37]

Cantor's theory was enthusiastically received by mathematicians, yet some of them saw problems with the vagueness of statements and so began the development of fuzzy logic to Zadeh. Fuzzy logic is thus based on set theory and the Cantor set, but is an expansion of this.[38] The basic idea is that membership can be by degrees; a set can thus have members that only partially belong to it. A set can also be empty. For example, the set of camels that wear pyjamas has 0 members, but because a fuzzy set, so to

---

[37]   See the foregoing McNeill and Freiberger ibid., 36.
[38]   Tanaka (n 28) 34–5.

speak, broadens determined sets, it is more common for nonfuzzy sets to have 0 members than for fuzzy sets to have 0 members.

To what extent does an object belong to a set? The complement of a fuzzy set is the degree membership needs to reach the value of 1.0. If two people, Bob and Linda, are in a room in which music is playing loudly, the set of irritated people in the room is Bob, 0.85 and Linda, 0.80. The complement is the set of non-irritated people in the room, which is Bob, 0.15 and Linda, 0.20, that is, the complement expresses to what degree each person does not belong to the set.

What sets belong to other sets? This is relatively simple to determine for fixed sets. As in the earlier example, large lakes includes all large Swedish lakes, which become a subset of large lakes, which in turn is a subset of lakes. In a fuzzy set, each object must belong to a subset to a smaller degree than the larger set, or belong to both equally. How much does an object belong to two sets? In fixed sets, the intersection constitutes a space shared by two sets (cf the above road intersection). In fuzzy sets, the sets share the degree of membership. A fuzzy intersection is the lower degree of membership that the two sets share in both sets. Using this, the intersection of, for example, men who are 'tall' and 'fat' can be calculated. How much does an object belong to one or the other set? The union of fuzzy sets is the reverse of the intersection. Instead of the lower degree of two fuzzy sets, it is the higher. The union is thus the higher degree of each individual's membership in one or the other set.[39]

The question on the use of fuzzy logic in interpretation and application of the law is, as far as I could determine, very sparse in legal literature. In interpreting the law, the premise is that a linguistic determination is made of the law's wording and that a division is made between the cases which are clearly covered by the wording of the law and cases which clearly lie outside this core area. Between these two is a grey zone in which the application of the law may presuppose extensive interpretation, while a restrictive interpretation may mean that the law will not be applied. In addition to these interpretive approaches, there are also analogical interpretation and application and interpretation and application e contrario.[40] It is easy to see that fuzzy logic could be used to describe a situation's degree of membership in a necessary condition in a legal provision. With fuzzy logic, it would furthermore be possible to handle competing laws in a completely

---

[39]   Cf the foregoing and McNeill and Freiberger (n 28) 36–7.
[40]   Regarding analogism, cf Jürgen Hollatz, 'Analogy Making in Legal Reasoning with Neural Networks and Fuzzy Logic' (1999) 7(2–3) *Artificial Intelligence and Law* 289.

different way than with traditional law interpretation and application methods, because it would be mathematically possible to describe how much a situation belongs to several different possible legal provisions.

### 4.6.3   Application of SAW and Fuzzy Logic – An Example

As promised above, Table 4.6 below will show the application of the simple additive model in combination with fuzzy logic on the agreement example in section 4.4 to demonstrate how this can be put into practice. To begin with, the outline below shows linguistic terms for scores and weights and their numbers when using the triangular function. Figure below shows that the lower the value is, the less membership, and the higher the value is, the higher the membership is.

To make the example more realistic, we will assume that the assessment is done with three judges on the bench. In Table 4.7 below, the judges' assessments for the various criteria are indicated by using the linguistic terms. The assessment that is shown in the table only refers to the criteria's scores with respect to modification, but a similar figure could of course be made for setting aside the clause.

The judges' assessments give the numbers in Table 4.8 after the use of the triangle as membership function.

*Table 4.6    Linguistic term for scores and weight*

| Linguistic term for scores and weight | | |
|---|---|---|
| Linguistic terms, score | Linguistic terms, weight | Triangulated fuzzy values |
| Very relevant VR | Very high weight VHW | 0, 75, 1.0, 1.0 |
| High relevance HR | High weight HW | 0.5, 0.75, 1.0 |
| Moderate relevance MR | Moderate weight MW | 0.25, 0.5, 0.75 |
| Low relevance LR | Low weight LW | 0, 0.25, 0.5 |
| Very low relevance VLR | Very low weight VLW | 0, 0, 0.25 |

*Multi-criteria analysis in legal reasoning*

*Table 4.7   Score assessment three judges on bench*

| Score assessment, three judges on bench | | | |
|---|---|---|---|
| Criteria | Judge 1 | Judge 2 | Judge 3 |
| A | VLR | LR | VLR |
| B | MR | HR | MR |
| C | HR | HR | MR |
| D | MR | MR | HR |
| E | LR | LR | MR |
| F | LR | VLR | LR |
| G | HR | HR | VR |

*Table 4.8   Matrix fuzzy scores*

| Criteria | Matrix fuzzy scores | | | |
|---|---|---|---|---|
| | Option | Judge 1 | Judge 2 | Judge 3 |
| A | Modify | 0, 0, 0.25 | 0, 0.25, 0.5 | 0, 0, 0.25 |
| - | Set aside | 0, 0, 0.25 | 0, 0, 0.25 | 0, 0, 0.25 |
| B | Modify | 0.25, 0.5, 0.75 | 0.5, 0.75, 1.0 | 0.25, 0.5, 0.75 |
| - | Set aside | 0.25, 0.5, 0.75 | 0.5, 0.75, 1.0 | 0.5, 0.75, 1.0 |
| C | Modify | 0.5, 0.75, 1.0 | 0.5, 0.75, 1.0 | 0.25, 0.5, 0.75 |
| - | Set aside | 0.5, 0.75, 1.0 | 0.75, 1.0, 1.0 | 0.5, 0.75, 1.0 |
| D | Modify | 0.25, 0.5, 0.75 | 0.25, 0.5, 0.75 | 0.5, 0.75, 1.0 |
| - | Set aside | 0.25, 0.5, 0.75 | 0.25, 0.5, 0.75 | 0.5, 0.75, 1.0 |
| E | Modify | 0, 0.25, 0.5 | 0, 0.25, 0.5 | 0.25, 0.5, 0.75 |
| - | Set aside | 0, 0, 0.25 | 0, 0.25, 0.5 | 0, 0.25, 0.5 |
| F | Modify | 0, 0.25, 0.5 | 0, 0, 0.25 | 0, 0.25, 0.5 |
| - | Set aside | 0, 0, 0.25 | 0, 0, 0.25 | 0, 0, 0.25 |
| G | Modify | 0.5, 0.75, 1.0 | 0.5, 0.75, 1.0 | 0.75, 1.0, 1.0 |
| - | Set aside | 0.5, 0.75, 1.0 | 0.75, 1.0, 1.0 | 0.5, 0.75, 1.0 |

*Table 4.9  Average values*

| Criteria and options | Average values | | | Recalculated value |
|---|---|---|---|---|
| A, Modify | 0 | 0.08 | 0.33 | 0.14 |
| A, Set aside | 0 | 0 | 0.25 | 0.08 |
| B, Modify | 0.33 | 0.58 | 0.83 | 0.58 |
| B, Set aside | 0.42 | 0.67 | 0.92 | 0.67 |
| C, Modify | 0.42 | 0.67 | 0.92 | 0.67 |
| C, Set aside | 0.58 | 0.83 | 1.0 | 0.80 |
| D, Modify | 0.33 | 0.58 | 0.83 | 0.58 |
| D, Set aside | 0.33 | 0.58 | 0.83 | 0.58 |
| E, Modify | 0.08 | 0.33 | 0.58 | 0.33 |
| E, Set aside | 0 | 0.17 | 0.42 | 0.20 |
| F, Modify | 0 | 0.17 | 0.42 | 0.20 |
| F, Set aside | 0 | 0 | 0.25 | 0.08 |
| G, Modify | 0.58 | 0.83 | 1.0 | 0.80 |
| G,Set aside | 0.58 | 0.83 | 1.0 | 0.80 |

The average values are calculated as follows: $(0+0+0) = 0/3 = 0 + (0 + 0 + 0.25) = 0.25/3 = 0.08 + (0.25 + 0.5 + 0.25) = 1.0/3 = 0.33$, and so on. The calculated values are shown in Table 4.9.

The weights of the criteria are then calculated in the same way. Table 4.10 shows the values using the triangular function. Note that the weights refer to the criteria without breakdown by option.

As above, there is an adjusted value here, Table 4.11 (linguistic values are omitted). This value is often referred to as a 'defuzzified value'. The normalized value is obtained by adding the defuzzified values for each criterion and then dividing each defuzzified value by the total: $0.08 + 0.5 + 0.67 + 0.58 + 0.33 + 0.33 + 0.67 = 3.16. = 0.08$ divided by $3.16 = 0.03$ (rounded), 0.5 divided by $3.16 = 0.16$, and so on.

Sometimes the normalized value for all criteria and options are calculated $R_{ij} = X_{ij}/max(X1, X2, X3, X4, X5, X6); i = 1, 2 \ldots$, and so on. Only the maximum values are used if there are no negative facts (in such cases, minimum values should also be calculated). However, this type of normalization has not been done because no negative values are deemed to be present in this case.[41] The simple additive model will thus ultimately be used in the following way. Modification: $(0.14 \times 0.03) + (0.58 \times 0.16) +$

---

[41]  Negative facts seems to be a difficult concept in MCA. It is sometimes hard to detect the difference between less of something and that something is negative.

*Table 4.10    Assessment matrix, criteria*

| Assessment matrix, criteria | | | |
|---|---|---|---|
| Criteria | Judge1 | Judge2 | Judge3 |
| A | 0, 0, 0.25 | 0, 0, 0.25 | 0, 0, 0.25 |
| B | 0.25, 0.5, 0.75 | 0.5, 0.75, 1.0 | 0, 0.25, 0.5 |
| C | 0.5, 0.75, 1.0 | 0.25, 0.5, 0.75 | 0.5, 0.75, 1.0 |
| D | 0.25, 0.5, 0.75 | 0.5, 0.75, 1.0 | 0.25, 0.5, 0.75 |
| E | 0, 0.25, 0.5 | 0, 0.25, 0.5 | 0.25, 0.5, 0.75 |
| F | 0.25, 0.5, 0.75 | 0, 0.25, 0.5 | 0, 0.25, 0.5 |
| G | 0.5, 0.75, 1.0 | 0.5, 0.75, 1.0 | 0.25, 0.5, 0.75 |

*Table 4.11    Defuzzified values*

| Criterion | Average value | Average value | Average value | Average value | Normalized weight |
|---|---|---|---|---|---|
| A | 0 | 0 | 0.25 | 0.08 | 0.03 |
| B | 0.25 | 0.5 | 0.75 | 0.5 | 0.16 |
| C | 0.42 | 0.67 | 0.92 | 0.67 | 0.21 |
| D | 0.33 | 0.58 | 0.83 | 0.58 | 0.18 |
| E | 0.08 | 0.33 | 0.58 | 0.33 | 0.10 |
| F | 0.08 | 0.33 | 0.58 | 0.33 | 0.10 |
| G | 0.42 | 0.67 | 0.92 | 0.67 | 0.21 |

$(0.67 \times 0.21) + (0.58 \times 0.18) + (0.33 \times 0.10) + (0.20 \times 0.10) + (0.80 \times 0.21) = 0.56$. Set aside: $(0.08 \times 0.03) + (0.67 \times 0.16) + (0.80 \times 0.21) + (0.58 \times 0.18) + /0.20 \times 0.10) + (0.08 \times 0.10) + (0.80 \times 0.21) = 0.58$. The final results differ slightly from the final results in section 4.4, where they were 57 and 47.5 respectively, but the input values are not completely identical. Because the difference is not significant anyway, it may be questioned whether fuzzy logic is necessary. This is difficult to comment on for this data. One advantage of fuzzy logic would anyway seem to be that lawyers feel that linguistic terms are easier to use for appraisal than numbers, and that there is a realism in the use of linguistic terms in the context of law because these capture the vagueness that indisputably exists in assessments better than numbers.

## 4.7 SUMMARY AND CONCLUSIONS

RB's rules and principles on procedure mean that process materials are 'packaged' into suitable parts in order to achieve an appropriate procedure and that only the voting rules are directly aimed at differences of opinion among the court members. MCA can be used in any decision situation and in judicial processes if there are not procedural rules that directly prevent this and this may be the case with voting rules. However, MCA can always be used to structure and analyse an extensive decision basis.

When the courts rule on a dispute, it is bound by the parties' claims. Furthermore, the options are decided by the parties because their claims determine which legal alternatives can come into question. This simplifies the decision-making process because the court does not need to seek and formulate options, which is the case when MCA is used in a planning process. The court also may not go beyond the claims. The starting point for the use of MCA and the simple additive model in judicial processes is furthermore that the parties in a case amenable to out-of-court settlement have alleged certain legal facts in the case as foundation for their positions. The claims, which correspond with the legal consequences, are thus the options or the legal alternatives the court must take a stand to and concrete legal facts are the criteria for assessment of the options.

In a trial, the plaintiff can, for example, claim a monetary amount and refer to several different legal grounds for this. In that case, they will be examined one by one, though not necessarily in order of priority, but the courts usually follow the party's ranking of the legal grounds and in some cases would even seem obligated to do so. The courts thus do not assess whether a claimed amount should be imposed after an overall assessment of all legal grounds for the claim, even if this could be possible and could provide a more satisfactory result. The way in which the examination is made in court and the voting rules thus prevent the court from making a total overall assessment of several alternative legal grounds. This does not mean that MCA cannot be used by legal representatives when planning a process that comprises multiple claims and several legal grounds. In such cases, an MCA analysis could consist of decision trees for each claim combined with a prognostic assessment of the probable outcome of each claim. In addition, different legal grounds can, in accordance with MCA, be regarded as alternatives, however not with respect to the final outcome.

In the party-controlled process of a case amenable to out-of-court settlement, where the court is bound by what the parties have alleged, the court can begin from the bottom with the parties' assertions in order to construct a decision tree. In a complicated case this could provide a good overview of the case. If the case is not amenable to out-of-court settlement (for example, 'the best interests of the child' in a custody dispute), the court can start from the top by determining desirable properties in the ruling, and if not directly looking in the process materials after things that can enable the objectives to be achieved, make the parties aware of legal facts that they may have overlooked, which could be of significance. The application of legal rules in individual cases may otherwise differ depending on what type of rules will be used. If the case is a criminal action and thus concerns the application of penal rules, the premise is that the application of law must be highly consistent with the existing conditions for criminality, as set down by the principle of legality. This does not mean that overall assessments cannot be made in criminal cases, but that if they are, they, as in the example above in section 4.5, usually concern what sentence will be imposed.

A local scale is defined by the options that are under consideration in the concrete decision situation. Because new options do not usually come into the picture after the main hearing has ended, a local scale has been used in this book. In the agreement and sentencing example, the swing method has been used and scoring and weighting referred to concrete legal facts. These have been said to express the legal value linked to the option's consequences with regard to the concrete legal fact. Consequences should in judicial processes be read as legal relevance; the legal value thus expresses the strength of the legal relevance.

The administration of justice means that courts apply legal rules in specific cases in order to resolve a legal dispute. Other concepts associated with the term 'administration of justice' and which express objectives or interests are, for example, behaviour modification, conflict resolution, foreseeability, impartiality and non-discrimination. In order to implement these overriding objectives, different principles for the interpretation and application of law are used in different areas of the law. As far as scoring and weighting in accordance with MCA is concerned, the aforementioned overriding objectives and law interpretation methods belong to the decision context and will impact the values that will be used in balancing of interests or overall assessments. Concerning the structural relationship between concrete legal facts, prerequisites, options and objectives in judicial processes, this is basically of the same nature as in the example given in the introduction of Chapter 1. The judge assesses the possible legal consequences of claims with respect to the legal facts that have been referred to, just as the house buyer evaluates potential houses with respect to the criteria he or she has decided. In the examples given in Chapter 2, it was noted that MCA can be used when buying a car, which should be inexpensive to own, safe and have an attractive design. A simple example was also given for the use of the simple additive model on the question of whether an agreement was 'unreasonable' under Section 36 of AvtL. Unlike the purchase of a car or house, however, the objective of a legal ruling may be difficult to define. What, for example, is the objective of the prerequisite 'unreasonable' in 36 AvtL? In this case, there are no clear purposes specified in law or preparatory work, but there are a number of examples of typical cases in the preparatory work where the provision could be applied. In legal balancing of interests, on the other hand, it is easy to see what interests are placed on the scales, for example the interest of camera surveillance in order to prevent crime versus the interest of privacy. However, it is no easy task to specify exactly what 'privacy' means and weighting can be even more difficult. The car buyer definitely has an easier task. The choice is to be made by the car buyer or the family. The decision only concerns them and their needs and preferences. They do not need to consider public interest or make the kinds of deliberations in general that a court must make. For a court, the task of determining objectives is thus significantly more difficult, even if the overall assessment basically follows the same patterns as for the car buyer.

As argued by Odelstad, it can be said that the purpose of an overall assessment or a balancing of interests is to achieve a 'total goodness'. The courts must then take into account such factors as law and order, non-discrimination and the presumed consequences of the judgement for other parties and even for the market, if it is a commercial dispute. The members of the court may have different opinions on how the law should be interpreted and applied and what function a rule has, as well as the functions of the administration of justice in general. Regarding values of this kind and the objectives of a judgment, it is therefore hardly possible to specify these in a decision tree so that they can be operative in an MCA analysis because they are far too diffuse and difficult to define, in any case as concerns overall assessments and balancing of interests. The decision tree used in this chapter has therefore been simplified. At the top of the decision tree are generally formulated objectives and – with regard to 36 AvtL – no specified purpose apart from the protection interest. The aforementioned means that the objectives are primarily built up and specified from the bottom up with the process materials in this specific case as a base. With respect to the foregoing, the starting point for the analyses performed is, as mentioned above, that appraisals of different kinds will impact the decision-makers' subjective scoring and weighting of concrete legal facts. The differences between different judges, however, would seem to usually not be significant because there is a high degree of consensus among professional decision-makers. Compare Lootsma:

> They [decision-makers] are prepared to estimate the weights of the criteria or their relative importance (weight ratios), regardless of how the performance of the alternatives has been measured and regardless of their aggregation procedure, so that they seem to supply meaningless information. The underlying reason may be that criteria have emotional or social values which neither depend on the actual decision problem itself nor on the method of analysis. Many decision makers want to be consistent over a coherent collection of decision problems. They want to employ a uniform set of criterion weights, to be used in a certain area (water management, environmental protection, national energy planning. . .), but in isolation from immediate context. Moreover, there is a good deal of distributed decision making in large organizations.[42]

Lootsma seems to mean that criteria in institutional decision-making is assessed mechanically without taking into account their relative importance and that this is due to underlying social values in the decision environment. In my opinion, Lootsma's reasoning goes too far, especially if the administration of justice is to be included. A distinction should be made between, on the one hand, legitimate sources for legal arguments in the legal source doctrine that also ranks these sources and, on the other hand, how these sources should be used in specific cases. However, legal sources, such as preparatory work, sometimes provide little guidance. They also say nothing about overall values. Yet, the legal source doctrine is a very important controlling factor that both simplifies the decision-making process and provides certain foreseeability and certain non-discrimination.

The simple additive model is linear and compensatory. The linearity expresses that a certain amount or quantity of something has the same value no matter where it is on the scale. Linearity in this strict sense does not exist in legal contexts and is also not required for the use of the simple additive model. Because a legal fact, at least in overall assessments and balancing of interests, is to a greater or lesser extent compensatory, there is a sort of linearity. Compensation means that high scores on one criterion can compensate for low scores on another. If, for example, in a case about negligent driving, a person was driving a car very fast on narrow road, it may not matter much if visibility was also obstructed. If the speed was lower, however, the obstructed visibility probably would have a greater importance, that is, have a greater relative importance in the assessment of negligence.

---

[42]    Lootsma (Ch 1 n 2) 33.

After having performed several calculations myself with MCA and particularly the simple additive model, I have found that it works best as an interactive decision support, that is, the input values are calculated and reconciled intuitively. If something does not feel right, one should try with other values. Furthermore, certain scorings and weightings can at first and in an intuitive assessment seem to have too little impact. The results in both the agreement example and the sentencing example may seem a bit surprising from the beginning according to my own intuitive assessment of individual legal facts. I had expected a clear outcome in favour of modification in the agreement example and an even clearer outcome in favour of suspended sentence in the sentencing example.

In the agreement example, virtually all individual legal facts have been given legal values. However, as noted in the text, for individual legal facts, the courts seem to apply the principle of all or nothing in accordance with the principle of successive relevance and successive verification, which appears to be incorrect if the purpose of the overall assessment is for all circumstances of significance to contribute to the overall assessment. Finally, this chapter introduced and presented fuzzy logic. We will return to fuzzy logic in Chapter 6.

# 5. Decision-making under uncertainty

## 5.1 INTRODUCTION

In Chapter 1, it was shown that one difference between overall assessments and balancing of interests is that a law-based balancing of interests refers to a license to take an action. Should camera surveillance be permitted? Should exemption be granted for a building within the shoreline-protected area? Is there extraordinary cause to sustain the petition for disclosure? These cases contain an uncertainty – that must be factored in when the decision is made – on what consequences the decision can be expected to have. If it concerns an application for camera surveillance intended to reduce crime, the decision-maker must assess whether, and in that case how much, crime will be reduced in the camera surveillance area and as a result of camera surveillance. The reduction in crime is the utility of the decision. The harm that a decision on camera surveillance may result in is that local residents may feel uncomfortable being under such surveillance. The interest in suppressing crime must be weighed against the privacy interest and this is done in the model that the Swedish Data Protection Authority calls the principle of preponderance of evidence in which utility and harm are placed in the scales.[1] Similar reasoning can be done concerning the weighting performed in a claim for declaratory judgement. Will this judgment eliminate the uncertainty of the legal relationship? What happens if it does not? A declaratory judgement over the entire legal relationship between the parties is beneficial because it could remove all uncertainty, but if uncertainty remains, there is a risk of additional processes that can be costly and cause inconvenience. Even in this case, a prognostic assessment must therefore be made along with the suitability assessment, containing utility and harm, the last perhaps primarily in regard to the financial costs of the process.

As stated in several places in this book, the additive model described and used, SAW, is based on there being no uncertainties or at least that this uncertainty is small with regard to the existence of criteria and the probability of an outcome occurring. The model is, in other words,

---

[1]    See section 1.3.5, above.

deterministic with regard to the outcome and the criteria. It has been said that a consideration of uncertainty can be added by calculating for each option the probability of it occurring.[2] It has also been argued that uncertainty in law can be handled with fuzzy logic.

In this book, overall assessments and balancing of interests have been discussed according to the definition given in Chapter 1. Below, a few basic assumptions are given concerning the underlying facts in prognostic assessments. Several of these have been touched on in this book: various environmental reviews, certain reviews under the Tenancy Act, 'the best interests of the child', claims for declaratory judgement, and so on. After an introduction to risk, hazard and uncertainty, benefit and probability will be discussed in relation to prognostic assessments.

## 5.2   RISK, HAZARD AND UNCERTAINTY

Decisions under certainty are a choice between options that lead to known consequences. In a decision under risk, the choice means that with a certain degree of probability, the option will lead to known consequences. If the decision is made under uncertainty, complete information is lacking on various options and/or the probability of different consequences. Uncertainty in decision-making is well illuminated in decision theory. It can have many causes, the most common being that something is difficult to investigate, lack of information, or diffuse or imprecise information,[3] which, incidentally, is not unusual in a legal context. In scientific contexts, uncertainty is usually classified as a probability problem.

If the decision-maker deems that the probability of rain in Paris tomorrow is 0.5, it axiomatically follows due to mathematical probability that the probability there will not be rain is 0.5 because the sum of these added together must be 1.0. Objections have been made against this approach because there is a difference between different types of probability. If, for example, a person who is not a wine expert is assessing the probability that a certain wine is red or white and determines that the probability the wine is red is 0.5, this can be a pure guess if this person does not know much about wine.[4] It is actually a possibility that it is red rather than a probability that it is red, which means that there is a difference between

---

[2]   See section 2.1, above.
[3]   Malczewski (Ch 1 n 4) 88, Belton and Stewart (Ch 1 n 2) 60ff.
[4]   Huber (Ch 4 n 29). The person in question can of course also assess the probability that the wine is either red or white.

this type of probability and the probability of getting a six when rolling a dice, because there is still a basis of knowledge for calculating probabilities when rolling dice.[5] Dempster (1968) and Shafer (1976) distinguish between these different types of probabilities. They make a distinction between the probability of outcomes in betting, which they argue are mathematical and two-sided, and how much the individual believes in this outcome. This 'belief function' does not, they argue, follow the principle of two-sided probability, but is instead one-sided. They call these levels 'credal level' and 'pignistic level'.[6]

Perhaps the most striking difference between the evidentiary theme method and the evidentiary value method for the evaluation of evidence, which I will return to in section 6.1.1, is that the probability under the evidentiary theme method is two-sided, but one-sided according to the evidentiary value method.[7] Thus, if the probability of A is 60 per cent, the probability of not A axiomatically becomes 40 per cent under the evidentiary theme method. In accordance with the evidentiary value method, on the other hand, the evidentiary value for A is 60 and uncertain with respect to not A (and counted as 0), if there is no contrary evidence. The reason for this is claimed to be uncertainty connected to how thorough the investigation were.[8] Another way to handle uncertainty is, as previously mentioned, by using fuzzy logic.[9] The uncertainty mentioned above in the wine example, called plausibility theory, is then labelled possibility theory.[10] This theory, which is based on Zadeh's work, uses rules from mathematical probability (e.g., the negation rule) and then become two-sided. However, it can be interpreted either way and instead yield a one-sided probability.[11]

According to Kaplan, risk can be technically defined as the answer to three questions: what can happen (risk scenario); how likely is the event; and what are the consequences. He calls this a triplet, where R=risk, S=risk scenario and X=consequences. Risk thereby becomes equivalent to the sum of all scenarios, the probability of them occurring and the con-

---

[5]   Ibid. The probability of a roll of a dice is based on the symmetrical conditions. Also see Nguyen and Walker (Ch 4 n 28) 251ff.

[6]   According to Huber, ibid.

[7]   These methods are described in more detail in section 6.1, below.

[8]   Per Olof Ekelöf and Robert Boman, *Rättegång IV* (6th edn, Norstedts Juridik 1992) 129.

[9]   Huber (Ch 4 n 29), Malczewski (Ch 1 n 2) 192, Belton and Stewart (Ch 1 n 2) 61ff, 165ff.

[10]   Huber, ibid., Jakob Arnoldi, *Risk. An introduction* (Polity Press 2009) 94, Nguyen and Elbert (Ch 4 n 28) 251ff.

[11]   Cf McNeill and Freiberger (Ch 4 n 28) 187ff.

sequences that may arise.[12] In this approach, risk is somewhat objective. The technical definition does not, however, answer the question of why certain events are undesired, which in a technical analysis is usually pre-determined. It also does not provide an answer as to why individuals have different opinions concerning what a risk is and what the importance of it is.[13]

Another approach to risk besides the technical that has emerged is known as the social constructivist perspective and is based on how people perceive risks.[14] According to this view, there are a number of flaws with the technical concept of risk.[15] It omits many negative elements that people generally associate with risk. There is also an interplay between human activities and consequences that is more complex and unique than what is contained in the technical concept of risk. Technical risk analysis should furthermore not be seen as value-free; values are reflected in how risks are described, measured and interpreted. Data compiled on large populations over a long period of time moreover omits often important individual differences.[16] There are proponents of social constructivist theory who argue that risk is entirely a social construction.[17] Although the objective definition of risk is still largely accepted, more and more researchers have observed a change in what people in modern society perceive as risks. This has given a qualitative dimension to the concept of risk. Here are some examples of the risk scenario:[18]

- involuntary exposure;
- lack of personal control;
- uncertainty regarding probability or consequences of an accident;
- lack of experience of the risk;
- time-delayed effects of exposure;
- genetic effects;
- accidents that seldom occur but which are catastrophic when they occur (Low Probability-High Consequence);

---

[12]   Stan Kaplan, 'The Words of Risk Analysis' (1997) 17 Risk Analysis 407, also see Jerry Nilsson, *Introduktion till riskanalysmetoder*, (2003) Rapport 3124, Lunds universitet, brandteknik, 11.
[13]   Nilsson, ibid.
[14]   Ibid., 9.
[15]   Arnoldi (n 10) 40ff.
[16]   Ibid., 46.
[17]   Nilsson (n 12) 11. 'This is clearly a postmodern view', compare section 6.2, below.
[18]   Harry J Otway and Detlof von Winterfeldt, 'Beyond Acceptable Risk' (1982) 14(3) *Policy Sciences* 247.

- advantages of political or administrative control measures that are not tangible;
- advantages of political or administrative control measures that benefit others;
- accidents caused by human factors (as opposed to nature-related factors).

There are thus different types of risk and risk scenarios. These can be nature-related (risk of earthquake), technological (transports, chemicals), social (war, sabotage) or lifestyle-related (drug use, obesity).[19] Risks can furthermore be categorized according to the consequences examined, such as individual risks (impact on an individual), professional risks (impact on a worker), societal risks (overall impact on the public), property and economic risks (commercial disturbances or damage to physical object) and environmental risks (impact on land, water, soil, flora, and so on). Another possibility is to divide the risks according to the method required to assess them.[20]

The probability of an accident occurring may be very low, but if the accident should occur, the consequences can be quite extensive and critical and instantaneous in nature. The cause–effect relationship can in such cases be clear and easy to identify. Human safety and the prevention of injury and damage are then central. The basis for damage assessment may be the number of casualties, injuries, lost workdays, property damage, or lost production or sales.[21] Accidents that occur infrequently but which are catastrophic if they occur are good examples of situations in which the risk is unknown and the situation is therefore perceived as dangerous rather than risky.

The change in the perception of risk and probability is attributed to the transition to an industrialized and high-tech society, which has given rise to risks that are extremely difficult to assess.[22] This also becomes apparent in all areas of law, sooner or later. New pharmaceuticals can lead to injury/or give rise to damages. High-tech society could also involve claims for damages due to delayed effects of a substance (for example in a workplace) or because a plane crash is alleged to have been caused by poor maintenance of the aeroplane, but which the airline claims was due

---

[19]   National Research Council (U.S.), Committee on Risk and Decision Making, *Risk and Decision Making Perspectives and Research* (2010) National Academies 13.

[20]   Nilsson (n 12) 9.

[21]   Ibid., 10. Also see Arnoldi (n 10) 67ff, 158ff.

[22]   Arnoldi, ibid., 48ff, 70ff refers to Ulrich Beck's classic book *Risk Society*.

to an unexpected failure in a technical system. New payment methods via the Internet can furthermore cause financial losses for businesses and consumers. Who is at fault? On whom, if anyone, should the burden of proof be imposed? Internet hate crimes can be difficult to prove due to, for example, the difficulties involved in proving who had access to a specific computer. How should the evidentiary problems be solved? A pregnancy assisted with reproductive technology results in a child with birth defects. Who is responsible? How should the evidentiary problems be handled? A pregnancy assisted with reproductive technology unexpectedly results in twins instead of a single birth. The legal father protests and wants to raise only one of the children (this has happened in Sweden). How should evidentiary issues, if any, be handled?

The evidentiary problems of a high-tech society can be difficult to solve with existing burden of proof theories, because high-tech damages are complex and often very difficult to foresee, both in nature and scope, and thereby also difficult to prevent. Instead, information on possible risks may instead be most important. If an accident occurs, the responsibility may be placed on the person who benefits the most from the technological system, or on the person who should have provided information but failed to do so. In some cases, however, it may be necessary to place the responsibility on the person who has and controls a machine, and that may be an ordinary citizen. A person who, for example, has a computer in his or her possession could be held responsible for the use of this computer by being obligated to safely protect the code that provides access to it. The person who has the code that provides electronic access to a bank account has, as a matter of fact, a legal responsibility to protect this code. Anecdotally, it can be mentioned that speed cameras, which are now in place along many traffic routes in Sweden, can result in speeding tickets only if the driver can be identified in the picture taken. In some other countries, however, the registered owner of the car is liable for the fine, regardless of who was driving the car at the time.

That technological progress leads to new evidentiary problems is of course nothing new. The invention of the telephone was revolutionary, and then it was realized that phone calls could be intercepted, which was ideal from a reconnaissance perspective. Today, text messages and email are used regularly as evidence in court. The DNA technology has also helped solve old crimes and settled old paternity cases. That RB is not adapted to the new technology is sometimes obvious. The following is one example of this. Finansinspektionen revoked HQ Bank's banking licence in 2010. Claims for damages were brought against shareholders, board members and auditors and the Economic Crime Authority (EBM) began a preliminary investigation. In the civil action, disclosure was petitioned for the 65 000 email messages in the bank's servers (even deleted ones) that were held by EBM. This claim was sustained on the whole by the District Court. EBM, however, considered that they could not release the requested material because of its scope.

Many people would probably consider the terms 'risk' and 'hazard' to be synonyms, but as indicated above, some researchers argue that these are actually two different things.[23] It has been argued that risk describes a situation in which a threat has materialized.

> Anyone who goes out on the roads on a major holiday is exposed to hazard, but a person who takes to the road in a motorcycle probably takes a greater risk than a person sitting in a car (author's translation).[24]
> The hazard is the condition or circumstances that gives rise to the risk. In this case, the hazard of poverty in retirement gives rise to a risk of not having enough retirement savings to avoid that poverty.[25]

However, Persson, who has commented on these examples, finds it difficult to see how they express a difference between hazard and risk.[26] That a hazard materializes must mean that it appears and becomes clearer. In the second example, hazard is a cause of risk. According to Persson, this is perhaps the most common understanding of hazard today. But must hazards always give rise to risks? Obviously, the concepts of hazard and risk are very closely related and difficult to distinguish between. However, hazard seems to be somewhat more general of a concept than risk. Persson therefore introduces two aspects of risk: risk as a risk object and risk as an outcome risk. Risks that are outcome risks are probabilities for negative events, while risks that are risk objects are not probabilities but rather give rise to these.[27] Persson further differentiates between outcome risks that can be affected and outcome risks that cannot be affected. The latter he attributes to the category of hazards.[28]

The crime 'creating danger to another' in section 3:9 of the Penal Code

---

[23]   The terms 'risk' and 'uncertainty' are much debated; see for example John Schuyler, *Risk and Decision Analysis in Projects* (2nd edn Project Management Institute 2001) 6ff. An overview of the concept of risk is provided in Peter Wahlgren, *Legal Risk Analysis. A Proactive Legal Method* (Jure 2013) 21ff.

[24]   Lars Nord and Jesper Strömbäck, *Hot på agendan: En analys av nyhets- förmedling om risker och kriser*. KBM:s Temaserie (2005) (7) 12.

[25]   Patrick Ring, 'Risk and the UK Pension Reform' (2003) 37(1) *Social Policy Administration* 72.

[26]   Johannes Persson, 'Risk fara och riskobjekt' in Johannes Persson and Nils- Eric Sahlin (eds) Risk & Risicio (nya Doxa 2008).

[27]   Ibid., 235.

[28]   Ibid.

is an example in which 'danger' (hazard) is an explicit necessary condition. In NJA 2008 p.1060, a person had dug down two wooden boards with nails hammered in face-up on a gravel road on his property with the objective of preventing further intrusion on the property, and was indicted for this. The accused had put up a warning sign on which it was written (in Swedish) 'STOP, proceed at your own risk'. Two policemen who passed this sign got out and decided to investigate (on foot). The District Court found the charge of creating danger to another to be substantiated and a majority decision in the Court of Appeals upheld the District Court's ruling. Two members dissented, stating that the hazard was not concrete. The Supreme Court, however, ruled that the hazard was concrete; a policeman, for example, could have stepped on one of the nails, but deemed that the risk of grave bodily injury was so low that it was not worthy of consideration. In NJA 1987 p.490, a doctor had mistakenly prescribed a dosage that was ten times too high for a one and half-year-old child who was having a skull X-ray. The District Court ruled that it was just a typing error on the part of the doctor, that the nurse should have checked the prescription 'to a reasonable degree' and that there were good opportunities to avert the danger because the treatment took place at a hospital. The Court of Appeals approved the claim and stated, among other things, that the nurse who performed the premedication could have averted the danger but deemed that the doctor's actions had endangered the life of the child. The Supreme Court found that it was not likely that the child would have died because the treatment was performed at a hospital and necessary countermeasures were taken, and therefore disapproved the case. In the first case, there is a concrete risk – an outcome risk. In the second case, it seems to fit better to use the term 'hazard'.

In 41:1 RB 'hazard' is a prerequisite in regard to evidence. The provision makes it possible to take evidence even if a trial is not in progress, if there is a hazard that the evidence will be lost. This situation may arise if, for example, a witness is of an advanced age and might therefore die before the trial. Even this 'hazard' can be compared with the distinction that has been attempted in decision theory between hazard and risk. At an advanced age, life is ending. There is therefore an increased hazard of death without there being anything concrete that says that the hazard will become a risk.[29]

As concerns the burden of proof, the word 'risk' is used; one of the parties must bear the risk for uncertainty regarding facts. The word

---

[29] The same applies for the necessary condition 'danger to another's life or health' (13:1 BrB), and 'jeopardises proof' in cases of falsifications (14:1 BrB).

'hazard' does not fit in linguistically in this context. There is no 'hazard' for uncertainty on facts. As already discussed 'hazard' is about consequences of events that are general rather than concrete, which we fear, which may even be catastrophic and over which we have no control. The burden of proof is, on the other hand, about facts that have more or less known legal consequences. The debtor must, for example, prove that he has paid. The guarantor must prove that there has been a loan. If the guarantor (plaintiff) cannot prove that he has loaned money, the plaintiff's petition will be disapproved. If the guarantor can prove this, but the debtor (defendant) cannot present evidence to the contrary, the plaintiff's claim will be approved. The consequences of uncertainty are thus rather easy to observe in these and most cases assessing events in the past, which the administration of justice in general is all about.

If the assessment is forward-looking, as is the case in balancing of interests and sometimes even in overall assessments, it can be difficult to assess what will happen. Is it in 'the best interests of the child' if the mother gets custody of the child? What could happen? Or what is the worst that could happen? In a prognosis, the burden of proof shifts object from past facts to also comprise hypothetical situations in the future and perhaps hazard for a specific individual – the child. Prognostic assessments are made in many different procedural situations and they can often be difficult to do. Will, for example, an intermediate judgment decide the entire case?[30] Will a declaratory judgment quash the uncertainty? The forecast is of course partly based on the contents of the legal rules applicable, but it is not possible to reliably predict how the factual situation between the parties will develop and it also is not the intention for the court to do a full investigation of the substantive situation in its prognosis.

In some forecast situations, the substantive rules provide no guidance at all. Will outdoor recreation or wildlife be affected in the worst possible scenario if permission is granted for an environmental project or will the impact be more negligible? This can depend on unknown factors. The permit is therefore ultimately about what risks the decision-maker is prepared to take. The greater benefit the project is expected to have, the higher risk the decision-maker might be prepared to take. As been demonstrated above risk or hazard in prognostic assessments are furthermore linked to substantive issues. However, this connection has brought very little attention in the literature on evidence, at least in Scandinavia, and will be discussed in the following section.

---

[30]   An intermediate judgment refers to an issue of relevance for the rest of the case, see section 4.2.1, above.

## 5.3 THE UTILITY OF A DECISION

The words risk and hazard are used when something bad or harmful might occur. People do not talk about good risks. If something good could happen, other words are used, like 'chance' or 'opportunity'. Utility is thus the opposite of harm. In an uncertain situation, the decision-maker therefore chooses the option that provides the most utility or at least is least harmful.

A rational decision-maker chooses the course of action that will best lead to the goal he or she wants to achieve. The decision-making process is often formalized in order to clarify it. Sometimes it is presented in the form of a decision tree.[31] This has also been done several times in this book. Important basic concepts are probability and expected utility, where the maximization of the expected utility is usually used as a criterion of a rational choice.

What constitutes a utility depends on a subjective estimation of the value of a certain outcome. How utility is assessed can thus vary between different individuals, for example the utility of receiving a certain monetary amount varies for different people depending on their financial situation. The utility rule means that the possible decision options are set up and that the consequences for each option are investigated. The probability of each option is then calculated. If the probability is known, the utility rule means that each option's expected utility is multiplied by the probability of its outcome. The products are then added together for each option. The option with the highest total is then chosen. The same approach is used if the options have an uncertain probability that must be assessed subjectively.[32] The medical journal *Läkartidningen* contains the example set out in Figure 5.1.

P represents probability and V represents value. The combined weighting of probability and value (utility) is shown in Figure 5.1. Waiting provides a higher combined utility $(0.8 \times 1.0 + 0.2 \times 0.7) = 0.94$ as opposed to $(0.99 \times 0.9 + 0.01 \times 00) = 0.89$.[33] Note that the probability in the example is two-sided; if the probability that the patient completely recovers by

---

[31]   Schuyler (n 23) 59.
[32]   Keeney and Raiffa (Ch 1 n 4) 132f, Goodwin and Wright (Ch 1 n 2) 121ff, Belton and Stewart (Ch 1 n 2) 96ff, Malczewski (Ch 1 n 4) 204. As there is seldom any objective measure of utility, the literature often uses the lottery method, which is a special technique for obtaining subjective measurements of a utility. The method yields values between 0 and 1, that is to say, the same as for probability, but with another meaning.
[33]   Ylva Skånér, *Läkartidningen* (1999) (96) 4190.

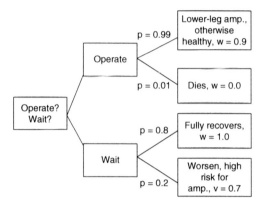

*Figure 5.1    Medical probability/utility assessment*

waiting is 0.8, the probability of the condition worsening must be 0.2. The expected utility value for the options with respect to each parent is also two-sided, but it can probably be constructed as one-sided. However, in the administration of justice it is an advantage if both probability and utility are regarded as two-sided, The court is under the obligation to make a decision, often in a relatively short time even in difficult cases. For the court the options are easier to take a stand in if the alternatives are clear, which they to a greater extent are if uncertainty is not deemed to impact on the probability or the utility.

A balance scale was used above to symbolize balancing of interests. The principle of preponderance of evidence can also be represented by a balance scale. It is sufficient that it tips over to one side or the other. How much is in the weighing pans does not matter as long as the scale gives a reading. If there is 1 kg in one of the scales and 1 gram more in the other, this is sufficient. If the frequency model is used, there must be more than 50 per cent in one of the pans. Thus, if there is 51 per cent in the plaintiff's pan and 49 per cent in the defendant's pan, the plaintiff will win. One question that may need some discussion is how the principle of preponderance of evidence can be used in both issues of evidence and issues of law. The question of whether it can be used in both issues of evidence and issues of law has already been discussed.[34]

As shown in Chapter 1, balancing of interests in law are made primarily with respect to decisions that in some way project into the future. The law-based balancing of interests requires that certain basic necessary

---

[34]    Sections 1.3 and 1.5, above.

conditions must be met. Whether the standard of proof for the fact must be 'plausible', 'probable', 'substantiated' or 'obvious' varies with regard to what might be stipulated in law or is clear from precedent or is otherwise considered appropriate. If the utility theory is used, an integrated assessment is made of probability and utility and the aforementioned standard of proof scale cannot be used. What becomes of interest instead is the integrated value of different outcomes. A probability of 50 per cent, if it is deemed to be too low, could possibly be compensated by a high utility value. If there are also multiple options and something must be chosen, the option with the highest integrated value should, in my view, be chosen in civil cases, even if the probability of the facts is relatively low.

If the existence of legal fact A is uncertain and this fact – along with other legal facts – has legal significance in an overall assessment or a balancing of interests, it should, under the views asserted in this book, have a probability of at least 50 per cent. If it concerns a procedural use of the principle of preponderance of evidence, this applies only to facts; the legal significance is another matter that is determined through a subsumption. As mentioned above, The Swedish Data Protection Authority seems, on the other hand, to use the principle of preponderance of evidence in both issues of evidence and issues of law. All facts and all legal arguments in favour of camera surveillance and their utility value are put in one weighing pan and all against it in the other. Leading up to the final weighting, there may have been several overall assessments, that is, aggregations on lower levels, and the products of these are placed in one or the other pan. How this principle of preponderance of evidence specifically works, though, is unclear.

Let us assume that camera surveillance is requested in order to reduce crime and thereby increase security in a shopping centre. Opposing this interest is the privacy interest – people in the area should not need to feel uncomfortable because of the surveillance. This balancing makes it significant what times the camera surveillance will be in force. If the crimes are mainly committed in the evenings and the cameras are switched on at 6:00 p.m., there will be more people outside than if they were switched on at 9:00 p.m. It also makes a difference if it is weekday or a weekend. The greatest utility from a crime-fighting standpoint is achieved if the cameras are on round the clock, but from a privacy standpoint, this might be unacceptable. The decision-maker must therefore try to find a time that balances the different interests and which is also proportional. The utility assessment can be difficult to make because different people perceive privacy intrusions in different ways.[35] According to the utility theory, the

---

[35] See section 1.3.3, above.

utility value is ascribed to something that with a certain probability may occur and which is good or bad or somewhere between good and bad. The probability does not, however, say what is good or bad.[36] In a legal context, both the assessment of probability and the utility are subjective. The utility of being able to shop at a shopping centre after 6:00 p.m., for example, thus means different things to different people. For someone who on moral grounds is opposed to a 'consumer society' and does not have anything against camera surveillance, it may even be the best option to keep the cameras on round the clock, even if this leads to a decrease in revenue in the area and retail workers getting laid off.

Can a balance point be calculated? It is not particularly difficult from a technical standpoint to apply the utility model in legal situations where both probability and utility must be assessed.[37] If, like in the example, an application is submitted for camera surveillance with the aim of reducing crime in a shopping centre, an assessment must be made of what impact camera surveillance will have, that is, how likely it is that crime will be reduced and if so, by how much. This probability can then be weighted together with the utility impact reduced crime will have, and then weighted against the harm from a privacy standpoint that camera surveillance is expected to bring.

If a significant number of people would choose not to shop at the shopping centre in the evenings because of the camera surveillance and would instead shop somewhere else, the impact of the camera surveillance would be economically measurable. If the probability of a significant reduction in crime (which becomes measurable retrospectively) is reduced significantly if the cameras are on round the clock, the utility from this aspect becomes very high. If this leads to an assessment that there is a risk of many people ceasing to shop after 6:00 p.m., the utility value of this option is low with respect to revenue in the shopping centre. By varying these parameters, the decision-maker can more easily assess the risk/benefit at different times of the day and find a suitable weighting. Because the exact values are not possible to specify, for either probability or for utility, it can be a good idea to put the values into ranges with minimum and maximum values.

Suppose that the probability of crime being reduced significantly if the cameras are switched on at 6:00 p.m. is estimated to be between 0.7 and 0.9

---

[36] Cf Keeny and Raiffa (Ch 1 n 4) 131ff and Howard Raiffa, *The Art and Science of Negotiation* (Belknap/Harvard 1982) 344ff.

[37] The utility rule comes up frequently in literature about negotiation, which usually entails risks of various kinds. A common example involves the calculation of the probability of winning a dispute and the financial value of the judgment; see Wahlgren (n 23) 76.

and also that people in the area feel safer, there are more people out after 6:00 p.m. and increased shopping. The utility value of this is estimated to be between 0.7 and 0.9. This gives us integrated values for probability and utility in a range between 0.49 and 0.81, which are then compared with the option of no camera surveillance. This option is estimated to have a probability of between 0.8 and 1.0 for continued high crime and fear among many people of being out after 6:00 p.m. and thus a reduced tendency to be out after that time. The utility value of this is estimated to be between 0 and 0.2. This yields a very low integrated value, so the choice seems simple. The reality is of course more complicated than this constructed example. Nevertheless, the weighting deals with probabilities and utility. Costs hardly even need to be taken into account in this case because camera surveillance is not a costly measure. However, other options should be considered, such as the presence of security guards, which is less intrusive to privacy. On the other hand, the assessment then becomes more difficult because the costs of security guards must then be taken into account in the assessment.

Another example of utility assessment is the following. The owner of a beachfront property located in the Stockholm archipelago wants to put in a dock and the question is whether exemption from shoreline protection should be granted.[38] In this case, the utility for the property owner is obvious. It can, however, be difficult to assess what significance a dock can have to outdoor recreation. How many people often pass through the area where the dock will be located? What will be the impact on outdoor recreation and the need for recreation sites in the area? Even if it is possible to obtain some data on the public interests, it is very difficult to weigh an individual interest against a public interest using numbers. Laws and guidelines based on political considerations may have conclusive significance in such cases.

## 5.4    PROBABILITY AND UTILITY IN AN INTEGRATED ASSESSMENT – AN EXAMPLE USING 'THE BEST INTERESTS OF THE CHILD'

When a position is taken on what is in 'the best interests of the child', an overall assessment must be made and this can involve a large number of factors. Unlike the example above in section 4.4 on an alleged 'unreasonable' agreement, determining what is in a child's best interest also deals with assessing something that has not occurred. The assessment instead concerns

---

[38]    Compare section 1.5.2, above.

a custody issue and in what environment it is likely to be best for the child to grow up. A forecast must thus be made. That the assessment projects into the future naturally does not mean that what has happened and facts on the current situation are not significant. On the contrary, such circumstances are a starting point for the assessment about the future.

Most forecasts concern simple and value-free themes, such as weather forecasts, the prognosis for an illness, which political party will win an election or which football team will win the World Cup. 'The best interests of the child', on the other hand, deals with the life of a child. If shared custody is not an option, would it be better for the child to live with the father or the mother? Obviously, this type of assessment becomes difficult unless there are clear indications that the child would have a better life if one or the other parent is entrusted with custody. If both of the parents are equally good, however, one might as well just flip a coin rather than apply a structured model for decision-making.

Let us assume there are two possible options: sole custody to the father or sole custody to the mother. They do not want joint custody and they are disputing who should have custody. The list of the general criteria in below shows what considerations are needed for achieving the objective of 'the best interests of the child'.[39] In the concrete decision-making situation, these general criteria will be compared with the concrete circumstances that have been presented and identified in the case. Each item on the list has been expounded on with an example, with the exception of item B, which is too vague to be made concrete. One should be able to follow these decision factors and their path to the goal, 'the best interests of the child'. They should in any case provide guidance in the assessment of 'the best interests of the child'.

A.  Care and protection: *The child is sometimes left unattended by the father, who has 'lost' the child several times at football matches.*
B.  People who they can receive love from and give love to.
C.  A stable and lasting relationship with their parents: *The father is often away.*
D.  To develop in an environment that meets their needs for stimulation: *The father does not think that children should have mobile telephones before they are 12 years old.*
E.  Parents help setting boundaries for their actions: *The father grounds the child, sometimes for a week, if the child has been disobedient.*

---

[39]   This list on children's needs is also given in section 1.4.1 above, though without being made more concrete.

F.   To feel that they are needed and that they can take responsibility: *The mother does everything for the child.*
G.   To be able to influence their situation: *The mother decides which other children the child can spend time with.*
H.   To gradually free themselves from their dependence on their parents: *The mother creates feelings of guilt if the child wants to be away from the home and spend time with other children.*
I.   Togetherness with both parents even if they are in conflict with each other. *The parents are not good at communicating with each other about the child and they do not speak with each other if they have been fighting.*

It is easy to see that the general criteria are very vague. Some of them are connected, such as F and G: to be able to affect their own situation, the child must have the chance to take responsibility, which in turn is a requirement for H: independence. Criterion E and also G can affect this, if the boundaries are too strict. This means that there is a dependence between several of the criteria in their general formulation with regard to the decision options (mother or father). It is, for example, hardly possible to rate the preference for criterion F for any of the options without knowing the preference score for criterion G. If the decision-maker thinks that F is a very important criterion, this should affect the assessment of the preference for the options with respect also to criteria G and H.

The aforementioned means that the decision-maker either has to use more precise definitions or combine some criteria into one criterion, possibly using one overlying criterion with one or more sub-criteria. Another possibility is that the decision-maker starts with the concrete circumstances in the matter or case and then inputs these under the general criteria. Everything that ends up in the same box can then be considered to be interdependent, while those in different boxes can be considered to be possible to assess independently of each other. Yet, another alternative is to view all factors as interdependent and use an MCA model, which is based on the existence of dependence. This model will then be rather complicated to use. However, the easiest way is probably to reformulate the criteria that the assessor deems to not meet the requirement for independence in order to eliminate the dependence, which usually works in most cases.

In Table 5.1 the forecast has been omitted, to simplify and show how it works, 100 points (out of 100 possible) has been given if the parent meets the criterion and less points (80) if it is deemed to be not fully met.[40]

---

[40]   Compare the simple example in section 4.3 on video conferencing or court session.

*Table 5.1    Simple additive model for custody decision-making*

| Custody | | | | | | | | |
|---|---|---|---|---|---|---|---|---|
|  | A | B | C | D | E | F | G | Total |
| Mother | 100 | 100 | 100 | 100 | 80 | 80 | 80 | 89 |
| Father | 80 | 80 | 80 | 80 | 100 | 100 | 100 | 91 |

Furthermore, criterion 'I' have been omitted from Table 5.1 since both parents are equally bad at communicating. This criterion will thus not be distinguishing. The mother has been given 100 points on all criteria except for criteria E, F and G. The father has been given 80 points on criteria A–D and 100 points on the rest. If the simple additive model is used by people in a group who are not familiar with the model, there is a risk of great variations because the preference score can and must be assessed subjectively. It can therefore in certain cases be appropriate to set limits for allocating points, that is, set upper and lower limits for the scores in order to avoid excessive fluctuations. It should be emphasized that this is a simplified example of the use of an additive method and that in concrete cases, there can be strongly divided opinions on both scoring and weighting. The advantage with a structured model is that it provides transparency and that it forces clear and explicit positions in difficult assessment questions – the decision-maker cannot hide behind vague and empty phrases or formulations.

A total of 100 weight points has been used (fixed budget), which have been allocated in the table as follows. 10 weight points each for criteria A, B and C, 15 weight points for criterion D, 20 weight points each for criterion E and F and 15 weight points for criterion G. As pointed out earlier, a total of 100 points to allocate yields a blunter result than if each criterion for each alternative is given a relative value between 0 and 100.[41] The importance of a more finely tuned and precise scoring and weighting can, however, be questioned when the necessary condition used, in this case 'the best interests of the child', is so vague.

If one assumes that the father does interesting things with the child and stimulates the child's independence and interests, A and B have been con-sidered to have less importance with respect to him. In this specific case, these criteria therefore have greater significance and the relative weight of each criterion can be decisive. The relative weight means, with the values

---

[41]    Section 2.3.7, above.

*Table 5.2    Linguistic variables model for custody decision-making*

| Option | Custody | | | | | | | | |
|---|---|---|---|---|---|---|---|---|---|
| | A | B | C | D | E | F | G | H | I |
| Mother | ● | ● | ● | ● | ● | △ | △ | △ | △ |
| Father | ○ | ● | ○ | ○ | ○ | ● | ● | ● | △ |

Contributes:   ● Strongly    ○ Moderately    △ Weakly

input in the example, that under the additive model the father receives 91 combined weighted points and the mother receives 89.

Another way to do a matrix is to use the linguistic variables instead of numbers. Table 5.2 above, shows how this can be done. Three ratings have been done: 'strongly', 'moderately' and 'weakly'. These ratings have been expressed with three simple symbols and indicate if each parent contributes 'strongly', 'moderately' or 'weakly' to 'the best interests of the child'.

In most cases, the actual situation will probably not involve so many problematic issues as in this hypothetical example. In real life, there are usually only a few circumstances that are difficult to take a position on. This is because there is a perception of what is 'normal' or 'common' which is based on experience and social codes and the fact that most cases fall within the 'normal'. The range of 'normal' or 'common' is of course not fixed. Something can be assessed as 'uncommon', 'less common', 'quite common', 'rather common' or 'less common'. It is, for example, 'common' for parents to help small children wash themselves. If, on the other hand, a father helps his healthy ten-year-old shower, this would be 'very uncommon' and not 'normal'. It is also 'very uncommon' and not 'normal' for a parent to shut their child in a dark wardrobe if the child has been disobedient, while it is common and 'normal' that parents help their children with their homework. Everything that is judged to be within the range of 'normal' does not pose any investigative problems, and yet sometimes a decision must be made on custody. In such cases, ratings are helpful, for example, in the form of a plus or minus sign, which are represented in the figure by the designations 'strongly' and 'weakly'. In addition, rules of thumb will probably be quite important.

The utility theory is used in Figure 5.2 below in a custody dispute in which a prognosis is connected to the example. Suppose that there is a suspicion that the father, who wants sole custody, sometimes uses recreational drugs, but otherwise lives in orderly conditions and that the mother, who wants to retain sole custody, does not set limits for the child. The forecast is limited to these two circumstances. Because of the mother's attitude, the child often misses school, and the school has reported on this. Instead,

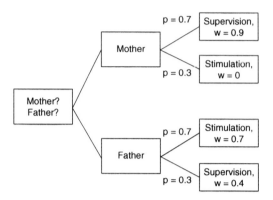

*Figure 5.2    Utility theory for custody decision-making*

the child is permitted to stay home and is pampered by the mother every time the child says he does not have the energy to go to school. The father claims that he does not take recreational drugs and the mother claims that the child has health problems and must be home more than other children. There is thus an uncertainty in the underlying facts. This uncertainty can possibly be remedied if there is sufficient substance in the supporting information, such as that the father voluntarily agrees to a drug test and the child undergoes a medical examination. Such investigations are not routinely performed, though, if everything else seems 'normal' and even if they are done there could still be uncertainty.

Figure 5.2 shows the two decision options: custody to the mother or father. The input values give the mother 63 combined weighted points and the father 61. The probability that the child will be 'supervised' if the mother is given custody has been given the value of 0.7. The expected utility of supervision has been given the value 0.9.

Anyone who wants to change an existing relationship has, under the stability theory, the burden of proof for demonstrating why there should be a change. Parties in a custody dispute who assert that custody should be changed from joint custody (the main rule in Swedish law) to sole custody under this theory carry a sort of risk in the sense that this request will not be granted in accordance with the party's wishes unless there is an investigation that more tangibly supports the claim.[42] If the parents, as in the

---

[42]    In custody disputes, as in many other civil cases, it is my opinion that the principle of preponderance of evidence should be the starting point because there is normally no reason to add a higher risk of uncertainty regarding the facts on either of the parents.

example above, have joint custody and the child lives with the mother, but the situation for the child is not satisfactory but also is not really bad, the option, moving sole custody to the father, may seem to be a better option for the child. However, the expected utility for the child should probably, taking the uncertainties into account, be deemed to be significantly better and just not a little bit better. Subjective values are of course never precise, but instead lie within a certain range. Therefore, the value 63 for the father is obviously too small for such a drastic measure as transfer of custody. If, however, the range is between 0.63–0.85, it might be sufficient if it lies in the upper range.

One difficulty that was criticized above is vagueness. Is it really possible to set numerical values on probability and utility for something as vague as 'supervision' and 'stimulation'? Clearly one can – as demonstrated in the example above – make clarifications, and these must be done regardless of whether a structured model is used or not, but vagueness can never be completely removed. Eliminating vagueness (if possible) would actually not be a good idea, because even vague words are informative. As shown in the previous chapter, in fuzzy logic, 'supervision' and 'stimulation' are sets that represent what parents do with their children. In the example, the father, mother and child are members in these fuzzy sets. Depending on the level of membership in the sets, it could mean that the child does not receive good 'supervision' and 'stimulation'.

## 5.5 UTILITY THEORY AND BURDEN OF PROOF

The utility theory raises questions on how courts make prognostic assessments. The classic and prevailing view on the application of law is the subsumption theory, which is designed for past events. The result of subsumption shows if and how the rule should be applied to the legal facts that – in disputes – are judged to have been investigated with sufficient certainty. Should the existence of a legal fact be uncertain, a burden of proof rule or the principle of preponderance of evidence should be applied. If, in an overall assessment or balancing of interests, the circumstance is deemed to have not been proven with sufficient certainty (whatever that would be), it will be removed from the decision basis and the subsumption will be performed on the basis of remaining legal facts.

An application of the utility theory in prognostic assessments means that the accepted and prevailing division into issues of evidence and issues of law cannot be made in the same way as with respect to past events. As seen, an application of this theory means that the probability of facts is connected with the expected utility of the outcome of the legal fact in question, $P \times V$.

The utility theory links probability and utility through simple multiplication. It thus represents an integrated model in which evidentiary value is multiplied by the estimated utility value. Two different types of input values, one probability and the other utility value, together create a new value, an integrated legal value. There are thus different types of legal values, both pure legal values, which were discussed earlier, and mixed legal values.

With subsumption theory, it can be difficult to explain how a concrete legal fact relates to the prognosis made in the application of, for example, the necessary condition 'the best interests of the child'. In the example above, it was stated that the father, who wanted sole custody, sometimes used recreational drugs and the probability of this was estimated at 0.7. The utility value of supervision was estimated at 0.7. The mother's supervision was given a utility value of 0.9, which is high, but supervision is also required in the home. The negative was that the child does not get any stimulation from the mother, which therefore was given the utility value of 0. In a custody dispute, the court must take a position on both the current situation for the child and the parents and the future situation for them. The facts in the current situation form the foundation of the prognosis, which refers to hypothetical situations: How will it be if the mother is given sole custody? How will it be if the father is given sole custody? Future events related to either of the parents (taking courses, going to therapy, and so on) can be included in the hypothetical assessment. Prognostic facts naturally have an evidentiary effect on the relevant prognostic evidentiary themes. At the same time these evidentiary themes clearly become hypothetical legal facts that must be compared with the prerequisite 'the best interests of the child'. How this actually is done is, just like the terminology, unclear.

Kaldal, who discussed the nature of prognostic facts in the assessment of 'the best interests of the child', argues that what constitutes a legal fact in the present situation changes character and becomes or can become evidentiary facts in the prognostic assessment.[43] Thus, according to Kaldal the same legal facts transform into evidentiary facts for 'the best interests of the child' in the prognostic assessment. In an article from 1987 on the assessment of insolvency, which includes a prognostic assessment with respect to the debtor's future ability to pay debts as they fall due, I argued that the legal facts that form the basis for the forecast are legal facts with evidentiary value.[44] The assertion that the debtor has other debts must in

---

[43]   Anna Kaldal, *Parallella processer. En rättsvetenskaplig studie av riskbedömningar i vårdnads- och LVU-mål* (Jure 2010) 191.
[44]   Bengt Lindell, 'Insolvensbedömningen' (SvJT 1989) 131.

fact be proven in a separate process; assertions of other debts thus concern a legal fact. Other circumstances, such as a claim by the debtor that he will receive a large inheritance and will therefore in future be able to pay his debts as they fall due, could supposedly qualify as evidentiary facts, but because there is also an allegation requirement for these details in the debtor's finances, the terminology is an adaptation to this requirement.

It is important to emphasize that a fact must not be either a legal fact or an evidentiary fact, but can also be both. That a single circumstance can fill different functions has been pointed out before.[45] If a person drove a car fast in foggy weather, this can be a concrete legal fact of significance in an assessment of fault or negligence, while at the same time the fog could be an evidentiary fact that the road was wet and an auxiliary fact for a testimony on the visibility conditions at the scene. We can call facts of different types polycentric, that is, they have different significance in different contexts and relationships. Such a fact can therefore in the same trial need to be referred to in its capacity as a legal fact in a certain respect, but not in another. And in a certain respect there can – still in the same trial – be a standard of proof and a burden of proof for such a fact, but not in another respect. Especially in overall assessments and balancing of interests, this phenomenon could occur quite frequently because there are often a great number of concrete circumstances. When a single fact in the same trial pops up in different places with different faces, things can definitely get messy. It seems clear that RB's systematic and conceptual apparatus is not built for these types of situations. If the terminological question in the prognostic assessment is based on the integrated value, which becomes a hybrid value, a legal fact does not change character and become an evidentiary fact, nor is it a legal fact with evidentiary value. It becomes something else because the integrated value is neither a pure evidentiary value nor a pure legal value; it is an evidentiary and a legal value merged together. In this book, however, the hybrid value is allocated to the category of legal values.

Because the utility model has existed in decision theory for at least 200 years, it may be asked why it does not seem to have had any bearing on evidentiary questions. Of course, this does not mean that judges do not use utility thinking intuitively and have done this at least as long as the theory has existed. Utility theory is simple, robust, has been in use for a long time in many areas and appears reasonable even in a legal context. Certainly, Bentham would agree to that. Judges, however, generally do not feel

---

[45]     Bengt Lindell, *Sakfrågor och rättsfrågor. En studie av gränser, skillnader och förhållanden mellan faktum och rätt* (Iustus 1987) 31.

on safe ground if intuition is formalized and clothed in a particularly symbolic language, which is virtually always the case in decision theory. This does not mean, though, that it is not used. There is every reason to believe that judges do use the utility theory mindset.

In the introduction to this chapter, several probability theory aspects of uncertainty were presented. In a legal context, however, there is an aspect that is not related to probability theory, but instead is substantive. In Chapter 1, it was said that the law-based balancing of interests and the principle of proportionality constitute substantive decision rules or at least important parts of a decision rule. This is also the case with the contractual law ambiguity rule. If it is unclear what a term of an agreement means, the risk of ambiguity is placed on the person who drafted the clause. However, the ambiguity rule is not generally considered to be a burden of proof rule, but rather just an interpretation rule. The principle of in dubio pro reo – ('when in doubt) – is applied in criminal cases. Other interpretation concepts and principles, such as restrictive interpretation and application, can also narrow the scope of application in such a way that uncertainty is avoided. Against this backdrop, one may ask why the burden of proof rules have been given such a place of honour as far as uncertainty is concerned. After all, these rules are also substantive. One difference seems to be that the burden of proof rules refer to facts while things like the ambiguity rule and the principle of in dubio pro reo more directly relate to the substantive issue. This difference is only superficial though. All uncertainty, whether it is called substantive or factual, is due to insufficient knowledge. And in many cases, the reason for this is that it is not possible to acquire the requisite knowledge. It does not matter, for example, how long the ambiguous rule is analysed; it still remains unclear.

## 5.6   SUMMARY AND CONCLUSIONS

Perhaps the most debatable aspect of utility theory in general, and maybe especially in a legal context, is the numerical determination of utility. As shown by the references, this problem has been noted in decision theory, but at the same time it must be pointed out that utility is actually scored according to the utility theory and is considered to provide decision support. And that is also how utility theory should be viewed in a legal context. It is not intended to solve a decision problem, but is instead a tool to help the decision-maker determine which option should be chosen. In a legal context, the problem is very much linked to vagueness. In the examples given, utility value is set on concepts such as 'stimulation' and 'supervision', but what is it really? As described earlier, one can use basic ideas in fuzzy logic to justify such an approach. We know without any definitions what 'obviously poor supervision' and 'very good supervision' are. If supervision is given a value of 0.5, this signifies a certain degree of membership in a set called 'supervision'. It is thus about the incorporation of a concrete case in a set that is vague because it is not possible to provide a complete definition.

In the book, MCA and the simple additive model have been used up until this chapter, when the utility theory has been used to weigh probability together with utility value. When MCA is used in overall assessments or balancing of interests and there is either no uncertainty or it is marginal, the product after the mathematical combined weighting becomes a pure legal value. No burden of proof or standard of proof applies for this value, which concerns the issue of law. If the model is used, however, there is reason to ask if the legal value should exceed a certain threshold in order to be considered. The answer to the question is that if MCA is used, the option that has the highest combined legal value should be chosen. If probability and utility is combined, the decision-maker should choose the option with the highest integrated legal value.

Uncertainty can be prevented or handled in other ways than through burden of proof rules, for example, by the way the legislative rules are written, through different types of formal requirements, or legal principles, such as in dubio pro reo. Regardless of how uncertainty is handled there are common denominators. One of these is that one of the parties must bear the risk of the uncertainty. The person who wrote the unclear rule bears the risk for ambiguity; the author of course had the possibility of writing a clearer rule. From a substantive standpoint, this risk distribution is therefore justifiable in the same way that it is justifiable to place the burden of proof on the party who has the best possibility of securing evidence. In a risk distribution, there does not need to be any blame, but there can be, such as when the burden of proof is placed on a person who has violated a safety regulation. The question of similarities and differences between burden of proof rules and other substantive rules, which was discussed earlier in the book, would be worth a closer examination.

# 6.  Evidentiary aspects

## 6.1  INTRODUCTION

The evaluation of evidence has been a controversial topic in Nordic jurisprudence for a long time, and particularly in recent decades. Two methods, the evidentiary theme method and the evidentiary value method, have been set against each other. These methods will be briefly presented below as they provide a framework for the following sections in the chapter.[1] A few other evidentiary theories in the Nordic countries and the concept of robustness will also be briefly described. Thereafter, in the following section, it will be asserted that the basic view that is still prevalent in Swedish evidence law doctrine, that the evaluation of evidence is an epistemological activity based on the use of sentences of experience and general deduction rules, appears too narrow as an explanatory framework for the intellectual activity labelled evaluation of evidence.[2] The next section will discuss how fuzzy logic can be used as a method in the evaluation of oral statements. This method of analysing and evaluating evidence deviates from the prevailing probability theory models and should be seen as an alternative or a complement to certain evidentiary situations.

As has been described in this book, MCA can be used on questions of law. In the book the method has been applied on the balancing of interests and overall assessments. MCA provides a structured way to deal with these assessments in the same way as methods for the evaluation of evidence, such as the evidentiary theme method or the evidentiary value method, are structured ways to handle questions of fact. The objective of using structured methods in both situations is to reduce the risk of

---

[1]  Here, only a selection of recent literature describing the evidentiary theme and evidentiary value methods will be mentioned: Løvlie, (Ch 4 n 28), particularly 314f, Magne Strandberg, *Beviskrav i sivile saker. En beviskravsteoretisk studie av den norske beviskravslaerens forutsetninger*, (Fagbogforlaget 2012), Christian Diesen and Magne Strandberg, *Bevisprövning i tvistemål. Teori och praktik* (Norstedts Juridik 2012) 39ff, Katrin Lainpelto, *Stödbevisning i brottmål* (Jure 2012) 81ff.
[2]  Sentences of experience refer to law of general experience or commonplace generalisations.

arbitrariness and safeguard law and order. However, as far as questions of law are concerned, it has been fully accepted that the balancing of interests and overall assessments are made intuitively and that the room for discretion is significant. Evidence, on the other hand, is not seldom calculated to the decimal point in legal doctrine because it should be exact. This attitude begs the question of why correct evaluation of evidence is deemed to be more important than correct application of law. The overall objective with this chapter is to demonstrate that the gap between evaluation of evidence and the application of law can be closed as far as the use of structured methods is concerned. In addition, using fuzzy logic on oral statements gives evidence an interesting twist.

### 6.1.1  The Evidentiary Value and Evidentiary Theme Methods

The provision on free evaluation of evidence in 35:1 RB means that both the evaluation of evidence and the presentation of evidence are free. Thus, the rule in question does not prescribe how different pieces of evidence are to be evaluated, nor does it prohibit the presentation of any kind of evidence that may be presented in a trial. The concept of evidence as an umbrella term includes a third element, namely the burden of proof, which includes the requirements on the probability that should be applied in the particular case.

In the same year that RB entered into force (1948), Ekelöf published a compendium on civil procedure in which he introduced certain computing rules for the aggregation of evidence.[3] It may seem like a paradox that new evidentiary rules – certainly of a different nature than the purely legal – were being recommended at the same time that Swedish law was finally formally released from the old legal evidentiary theory. The reason for this was that Ekelöf wanted to capture the law of evidence in a system of thought that would reduce the risk of arbitrariness. Such law and order aspects were admittedly also behind the legal evidentiary theory, but were now given a new twist in which the value of individual pieces of evidence would be determined freely, while the actual compilation of several items of evidence, whose value would be decided intuitively, would follow certain decided logical rules.

In accordance with the evidentiary value method, the focus is on the relationship between the evidentiary fact and the evidentiary theme. The question is raised why an evidentiary fact constituted proof that a certain

---

[3]  Per Olof Ekelöf, *Kompendium över civilprocessen,* del II (Juridiska föreningen Uppsala 1948) 348.

event has occurred.[4] In that context a requirement on a causal relation between the evidentiary fact and the evidentiary theme has been laid down.[5]

The basic concepts of the method were formulated by Ekelöf.[6] They have since then been expounded upon by others, including Halldén, who says that in evidence evaluation, the judge must take a position on the ascertainment of an effect 'd', a hypothesis on a causal link 'i' and a hypothesis on an original cause 'h'.[7] Under the evidentiary value method, the focus is on the value P (i/d), that is, the probability that the causal mechanism worked.[8] There are, however, other evidentiary relationships than the causal, implication for example,[9] but the causal is perceived as the most important and most common evidentiary relationship.[10]

An example of a causal relationship is the requirement that a witness's observations must have been caused by the observed event. If a witness has concocted a story that happens to be consistent with the evidentiary theme, it still does not have evidentiary value because the theme has not caused the testimony.[11] Thus, the concept 'evidentiary value' is important since it, according to Ekelöf, means that there must be a causal link.[12] Without evidentiary value, there is no evidence, or at least not a good piece of evidence. In practice, however, the term evidentiary value seems to be

---

[4]   Stening (Ch 3 n 36) 25, Robert W Goldsmith and Sven Ingmar Andersson, 'Bevisvärdemetoden versus temametoden vid juridisk bevisvärdering' (TfR 1978) 72, Sören Halldén, Indiciemekanismer (TfR 1973) 56, Per Olof Ekelöf, Henrik Edelstam and Lars Heuman, *Rättegång IV* (7th edn Norstedts Juridik AB 2009) 184–5, Lindell (Ch 5 n 45) 144ff.

[5]   Ekelöf and Boman (Ch 5 n 8) 133. Halldén, ibid., 56, Gärdenfors, 'Evidentiary Value' in Peter Gärdenfors, Bengt Hansson, Nils-Eric Sahlin and Sören Halldén (eds) *Evidentiary Value: Philosophical, Judicial and Psychological Aspects of a Theory. Essays dedicated to Sören Halldén on his Sixtieth Birthday* (C.W.K. Gleerups 1983).

[6]   In addition to in *Rättegång IV*, Ekelöf also wrote about the method in other publications, including in Wolfgang Grunsky, Rolf Stürner, Gerhard Walter und Manfred Wolf (herausgeber) *Festschrift für Fritz Baur*, Zetschrift für Zivilprozess (1978) and *Evidentiary Value* (n 5). Ekelöf collaborated with philosophers in his evidence law research, including Sören Halldèn († 2010), who was a professor of theoretical philosophy at Lund University.

[7]   Halldén (n 4) 56.

[8]   Ibid.

[9]   Goldsmith and Andersson (n 4) 74.

[10]   Gärdenfors (n 5) 47.

[11]   Ekelöf, Edelstam and Heuman (n 4) 184.

[12]   Per Olof Ekelöf, 'My Thoughts on Evidentiary Value', *Evidentiary Value* (n 5) 9.

used to indicate that a circumstance has an evidentiary value, regardless of whether there is deemed to be a causal connection or not.

The evidentiary theme method is directed at the value P (h/d), that is, the probability for the evidentiary theme given the presented evidence.[13] The evidentiary theme method thus does not set any requirement for causal link. Among other things, this means that the probability will not be 0 if a witness concocts a story that happens to be consistent with the evidentiary theme, because there can still be a probability for the evidentiary theme. This difference is connected to another difference between the methods, which concerns the importance of a theme's original probability, which usually means the evidentiary theme's probability before any evidence has been taken to support it.[14] In this context the probability ex ante also should be observed. The theme's original probability in this sense does not, however, mean the theme's original probability before any evidence whatsoever has been taken to support it, but rather the theme's probability before a certain evidentiary fact is taken into account and other evidence has already affected the theme's original probability.[15]

In the use of the evidentiary value method, the original probability for the theme is said to have little significance because there is usually no causal mechanism.[16] Under the evidentiary value method, however, the original probability can be very important to the evidentiary value of the individual evidence, particularly when it is very high or very low.[17] In practice this means that the difference between the methods, as far as the original probability is concerned, is only that in the evidentiary value method, original probability only affects the evidentiary fact's evidentiary value for the theme, while in the evidentiary theme method, it instead affects the theme's probability.[18] Because the original probability is taken into account in the application of the evidentiary theme method, the starting point is furthermore that the probability for A and not-A are equal, 50/50, while in the evidentiary value method the starting point is 0 because it disregards the original probability. In addition, and as mentioned above in section 5.2,

---

[13] Proponents of the evidentiary theme method include Per Olof Bolding, *Bevisbördan och den juridiska tekniken* (Uppsala 1951) 55 and Torstein Eckhoff, *Tvilsrisikoen* (Tanum 1943) 11 and also, 'Temametode och verdimetode i bevisvurderingen' (SvJT 1988) 321 Also see Lindell (Ch 5 n 45) 145.
[14] Stening (Ch 3 n 36) 42, Goldsmith and Andersson (n 4) 80.
[15] Stening, ibid., 42.
[16] Ekelöf, Edelstam and Heuman, *Rättegång IV* (n 4) 170, 190. Cf Anders Stening, 'Konflikt mellan två bevismodeller' (SvJT 1979) 295.
[17] Stening (Ch 3 n 36) 86.
[18] Lindell (Ch 5 n 45) 168.

the evidentiary value method does not assign any probability to the negation of the evidentiary theme, provided no contrary evidence is presented. If such evidence exists the probability could for example be 50 per cent probability for the theme, 30 per cent against while 20 per cent is uncertain, which corresponds to the Dempster-Shafer theory.[19] The evidentiary theme method, on the other hand, always gives a two-sided probability.

As a result of, among other things, the concentration on evidentiary relationships and the way of structuring the evidence, the evidentiary value method is argued to entail a stricter and more careful evaluation of evidence than the evidentiary theme method.[20] Because the assessment under the evidentiary value method is focused on evidentiary relationships, the presented evidence will be divided up into evidentiary facts, auxiliary facts and sentences of experience where each and every auxiliary fact and evidentiary fact will be analysed individually with respect to the relevant sentence of experience.[21] Against this way of dividing up the body of evidence, it has been argued that an excessively far-reaching analysis can lead to an overall assessment being considerably impeded and that it is not sufficiently taken into account that commonplace generalizations may refer not only to individual facts, but rather to multiple facts combined. If the requirement is then set that each circumstance must be evaluated individually, independently of other factors, the consequence could be that the facts are not seen in the context in which there is a sentence of experience that gives them significance. It has therefore been argued that the courts when evaluating evidence should look for the sentence of experience that explains as many factors as possible in the course of events, even if this from a probability standpoint is weaker than a competing sentence of experience that only explains part of the disputed factors in the course of events and which therefore leaves important questions unanswered.[22] This sought inductive empirical statement has been called the optimal.[23]

---

[19]   Cf Clermont, *Death of Paradox* (Ch 1 n 14) 1106, which seems to interpret fuzzy logic to support a one-sided probability where there is no counter evidence.

[20]   Goldsmith and Andersson (n 4) 78–9.

[21]   Stening, Bevisvärde (Ch 3 n 36) 48, 72, Ekelöf, Edelstam and Heuman (n 4) 193ff. Of course, sentences of experience do not exist for every individual piece of evidence. According to Stening, the decision-maker then must construct a sentence of experience based on how it is likely it would look, if it existed. These fictious frequencies represent norms because they are based on expectations, usually with respect to human behaviour. Because of this it has been argued that fictious sentences of experience indeed are norms, in addition arbitrary norms, Lindell, *Civilprocessen* (Ch 3 n 17) 518ff.

[22]   Lindell (Ch 5 n 45) 114.

[23]   Ibid., 249ff.

The evidentiary value method comprises three different evidence situations: chain evidence, corroborating evidence and countervailing evidence. A chain of evidence refers to several links in a chain where A has evidentiary value for B and B evidentiary value for C, and so on. The longer the chain becomes, the lower the final evidentiary value will be, provided each link in the chain is not proven with absolute certainty. Corroborating evidence refers to the occurrence of multiple evidentiary facts supporting the same evidentiary theme. In countervailing evidence, there is evidence of a contradictory theme that can exclude the existence of the main theme. Under the evidentiary value method, the strength of the contrary evidence is deducted from the strength of the primary evidence.[24] All decision situations make use of mathematical formulas derived from probability theory. The evidentiary theme method uses Bayes' theorem for combined weighting of statistics and regular evidence and is not as articulated and clear as the evidentiary value method for other situations.

According to both the evidentiary value method and the evidentiary theme method, evidence must be mutually independent. That evidence must be mutually independent means that when assessing evidence A, the judge should not let himself be affected by his knowing that the theme is proven by evidence B.[25] The requirement for independence clearly also means that different evidentiary facts must be distinctly separated from each other in order to avoid double counting. This separation can be difficult to do, as can the separation from an auxiliary fact. As shown in section 2.3.3, MCA also has an independence requirement. This requirement for independence is, unlike the evidentiary independence requirement, subjective. The reason why the evidentiary independence requirement is objective would seem to be because evaluation of evidence concerns assertions on facts, that is, things that are true or false, and that are conducted in judicial processes in a way that a reading of the reasons for the court's evidentiary assessment can be understood and accepted by the parties and other people as convincing. MCA, on the other hand, is about assessing what is best and what is worst, it being understood that different people have different values, which will affect the scoring and weighing of the criteria.[26]

---

24   Ekelöf, Edelstam and Heuman (n 4) 206–7.
25   Stening (Ch 3 n 36) 41.
26   Compare sections 3.5 and 2.3.3, above.

### 6.1.2   A Few Other Approaches and Robustness

Professor Henrik Zahle argues that it is not consistent with frequency theory that the parties choose the evidentiary themes (in cases amenable to out-of-court settlement) and evidentiary facts, because the body of evidence then does not meet the requirements for randomness and representativeness advanced by the frequency theory. He furthermore argues that the parties' behaviour is significant to the assessment of burden of proof issues and talks in this context about normative behavioural assessment.[27] For example, there is in certain cases manifest standard evidence, such as a debtor's receipt of payment. The idea is that the judicial system places demands on the perpetuation of evidence by the debtor and that a debtor who has failed in this respect therefore bears the risk of having to pay again.[28]

Nygaard places subsumption of legal facts under prerequisites on par with subsumption of evidentiary facts under a standard of proof.[29] Cohen rejects the mathematical probability concept as too narrow and argues that a comparison should be made between the individual case and a normal case (de ceteris paribus) to produce a measurement of the probability. He calls this inductive probability.[30] The normality assumption can, however, be criticized for leading to arbitrariness because it presupposes an estimation of how much the assessor does not know and about what is 'normal' in that specific type of evidence situation.[31] Diesen, on the other hand, argues that the normality assumption only means that inductive empirical statements should be taken into account.[32] Yet, none of these would seem to provide an answer to what is normal in that specific evidence situation. Diesen's own views on the evaluation of evidence in criminal proceedings could be said to take an intermediate position. He takes his starting point in the standard of proof and concentrates on the stage that comes after

---

[27]   Henrik Zahle († 2006) was a prominent Danish professor, first in public law and thereafter in jurisprudence. He was also a judge in the Danish Supreme court for some years.

[28]   Henrik Zahle, *Om det juridiske bevis* (Jurisforbundets forlag 1976) 12, 299, 398. Also see Zahle, Bevisret, Oversigt (DJØF 1994).

[29]   Nils Nygaard, 'Overviktsprinsippet ved bevis for faktisk årsakssammenheng' i Festskrift til Torstein Eckhoffs 70-årsdag (Tano 1986) 491. Similar, Lindell (Ch 3 n 17) 530ff.

[30]   L Jonathan Cohen, *The Probable and the Provable* (Clarendon Press 1977) 212ff.

[31]   Lindell (Ch 5 n 45) 354–55.

[32]   Christian Diesen, *Bevisprövning i brottmål. Teori och praktik* (Norstedts Juridik 1993) 23.

the actual evaluation of evidence, namely the presentation of alternative hypotheses. His model can therefore more accurately be characterized as a method for decision-making than as a method for the evaluation of individual evidence. Finally, narrative evidence evaluation, originating from postmodernism, means that the truth is sought through a comparison or construction of stories instead of through a critical analysis of the presented evidence.[33]

Robustness means that a probability judgment can be more or less secure depending on how thorough the investigations were. It is possible to achieve a high degree of probability value on a meagre investigation, but this probability is not robust because it must be expected that the probability will change when additional assessment materials come into play. If, on the other hand, thorough investigations have been performed, it is not likely that the probability will be significantly changed by further investigation.[34] Because robustness is connected with the investigation, it is also associated with a legal system property.[35] What is meant by this is that the legal system is built in such a way that a meagre investigation must sometimes be accepted, for example in sequestration, stay of execution and interim judgments. In other cases, however, the system of judicial proceedings requires that exhaustive investigations are performed, such as in paternity investigations, custody disputes and in other civil cases not amenable to out-of-court settlement. Of course, the same applies in criminal proceedings, particularly for more serious crimes. Because the assessment of a legal question requires knowledge of facts, the assessment of legal issues also risks becoming less robust if little investigation has been done.

According to Ekelöf, the evidentiary value model requires that account should be taken of the robustness of the case when determining the evidentiary value.[36] Under this approach, if robustness seems low, evidentiary value also drops. Robustness is also included in Cohen's normality assumption and therefore also influences his inductive model on evidentiary value. Because the assessment of the investigation's completeness

---

[33] See for example Terence Andersson, David Schum and WilliamTwining, *Analysis of Evidence* (2nd edn Cambridge University Press 2005) 262ff. Modern research shows that stories appeal to emotion and intuition instead of logic and rationality, which can entail tangible risks from a rule of law perspective, particularly in countries that have juries.

[34] See John Maynard Keynes, *A Treatise on Probability* (Macmillan 1973) 82, who differentiates between probability and 'weight'. Also see Lindell (Ch 5 n 45) 353 and the literature cited there.

[35] Also see Torleif Bylund, *Tvångsmedel I*, (Iustus 1993) 99.

[36] Ekelöf and Boman, *Rättegång IV* (n 5) 129.

depends on how much investigation the judge thinks should be required, this matter verges on legal policy. Thus, because the requirement for robustness clearly is a normative issue, it will be mixed up with the epistemological question of how strong the evidence is. Regarding cases amenable to out-of-court settlement, the courts should furthermore never make any deduction from the evidentiary value due to poor robustness because the parties themselves, in accordance with the maxim of party disposition, decide on the investigation and thereby also how extensive it will be. Consequently, if the parties decide not to make further investigations or one of the parties for some reason does not want to present more evidence, the court should not make evidentiary deductions because of this since it would violate the principle of party disposition. It has therefore been suggested that probability and robustness should be measured against two separate scales, but only in criminal cases and disputes not amenable to out-of-court settlement, in which the judicial system can supplement the investigation of its own motion.[37]

## 6.2 THE EPISTEMOLOGY OF EVIDENCE EVALUATION

There is no doubt that the approach to knowledge of the law of evidence is essentially based on modernism, that is, our knowledge of reality depends on observation and empirical evidence. The frequent references in evidentiary law literature to facts and sentences of experience confirm this. What cannot be observed, measured or weighed and preferably broken down into brute facts in the real world does not fit with the prevailing theoretical models for the evaluation of evidence, at least not with the evidentiary value and the evidentiary theme models. Under a postmodern approach, however, reality is a social construction, created by an interaction between people and through language or other forms of communication. The premise of modernism is that reality is outside us; we see it and describe it, more or less precisely. This is also the traditional scientific and prevailing approach, in which observations should be able to be repeated and empirically substantiated. Under the postmodern approach, on the other hand, it is not possible to separate ourselves from reality as observers of it. We are a part of reality, which we interpret, understand and create through

---

[37] Bengt Lindell, 'Några bevisrättsliga frågor' (TfR 1989) 237. In cases amenable to out-of-court settlement, the body of evidence presented by the parties must be considered to be the complete body of evidence.

discourse. The word 'discourse', which comes from Latin and means 'to and from', is frequently used in the postmodern language, primarily in semantics, but has a broader meaning. It represents communication and conversation and larger units that shape our view of reality and make it understandable. Another word that seems interchangeable with discourse is context, if context is seen as a coherence that creates understanding.

The difference between modernism and postmodernism is both deep and antagonistic, but the situations vary. It is, for example, not credible to claim that Gotland is a social construction.[38] If, on the other hand, it is said that 'Carl is rowdy and disruptive at school', this could be because a narrative about Carl has been created that he is 'rowdy and disruptive' and after a time, this narrative about how Carl is will become cemented and part of our perception of Carl. There are indeed undeniably differences between the assertion that Gotland is an island and the assertion that Carl is 'rowdy and disruptive' at school. Gotland exists on a map, identified by latitude and longitude, and aeroplanes land on Gotland, which they certainly would not be able to do if Gotland was a social construction. Faced with examples such as these, postmodern proponents not infrequently invoke quantum physics and how the smallest real world components look and behave. Put under the magnifying glass through the use of scientific methods, 'reality' is broken down, for example in accordance to the string theory, into vibrations and multiple realities, which we do not see because they have curled up into 11 dimensions. However, the judge does not need to be trained in quantum physics and string theory to be able to make judgments. In the reality that we live in every day, we manage just fine with modernistic ideas. It is also a requirement that a court decision can be legitimized, which means that there may not be as many constructed realities as there are people on earth.

The notion that reality is a social construction should therefore not be taken too far. Wetherell and Potter have argued that New Zealand is discursively constituted and that you die if your aeroplane flies into a mountain, whether you think that the mountain is the result of a volcanic eruption or a petrified mythical whale. That the material reality can get in the way of an aeroplane makes it, in their view, no less discursive when the reason for the death is constituted from our discursive systems.[39] It is not easy to understand what they mean. They do not seem to deny that there is

---

[38]   The largest Swedish island, located in the Baltic See.
[39]   Margaret Wetherell and Jonathan Potter, 'Discourse Analysis and the Identification of Interpretative Repertoires' in Charles Antaki (ed.) *Analysing Everyday Explanation. A Casebook of Methods* (Sage Publications Inc 1988).

a physical reality outside the discourse, but seem to think that this is given meaning through discourse.

Carl exists, in the same sense that Gotland exists, but the assertion that he is 'rowdy and disruptive' is not about existence. The opinion about him is furthermore vague and judgemental. And this vagueness is not possible to eliminate entirely because language is vague. However, the perception of Carl can be changed, even if it may be difficult. Narrative evaluation of evidence, which is a postmodern phenomenon, is based on creating narratives that have a beginning and an end and which seem coherent and reasonable and therefore convincing. In addition, the premise for narrative mediation is that conflicts are caused by narratives; for example, a narrative saying that Carl is 'rowdy and disruptive' and that the conflict surrounding Carl can be removed if the narrative about Carl is taken away and replaced with another narrative about how Carl is. This approach underlies narrative mediation as a method of handling conflicts.[40]

Postmodern theories have challenged and questioned predominant and established notions of what knowledge is and how knowledge is created.[41] As a scientific contender, postmodernism has endured harsh criticism.[42] If all of our knowledge were based on social constructions in different types of context, scientific discussions would be meaningless. Postmodernism also does not seem to have had any significance in natural science and technology and has therefore been ignored in these scientific fields. In the humanities and social sciences, it continues to have academic significance, however, as it seems, less and less.

Viewing evidence with modernist glasses from a postmodern perspective, it could be argued that evidentiary facts, auxiliary facts, commonplace generalizations, burden of proof and standard of proof mould the discourse. Particularly auxiliary facts, which Lindblom describes as a sort of catch-all,[43] takes up, for example, how questions are posed and that some doors may be closed because the questions have steered the

---

[40] See Hans Boserup, *Mikrostyring i mediation* (Uppsala Universitet 2015) and John Winslade and Gerald D Monk, *Narrative Mediation. A New Approach to Conflict Resolution* (Jossey Bass 2000).

[41] See for example, Daniel Litowitz, *Postmodern Philosophy and Law* (University Press of Kansas 1997).

[42] Alan Sokal and Jean Brichmont: *Fashionable Nonsense. Postmodern Intellectuals' Abuse of Science* (Picador 1998). Alan Sokal, a physics professor, tricked the postmodern journal *Social Text* with a parodical article in which he argued, among other things, that gravity is a social construction; 'Transgressing the Boundaries: Toward a Transformative Hermeneutics of Quantum Gravity'.

[43] Per Henrik Lindblom, Review of Stenings dissertation Bevisvärde (SvJT 1977) 280.

decision-making in a certain direction. The optimal commonplace generalization, a concept that I myself have used, can furthermore be perceived as a total discourse. It could thus be argued that postmodern tools already exist in a modernist approach, but that other terms and concepts are used and that even the approaches are different.

It is, however, difficult to get away from the perception that the positivist approach is not able to adequately explain what evaluation of evidence actually is; the explanatory framework is too narrow. The question is whether postmodernism has anything to contribute. I believe that it can, for certain explanations. The legal system creates explanations for events, such as crimes, which are constituted by the law and the legal system's principles. Moreover, the procedural formal concept of truth can create 'truths', which become a product of the legal system.[44] Both the law and the formal concept of truth have been around a lot longer than postmodernism, but postmodernism has brought additional interesting aspects concerning explanations, though not for explanations with cause–effect relationships based on there being a generative causal and law-bound mechanism.

## 6.3  EVALUATION OF TESTIMONIES

In the 1990s, the Supreme Court began using certain criteria for the assessment of testimony credibility in sexual offence cases, particularly in rape cases where the only evidence usually are the statements of the victim and the accused. A testimony under these criteria must, among other things, be coherent, consistent and contain unique details. For evaluating testimonies, the evaluation of evidence is thus in these cases about assessing whether a testimony, in its content, is such that it can be deemed credible in accordance with predefined criteria. Determining this does not require any probability assessment. That the testimony has been submitted, what content it has and how it has been submitted are indisputable. The first stage of the evaluation of evidence thus deals with checking the testimony against the predefined criteria. If these have been met, the testimony is credible. Fuzzy logic, along with MCA and the simple additive model, will be applied to testimonies later in this book. First, however, the truth criteria will be described in more detail.

---

[44]  Regarding the legal concept of truth and the minimalistic realistic concept of truth, see Magne Strandberg 'Bevisrettens sannhetsmålsetning' in Simon Andersson and Katrin Lainpelto (eds) *Festskrift till Christian Diesen* (Norstedts Juridik 2014).

### 6.3.1   Truth Criteria

A number of authors have written about the criteria that the Supreme Court uses in the evaluation of testimonies made by victims in sexual offence cases. Lena Schelin has identified five truth criteria (reality criteria) by studying the judgments rendered by the Supreme Court and found that the following criteria for a true testimony were used:

- long statement;
- coherent statement;
- clear statement;
- detailed statement;
- stable statement over time.

Schelin also found six control criteria:

- the existence of elements in the statement that are difficult to explain;
- the ability to explain the existence of weaknesses in the statement;
- how the statement was conveyed (solemnly, spontaneously, circumspectly, gestures and facial expressions);
- the statement gives a credible impression;
- the statement has the quality of giving the impression of being experienced first-hand;
- no part of the statement contains inaccuracies (are 'contaminated').[45]

The truth criteria were compiled from several rulings and thus do not constitute a fixed set of criteria that are all always used in cases where two testimonies – the accused's and the injured party's – contradict each other. Instead, the individual circumstances in the case determine which criteria are used in the judgment.[46] The criteria that the statement gives a credible impression and has the quality of being experienced first-hand are general control criteria and thus cover the entire testimony. According to Willén and Strömwall, who scientifically examined the Supreme Court's established practice in the area, these criteria are given great importance.[47]

---

[45]   Lena Schelin, *Bevisvärdering av utsagor i brottmål* (Norstedts Juridik 2007) 163ff.

[46]   Helena Sutorius and Christian Diesen, Bevisprövning vid sexualbrott (2nd edn Norstedts Juridik 2013) 82ff.

[47]   Rebecca M Willén and Leif A Strömwall, 'Offenders Lies and Truths: An Evaluation of the Supreme Court of Sweden's Criteria for Credibility Assessment' (2012) 18(8) *Psychology, Crime & Law* 745.

Schelin names two structured models for the analysis of testimonies: criteria based content analysis (CBCA) and reality monitoring (RM), which are based on certain criteria for truthfulness. These have little scientific support, however, and the majority of the criteria set by the Supreme Court have no reliable scientific support whatsoever.[48] Because the testimony analyses are done according to certain predefined criteria of truth, they are, as mentioned previously, not in themselves a probability assessment but rather this is the result of an assessment of the criteria, which is typically considered to indicate a true testimony. One could say that the testimony analysis according to the truth criteria is an indirect probability assessment that must be supplemented with a direct probability assessment. Even if all the criteria have been met, the evidence can still be deemed insufficient. This is obvious if the person giving the testimony gives a statement concerning circumstantial evidence. That the accused was seen carrying an axe can thus be a weak item of circumstantial evidence for a charge of vandalism. If the testimony that the accused had an axe is assessed to be both credible and reliable, the item of circumstantial evidence may still have a weak evidentiary value for the relevant evidentiary theme. It is dependent upon whether, with respect to the circumstances in the case, there is a sentence of experience that can be connected between carrying an axe and vandalism, and if so, how strong this sentence of experience is deemed to be.

Another situation in which circumstances outside the testimony can become significant is if a witness has a relationship to the party or the matter at issue. If the witness receives high scores in a credibility assessment, there will then be an uncertainty that cannot be evaluated within the content of the testimony. It is thus conceivable that high scores for credibility would not necessarily mean high reliability. However, if credibility is high, this usually also means that reliability is also high, because biases of different types tend to leave traces behind that can be discovered in a credibility assessment, for example the witness's account of some item is doubtful or not coherent in some enigmatic way. On the other hand, the witness can of course also be a skilled liar.

In the use of truth criteria, a distinction must be made between different situations. The police officer who finds herself in court talking about the way the accused hit her usually does not remember details and the testimony is often short. The same applies if a temporary eyewitness says that he saw some men break into a shop. The truth criteria are in the first place not intended for this type of testimony but, as mentioned above, for

---

[48]   Schelin (n 45)182ff.

testimonies in cases involving sexual assault and domestic violence. This may explain why the conditions of origin of the testimonies do not seem to be among the control criteria. Was it dark, for example, when the observation was made? From what distance did the witness make the observation? The conditions of origin for a testimony would seem to usually be more important and of a different nature when the situation does not involve a relational crime.

Altogether there are strikingly many truth and control criteria. If the aim is that they should contribute to a more reliable evaluation of evidence, it might be questioned whether the amount of criteria is too large. The criteria furthermore relate both to the testimony itself and to how it was given (criteria outside the testimony), as well as to other factors than how it was given. As I will shortly come to, the criteria are also vague and there is therefore a high risk of overlap.

The use of MCA presupposes that the criteria are understandable, operational, not redundant, precise, concrete and mutually independent.[49] Generally, the objective is to limit the number of criteria. In a decision tree, concrete criteria should be at the bottom. These should be useful for finding the 'truth'; in other words, they should indicate what is 'true'. However, very vague criteria are difficult to use. In addition, vague criteria also make the requirement for independence difficult or even impossible to uphold. Deficits in independence also lead to a risk of double counting of the criterion's importance, so that the testimony is either assessed as more credible or less credible than it actually is. To test the independence criterion, the decision-maker must ask herself if she can assess one criterion vis-à-vis the objective of finding 'the truth' without being affected by how she assessed the importance of another criterion (for 'truth'). Can, for example, a testimony be 'clear' without being 'stable' or 'coherent'? Or can a testimony be 'clear' and still contain 'elements that are difficult to explain'? This latter is a control criterion according to Willén and Strömwall. If the testimony is judged to be 'clear', however, this control criterion can be redundant. 'Credible impression' has also been set as a control criterion, a general one. One wonders, though, how a credible impression can be a control criterion when the truth criteria are aimed at determining precisely whether or not a testimony is credible. One problem is thus, once again, the vagueness of the criteria. One way to remedy vagueness is through further clarification, that is, by breaking down the criteria into smaller parts and removing that which despite clarification does not meet the requirement for independence.

---

[49]   See section 2.3.3, above.

It has not been investigated whether the truth criteria are mutually independent or how they are separated from the control criteria, particularly from the general control criteria. Because of the vagueness of the criteria and the fact that they are set up as separate criteria, there is indeed a risk of them being double-counted. Willén and Strömwall have admittedly used the statistical method multiple analysis of variance (MANOVA) in their study to check the influence between different criteria, but as they themselves point out, it is a problem that the criteria are so vague.[50]

Because there are no scientifically substantiated criteria that reliably show the difference between a true and a false testimony, the question arises of where the criteria come from and what basis they have. They seem to me to be norm-based. We expect a true testimony to be 'long', 'coherent', 'detailed', 'stable over time' and not contain 'contradictions or other details that are difficult to explain'. But where do these norms, these expectations, come from? And, above all, should they – and if so, to what extent – form the basis for an assessment of what is 'true'? Perhaps the criteria are culturally conditioned; perhaps we have heard stories read to us when we were small which had a beginning and an ending, which were coherent and also exciting, peppered with details.[51] One hypothesis is that there is an ideal of a true testimony. The ideal of a true testimony is the product of the culture we live in, including the stories we were read as children, which has created norms, that is, expectations of content and the performance of a 'true' testimony. What the reality is, however, is something we know very little about when it comes to the assessment of credibility. From a cynical perspective, one could say that this does not matter in a courtroom because what matters there is getting the court to believe a hypothesis, not presenting evidence of how 'reality' is or was created.

As previously mentioned, in law of evidence contexts, reference is usually made to sentences of experiences or commonplace generalizations. Does a judge then have experience that testimonies which are 'long', 'coherent', 'clear', 'detailed' and 'stable' are 'true'? It is doubtful that anyone could brag about rich experiences in this area. Each one of us could go back through our own experiences and try to answer that question. Most will try to recall situations where the question of credibility arose or where an explanation for something was questioned, but the results would likely be rather meagre. This could be explained in that the credible testimony is an idealized testimony, which rarely puts in an appearance in the real world.

---

[50] Willén and Strömwall (n 47) 755.
[51] Cf Sven-Åke Christiansson and Marika Ehrenkrona, *Psykologi och bevisvärdering. Myter om trovärdighet och tillförlitlighet* (Norstedts Juridik 2011) 83.

And when the perfect 'ideal' testimony pops up in a real situation, such as in a trial, it is almost too good to be true, so good that one almost becomes suspicious. When the ideal testimony is confronted with the specific case, the criteria also become very difficult to apply because of their vagueness. The criteria therefore need to be padded using additional assumptions that seem reasonable in the specific case. This padding and the clarified credibility criterion of the specific case is a context-bound construction that is accepted if it appears reasonable. One could then justifiably claim that 'legal truth' is created in the courtroom through what happens there. In this sense, postmodernism has made contributions that supplement the concept of legal truth.

## 6.4   DIFFERENT ASPECTS OF EVIDENCE

There are several different aspects that could be applied to an item of evidence, including the testimony's credibility according to the truth criteria outlined above. If, however, four credible and reliable witnesses say that the perpetrator was at the scene of a crime, it does not generally make a difference if a fifth reliable witness emerges and says the same thing. The evidentiary value of this witness might be as high as for the first four witnesses, but his evidence has little weight. The fifth witness may even be dismissed as unnecessary under the provisions of 35:7 RB, because there are already four witnesses.

If a testimony concerns a single temporary event the criterion 'coherent statement' becomes easier to both meet and assess than if it was a prolonged course of events consisting of many elements.[52] This truth criterion should then reasonably have less weight even if it is met, than it would if it involved a complicated course of events. Even if the truth criteria were mutually independent, it depends on the context what importance they should be attached in an overall assessment. It may also be the case that two witness testimonies on an evidentiary theme are judged to be equally strong based on an assessment founded on sentences of experience but that one of the testimonies is still judged to have a higher weight. This could be due to the witness's appearance and behaviour, for example one witness speaks distinctly with feeling and gestures, while the other witness speaks quietly, slowly and indifferently. It could also be that one testimony that is given in an alert, animated and engaged manner compensates for certain deficiencies in coherence and clarity that are not found in the slow and

---

[52]   Sutorius and Diesen (n 46) 119.

seemingly indifferent witness. For these types of subjective assessments, there are no sentences of experience that the evaluation can build on. There are no scientific studies supporting the assumption that the one testimony should be more credible than the other. If such an assessment is done anyway, this is due to other reasons than the existence of sentences of experience (compare the ideal above).

It is important to emphasize that a testimony is assessed within a legal context. In criminal cases, the frame for evaluation is set by the definition of the crime. This excludes parts of the story that in the court's view are not significant to the assessment because they are not legally relevant. In this way, the evaluation of evidence is legally controlled. Substantial points are only those with significance for the assessment of the crime. A testimony can thus be 'coherent' and 'clear' or 'detailed' outside the framework of the crime, but disconnected and less detailed in the areas that are considered legally relevant. The framework for assessment is also set from the outset by the police and prosecutors, because the assessment of deviations in a testimony is made on the basis of what the witness said the first time. Of importance in the examination of a witness is thus which questions were asked the first time. Each question that is asked to the injured party precludes other questions, other interpretations and other 'constructs of reality', that is, possible explanations. The person who has the power to ask questions and lead an interrogation will thus be able to steer the outcome of an interrogation and the answer to the question of what happened and how it happened by creating the framework for the assessment. With other questions, the outcome may have been different. The judge's own background, capacity to feel empathy, and ability to listen and evaluate also plays a role in what he or she considers to be credible and reliable and what she does not.

Certain evidentiary themes are more important than others. Those that involve the core of a legally relevant course of events have greater importance than those on the outskirts. Legal premises also determine what the final evidentiary theme is and what is instead circumstantial evidence. The direct evidence is considered to meet the final evidentiary theme, while circumstantial evidence additionally requires a conclusion from the circumstantial evidence to the final evidentiary theme or sometimes to another item of circumstantial evidence and from there to the final evidentiary theme. The circumstantial evidence is therefore usually viewed as weaker than the direct evidence. Should the direct evidence switch places with an item of circumstantial evidence through the way in which the applicable legal rule's area of significance is decided, this could have significance for the evidentiary value. Even the standard of proof is legally determined, both generally and in the specific case. This means that the evidential significance for the same evidentiary fact varies according to the applicable standard of proof. An evidentiary fact with evidentiary value 0.6 has a greater relative evidential significance if the standard of proof is 'presumable' than if it is 'substantiated' or even 'obvious'.

According to the evidentiary value method, a testimony should be seen as an 'event'.[53] Statistical calculation rules are applicable precisely to events, which – after some modifications – are used by the evidentiary value method. If the probability of an event is 0.8, and the probability of another event is 0.5, the probability of both events occurring according to the statistical multiplication theorem is $0.8 \times 0.5$, or 0.4. If two events could potentially occur and one is looking for the probability of either occurring, the probability for one event is added to the probability for the other event according to the statistical addition theorem. The probability of both events occurring is subtracted from this sum. Thus, if the probability that tomorrow will be sunny and that my sister will come to visit are 0.8 and 0.7 respectively, the probability that it will either be sunny or that my sister will come to visit will be 0.93. If two witnesses give statements on the same theme, this same formula is used. The testimonies are viewed as 'events' and receive under the collaboration formula a combined weighted evidentiary value for the theme. The computing rules are not difficult to understand. However, they are used on the outcome of an assessment, but say of course nothing of what qualities a testimony should have to be considered credible. However, as will be demonstrated below, fuzzy logic can also be used on credibility assessments.

## 6.5	FUZZY LOGIC – AN EXAMPLE OF APPLICATION

Fuzzy logic was introduced in Chapter 4, to which reference is made for the following application.

Some of the truth criteria are, as previously discussed, vague bordering on obtuse, unless they are clarified. The criterion 'long testimony' is an example of this. If a testimony lasts 15 minutes and 27 seconds, it may under the circumstances be considered 'long', but why would a testimony lasting 15 minutes and 26 seconds be considered 'short'? And what would be the benefit or utility of such a definition? 'Long' is a typical example in which there are transitions between 'short', 'rather short', 'average', 'rather long', 'long' and 'very long' testimonies.

---

[53]	Stening (Ch 3 n 35) 79–80.

The simplest membership function, the triangle, will be used in this example. If this is used for the criterion 'long testimony', it would produce a similar figure as that in Figure 4.8 in section 4.6.2 for tall men. In the use of fuzzy logic, the criteria 'long', 'coherent', 'clear', 'detailed' and 'stable' are thus seen as different sets. A testimony then has a membership in each of these sets. It was noted earlier that probability assessment is not built in to the simple additive model. However, the assessment of truth criteria is not a probability assessment as such, but rather the evidentiary values of the testimonies are instead a result of how well they meet the truth criteria. For this reason, a probability assessment does not need to be connected to the analysis, but can be done if, for example, the witness gives a statement on circumstantial evidence. Correspondingly, when considering the reliability of the victim's testimony in a rape case, a probability assessment can be added.

Using fuzzy logic together with MCA requires fixed or nonfuzzy sets. The set 'detailed' could be decided by the number of details in the testimony and the criterion 'long' could be measured in time. 'Stable' could describe the nature and degree of changes in the testimony, 'coherent' could consist of the chronology of the narrative and 'clear' could include dissonance in the testimony. All of these qualifiers are vague, but better than nothing at all. Fixing the criteria in a uniform way would seem to be impossible. Even after clarification, there will thus be a discretionary element in the assessment of the degree of membership. One alternative to clarification is to assess the degree of membership solely subjectively by deciding the degree of membership for each truth criterion directly and intuitively.

The aim of the following is to show the different steps involved in fuzzy logic when it is used together with the simple additive model and the assessment is made by one person. The example is structured as follows: There are five witnesses: W1, W2, W3, W4 and W5. The objective is to determine which witness is best with respect to the five truth criteria (Tc):

Tc 1: long testimony
Tc 2: coherent testimony
Tc 3: clear testimony
Tc 4: detailed testimony
Tc 5: stable testimony over time

The witnesses are scored and weighted, Table 6.1, using the following scores and corresponding linguistic variables with the triangle as the membership function.

Tables 6.2 and 6.3 below show the assessment of each witness using the

*Table 6.1   Linguistic terms for scores and weights*

| Linguistic terms for scores and weights | | |
|---|---|---|
| Weight | Score | Triangulated numbers |
| Very high (VH) | Very good (VG) | 0.75, 1.0, 1.0 |
| High (H) | Good (G) | 0.5, 0.75, 1.0 |
| Regular (R) | Moderate (M) | 0.25, 0.5, 0.75 |
| Low (L) | Poor (P) | 0, 0.25, 0.5 |
| Very low (VL) | Very poor (VP) | 0, 0, 0.25 |

*Table 6.2   Score assessment of witnesses, linguistic*

| Score assessment of witnesses, linguistic | | | | | |
|---|---|---|---|---|---|
| | W 1 | W 2 | W 3 | W 4 | W 5 |
| C 1 | B | MB | M | D | D |
| C 2 | B | B | MB | M | MB |
| C 3 | M | B | B | MB | M |
| C 4 | B | MD | M | D | M |
| C 5 | B | M | D | MB | B |

linguistic criteria for criteria Tc 1-Tc 5. The triangulated values are shown in Table 6.3.

Average ('fuzzy') scores are calculated. Average scores are calculated as demonstrated in section 4.6. Fuzzy average scores are then calculated for each witness, Table 6.4.

Linguistic assessments of weighting are performed in the same way as for scoring. This figure therefore does not need to be revised. Instead, the weighting is shown directly by the matrix. This weighting is shown below, Table 6.5.

*Table 6.3   Score assessment of witnesses, matrix*

| Score assessment of witnesses, matrix | | | | | |
|---|---|---|---|---|---|
| | **W 1** | **W 2** | **W 3** | **W 4** | **W 5** |
| C 1 | 0.5, 0.75, 1.0 | 0.75, 1.0, 1.0 | 0.25, 0.5, 0.75 | 0, 0.25, 0.5 | 0, 0.25, 0.5 |
| C 2 | 0.5, 0.75, 1.0 | 0.5, 0.75, 1.0 | 0.75, 1.0, 1.0 | 0.25, 0.5, 0.75 | 0.75, 1.0, 1.0 |
| C 3 | 0.25, 0.5, 0.75 | 0.5, 0.75, 1.0 | 0.5, 0.75, 1.0 | 0.75, 1.0, 1.0 | 0.25, 0.5, 0.75 |
| C 4 | 0,25, 0.5, 0.75 | 0, 0, 0.25 | 0.25, 0.5, 0.75 | 0. 0.25, 0.5 | 0.25, 0.5, 0.75 |
| C 5 | 0.5, 0.75, 1.0 | 0.25, 0.5, 0.75 | 0, 0.25, 0.5 | 0.75, 1.0, 1.0 | 0.5, 0.75, 1.0 |

*Table 6.4   Average values*

| Average values | | | | | |
|---|---|---|---|---|---|
| | **W1** | **W2** | **W3** | **W4** | **W5** |
| C 1 | 0.75 | 0.92 | 0.5 | 0.25 | 0.25 |
| C 2 | 0.75 | 0.75 | 0.92 | 0.5 | 0.92 |
| C 3 | 0.5 | 0.75 | 0.75 | 0.92 | 0.5 |
| C 4 | 0.5 | 0.08 | 0.5 | 0.25 | 0.5 |
| C 5 | 0.75 | 0.5 | 0.25 | 0.92 | 0.75 |

Average scores for the weights, see Table 6.6, are calculated as shown in section 4.6.

The weights for each witness are then normalized as shown in section 4.6. This provides the following weight table, Table 6.7.

To obtain the final results, the simple additive model is then used. For each witness and each criterion, the average scores are multiplied by the normalized weights, which have been determined for each witness. The results are then added together. For example, for witness 1 this becomes $(0.25 \times 0.75) = 0.19 + (0.20 \times 0.75) = 0.15 + (0.14 \times 0.5) = 0.07 + (0.20 \times 0.5) = 0.1 + (0.20 \times 0.75) = 0.15$. The final result for witness 1 is thus: $0.19 + 0.15 + 0.07 + 0.1 + 0.15 = 0.66$. Witness 2 receives a final score of 0.66,

*Table 6.5   Weighting of witnesses, matrix*

| Weighting of witnesses, matrix | | | | | |
|---|---|---|---|---|---|
| | **W 1** | **W 2** | **W 3** | **W 4** | **W 5** |
| **C 1** | 0.75, 1.0, 1.0 | 0.75, 1.0, 1.0 | 0.5, 0.75, 1.0 | 0,5, 0.75, 1.0 | 0,25, 0.5, 0.75 |
| **C 2** | 0.5, 0.75, 1.0 | 0.5, 0.75, 1.0 | 0.75, 1.0, 1.0 | 0.5, 0.75, 1.0 | 0.75, 1.0, 1.0 |
| **C 3** | 0.25, 0.5, 0.75 | 0.75, 1.0, 1.0 | 0.25, 0.5, 0.75 | 0.75, 1.0, 1.0 | 0.5, 0.75, 1.0 |
| **C 4** | 0.5, 0.75, 1.0 | 0.25, 0.5, 0.75 | 0.5, 0.75, 1.0 | 025. 0.5, 0.75 | 0.25, 0.5, 0.75 |
| **C 5** | 0.5, 0.75, 1.0 | 0.5, 0.75, 1.0 | 0.25, 0.5, 0.75 | 0.75, 1.0, 1.0 | 0.5, 0.75, 1.0 |

*Table 6.6   Average values, weight points*

| Average values, weight points | | | | | |
|---|---|---|---|---|---|
| | **W 1** | **W 2** | **W 3** | **W 4** | **W 5** |
| **C 1** | 0.92 | 0.92 | 0.75 | 0.75 | 0.5 |
| **C 2** | 0.75 | 0.75 | 0.92 | 0.75 | 0.92 |
| **C 3** | 0.5 | 0.92 | 0.5 | 0.92 | 0.75 |
| **C 4** | 0.75 | 0.5 | 0.75 | 0.5 | 0.5 |
| **C 5** | 0.75 | 0.75 | 0.5 | 0.92 | 0.75 |

witnesses 3 and 4 have a final score of 0.62 and witness 5 has a final score of 0.65.

The truth criteria originate from rape and domestic violence cases, but in principle they can be used for any oral testimony. In this example, I imagine that if five witnesses were to be examined on the same evidentiary theme in a complicated case (other than domestic violence or rape), scoring could be done after the immediate impression that the witnesses have given and that the concrete assessment with weighting will come in as a second stage. If the witnesses turn out to have similar scores on most of the truth criteria, the remaining criterion or criteria will be decisive. It can furthermore be assumed that the truth criteria are to a certain extent com-

*Table 6.7   Normalized weight points*

| Normalized weight points | | | | | |
|---|---|---|---|---|---|
| | **W 1** | **W 2** | **W 3** | **W 4** | **W 5** |
| **C 1** | 0.25 | 0.24 | 0.22 | 0.20 | 0.16 |
| **C 2** | 0.20 | 0.20 | 0.27 | 0.20 | 0.29 |
| **C 3** | 0.14 | 0.24 | 0.15 | 0.24 | 0.16 |
| **C 4** | 0.20 | 0.13 | 0.22 | 0.13 | 0.16 |
| **C 5** | 0.20 | 0.20 | 0.15 | 0.24 | 0.24 |

pensatory so that a lower degree of membership in one set can be compensated by a higher degree of membership in another. These compensatory weightings become clearer and easier to do with the help of fuzzy logic. An alternative to fuzzy logic is to use MCA without linguistic variables and instead set the values within ranges, that is, evidentiary value is given a minimum and a maximum value. However, this method does not address vagueness in the same way.

The use of fuzzy logic in legal evidence evaluation is as yet uncommon.[54] It is time-consuming to use manually, even in the relatively simple example above, because it requires calculation in several stages. It is therefore not a realistic option for practical use without software, that is, without a computer program that performs the calculations.

There have been (and still are) objections to fuzzy logic, but no one today could deny its scientific value when there is vague and imprecise information that must be dealt with. Through fuzzy logic, vagueness becomes legitimized in a completely different way than if just intuition and feeling are used. Fuzzy logic confirms that vagueness is information bearing and prescribes a structured way for handling and using this information. The transitions and overlaps are specified by degrees of

---

[54]   Cf however, Gerald T Seniuk, 'Credibility Assessment, Common Law Trials and Fuzzy Logic' in Barry S Cooper, Dorothee Griesel and Marguerite Ternes (eds) *Applied Issues in Investigative Interviewing, Eywitness Memory and Credibility Assessment* (Springer 2013) and Clermont, *Death of Paradox* and *Conjunction of Evidence* (both Ch 1 n 14).

membership, which can be assessed discretionarily if concrete calculations are not made. Even if the degree of membership is subjectively
determined, this subjective assessment is performed using a structured
approach, which is better than pure intuition, while at the same time
intuition is essential for it to work.

### 6.5.1   The Standard of Proof is Linear

Regarding which party should bear the burden of proof and the level of
the standard of proof, the substantive rules do not always provide an
answer to this important question, which for a long period of time has
been debated in Sweden. Olivecrona argues that the decision of the assignment of burden of proof should conform to the objective of the applicable
substantive rule.[55] This idea was pursued by Ekelöf, who advocated a
teleological interpretation and application of the substantive rules for
determining on whom the burden of proof should be placed and how
high the standard of proof should be. Regarding the standard of proof, he
argues that this should normally be 'substantiated' in a four-point scale:
'presumable', 'probable', 'substantiated' and 'obvious'.[56] 'Substantiated/
demonstrated' is thus considered to be the normal requirement for the
strength of evidence in civil cases in Sweden. However, the required degree
of proof is lower in cases where the evidentiary theme is hard to prove, for
example when it is about causal connections.

   Some other authors argue that the standard of proof should be more
nuanced and that the principle of preponderance of evidence should
be the starting point for a discussion on how the risk of an erroneous
judgment should be distributed among the parties.[57] The principle of
preponderance of evidence, which means that that party with the strongest evidence wins the case, regardless of how much stronger this evidence
is, is not a burden of proof rule. However, should it not be possible to
determine which party has the strongest evidence (though this is a very
unlikely situation), the court must decide how much evidence should
be required and then a burden of proof will also emerge. The difference
between the different approaches to burden of proof and standard of
proof is connected to a fundamental difference of opinion regarding the
functions of the administration of justice. Ekelöf and Olivecrona stress

---

[55]   Karl Olivecrona, *Bevisskyldigheten och den materiella rätten* (Uppsala 1930)
130.
[56]   Ekelöf and Boman (n 5) 140.
[57]   [57] See, for example, Bolding (n 5) 94 and also *Går det att bevisa?* (Norstedt
1989) 95ff, Eckhoff (n 13) 60ff and Lindell, (Ch 5 n 45) 284, 287.

the importance of behaviour modification, while Bolding and Lindell instead argue that the administration of justice should first and foremost be conflict resolution.

In accordance with the behaviour modification model, the required degree of proof should thus be rather high. In for example actions concerning payment of a debt, it should be 'substantiated' in order to impose pressure on debtors to pay. As a consequence of the high standard of proof, the debtor should realize the futility of making ungrounded or loosely grounded objections in the hope of evading payment. This in turn is assumed to create good payment morals and a willingness among lenders to lend money, something that benefits economic turnover in society. The argument that the risk of paying the same debt twice if the required degree of proof is high is met with the argument that some debtors must be sacrificed on the altar of credit in order to achieve behaviour modification.[58] Supporters of conflict resolution theory oppose this reasoning. While conceding that a high standard of proof creates a certain pressure to pay and that unnecessary processes could thereby be avoided, they point out that confidence in the moral enhancement function of the administration of justice is exaggerated and that in some cases it may even be considered offensive to sacrifice debtors on the altar of credit instead of achieving justice in the individual case. Therefore, if there are no special circumstances in favour of a placing the risk of uncertainty on one or the other of the parties, this risk should be distributed equally between them, which according to conflict resolution theory will be the result if the principle of preponderance of evidence is applied. In addition, this principle – which is intended only for civil actions – has the effect that in the long run, more substantially correct judgements are achieved than if burden of proof rules are used.

Regarding how high the requirement of the degree of proof is in different types of actions in practice, it is difficult to say how high these actually are. This is because expressions such as 'probable' and 'substantiated' are so vague. They can either denote that the theme has been proven, in which case nothing can be concluded about the particular degree of proof that has been applied, or they can refer to a special degree of required proof.[59]

In Figure 6.1 below, it will first be shown that the standard of proof under the axiomatic models available is linear and then that fuzzy logic can also be used on these. 'Presumable' has been said to represent at least 60 per cent probability, 'probable' at least 75 per cent, 'substantiated/

---

[58] Ekelöf and Boman (n 5) 91.
[59] Lindell (Ch 5 n 44) 335ff.

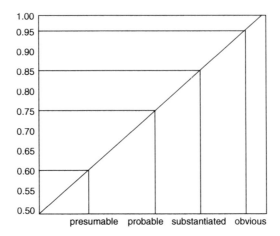

*Figure 6.1　Linear probability scale*

demonstrated' at least 85 per cent and 'obvious' at least 95 per cent.[60] This means that 'presumable' lies within a range of 60–75 per cent, 'probable' in a range of 75–85 per cent, 'substantiated' in a range of 85–95 per cent and 'obvious' in a range of 95–100 per cent. If the evidentiary value is 84.9 per cent, it is thus not 'substantiated'. That this tenth of a point would be of decisive significance does not seem from this perspective to be reasonable.[61] One problem for the decision-maker is naturally that she cannot know where she is on the standard of proof scale. There is no green lamp that starts blinking right at 85 per cent. Nor can the decision-maker have any exact understanding of where the evidentiary value lies. How can she then know where the limits are?

Figure 6.1 shows that the scale for evidentiary value and standard of proof is linear. That the scale is linear means, among other things, that an increase in the value of one piece of evidence from, say, 0.60 to 0.70, is worth the same as an increase from 0.75 to 0.85 or an increase from 0.90 to 1.0. Even if this is apparent because the scale is linear, an increase from 0.75 to 0.85 in practice or in the real world has a greater value than an increase from 0.60 to 0.70, if the standard of proof is 'substantiated', because this brings the party up to the minimum level of the applicable standard of proof. Furthermore, it is usually easier to increase the value of

---

[60] Per Olof Ekelöf, *Rättegång IV* (1977 4th edn P A Norstedt & Söners Förlag) 31. Corresponding values for the evidentiary value method are shown to be 25, 30, 75 and 90.

[61] Of course, in the real world this tenth of a point would not be detectable.

the evidence from a low level than from a high level. Increasing the value from 0.55 to 0.6 is thus generally easier than increasing it from 0.95 to 1.0. This latter increase can therefore be more valuable than an increase from 0.55 to 0.6; in a criminal trial the last piece is crucial. If the standard of proof is 0.95, there is a risk that five out of a hundred convictions are incorrect. If it would be possible for the prosecutor to boost up the value just a little bit, for example from 0.90 to 0.95, this obviously has great significance compared with an increase from 0.55 to 0.6 in the same case. Moving up a level to another standard of proof can be done through so-called 'positive auxiliary facts' or through further evidence for the same theme. The question for the plaintiff is what sacrifices he or she is willing to make to try to move the evidence up to a higher plateau. This can take time and cost money. The answer depends in part on how much is at stake. If the dispute concerns a large sum of money, it can be worth the sacrifice. With a game theory perspective, the plaintiff could be prepared to pay more for an increase in the evidentiary value from 0.80 to 0.85 than for an increase from 0.75 to 0.80. And if the plaintiff had a surplus value, say if the evidence was worth 0.95, then he or she could sell the surplus value to someone else in need on a fictitious market trading with evidentiary values.

The linearity of the evidentiary value scale presupposes of course that an evidentiary value has linear properties. This linear thinking exists in different models for evidence evaluation, such as the evidentiary value method and the evidentiary theme method. Under the evidentiary value method, there is an evidentiary value that can be increased or decreased by positive or negative auxiliary facts. As has been argued in other contexts, however, a witness testimony does not have its own original evidentiary value, but rather the evidentiary value of a testimony arises if it meets certain conditions.[62] These include, for example, the conditions of origin, for example if the observation made by a witness was made from a far distance. We know from experience that people do not see as well from a long distance as they do from a short distance; ergo the longer the distance, the less reliable the testimony. From a very far distance, the testimony has no evidentiary value at all. This relationship between distance and the ability to see is thus linear until it drops off, because people cannot make good and careful observations from too long distances. Enmity between the witnesses and the party or the accused – which affects the witness's reliability – would also seem to be a sort of linear relationship; the stronger the enmity the lower the reliability. Yet, because enmity is a vague social concept, its linearity is difficult to determine.

---

[62]   Lindell (Ch 3 n 17) 532.

What about the above truth criteria then, for example, 'long', 'coherent' and 'detailed' testimony? Conceptually, these criteria should fall into the same category as auxiliary facts because the criteria do not have any evidentiary value of their own and there is no other evidentiary concept available. If the statement is an evidentiary fact, its content and the manner in which it was given will thereby be what determines the evidentiary value. The statement in itself thus becomes the evidentiary fact around which the truth criteria gather, even if has not been analysed from the start using the truth criteria and it is thus not initially possible to say if the statement is good or completely lacks evidentiary value.

That the scale is linear in the sense that an increase in the value of one piece of evidence from, for example, 0.60 to 0.70 is worth the same as an increase from 0.75 to 0.85 does not mean that it is always possible to achieve high evidentiary values. Certain things are difficult to investigate. For this reason, probability may stop at about 50 per cent despite considerable investigative efforts. It would then become tempting to argue that this 50 per cent is worth more than a probability of 50 per cent that was easy to reach. The difference between these situations, and which is about robustness, is important. The question is how it should be addressed. According to the evidentiary value method, poor investigation will, as mentioned above, decrease the evidentiary value. However, thorough investigations do not increase the probability. Instead, lowering the required degree of probability is deemed to be an option when the investigation is poor. Another possibility is to give a piece of evidence based on thorough investigations a high weight and – conversely – give low weight to another piece of evidence, if little investigation was done, even if both pieces of evidence would have a high probability value.

In the introduction to this chapter it was said that the evidentiary theme method and the evidentiary value method appear to be far too narrow for describing in a fair and true manner the intellectual activity called the evaluation of evidence. The explanation for this would seem to be that the methods are epistemological in the sense that they are based on our knowledge of reality. This knowledge is expressed in terms of evidentiary facts, auxiliary facts and sentences of experience. The problems with the models in question – and the epistemological models for evidence evaluation in general – is that our knowledge of reality is limited and that language is vague. The sentences of experience that the courts commonly use are thus vague and the legal language is not exact. As a result, sentences of experience are constructed and this construction is essentially based on expectations based on hypothetical situations. At the same time, the evaluation of evidence should be objective and connected to the knowledge base that exists or is assumed to exist. Fuzzy logic is designed for vagueness and is therefore better able to express uncertainty than frequency theories of any type. In many ways, MCA together with fuzzy logic therefore seem to be better suited for vague and imprecise information than the evidentiary theme and evidentiary value methods, at least in their current forms.

### 6.5.2   The Standard of Proof is 'Fuzzy'

As we have seen, the standard of proof is 'fuzzy'. 'Presumable', 'probable', 'substantiated' and 'obvious' are vague concepts. In accordance with fuzzy logic each of the standards expresses a required degree of proof. Something may, for example, be more or less 'presumable'. In Figure 6.2 below, 'presumable' falls into the range of 60–70, 'probable' between 70–80, 'substantiated' between 80–90 and 'obvious' between 90–100 (Ekelöf's ratings have thus not been followed). Because the standard of proof is fuzzy, there are overlaps between these minimum and maximum values. 'Presumable' thus begins in the figure at 50, but with a very low degree of membership in this standard of proof.[63] The highest degree of membership in this fuzzy set lies at probability 65; the degree of membership then increasingly declines and stops at 75. 'Probable' begins at 65

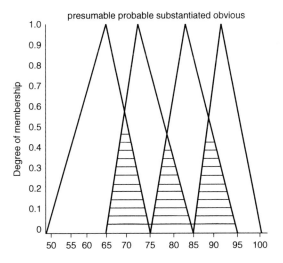

*Figure 6.2    Fuzzy probability scale*

---

[63]   Note that degree of membership is not the same thing as probability value. A low degree of membership can mean a high degree of probability in a standard of proof.

with a very low degree of membership and peaks at 75 – where 'substanti-ated' begins with a low degree of membership – and then drops at 85. 'Substantiated' ends at 95 with a low degree of membership in 'obvious' and reaches its highest point at 85, where 'obvious' begins with a low degree of membership. 'Obvious' reaches its peak at 95. The principle of preponderance of evidence, which does not denote a standard of proof, would, if it were input in the figure, land between 40–60. Thus, because the area is 'fuzzy' it is understandable that in practice, it can be impossible to determine if the evidence in a case, for example, only entails preponder-ance or if it reaches up to the standard of proof 'presumable'. There is thus realism in fuzzy logic that is difficult to deny, which makes it suitable to use, at least in certain legal contexts.[64]

Figure 6.2 is not perfect, but it illustrates how fuzzy logic can be used to describe vagueness in the standard of proof. The figure also shows that fixed values are necessary in order to determine fuzzy areas, but also that the judge in practice does not know more than that he or she is somewhere in a 'fuzzy' area. It is hardly possible to give any recommendations for what a judge should do if the membership in the proposed standard of proof seems problematic. However, because vagueness is the reason for this span, it can be said that in a criminal case, the degree of membership in the set 'obvious' should not, for reasons of legality and rule of law, be as low as, for example, at 0.80. A deciding factor for the choice that is made in a fuzzy area could thus be what legal area it concerns. For a civil case, it may in some cases be sufficient with only membership in that specific standard of proof. In addition, the manner in which the substantive rule is interpreted could be of importance. If a rule is given a broad interpreta-tion, this can maybe justify a low probability and a low degree of member-ship in the relevant standard of proof being sufficient.

## 6.6   SUMMARY AND CONCLUSIONS

There are different theories for the evaluation of evidence. The majority are based on modernism and empirical evidence but there are others, for example normative evaluation theories (e.g. Zahle) and even narrative theories. Theories are general, but in a legal context they can take differ-ent forms in different areas of law. One method for evidence evaluation in criminal cases might not fit in a civil case and a method adapted for civil cases may not fit in an administrative case. The situation can also be dif-

---

[64]   Cf Seniuk (54) 25ff.

ferent in different types of cases in the same branch of law. A distinction must also be made between descriptions about how evidence is evaluated in different branches of law and a theory that prescribes how this should be done. Evidentiary law theories are consistently normative (recommending how it should be) and can be specially designed to meet certain requirements for law and order, such as the evidentiary value method.

In this chapter, different aspects have been established concerning evidence and individual items of evidence. In accordance with MCA, criteria are assigned a weight. Weight would seem in modern evidentiary law literature to be linked solely with robustness, but weight represents more than the scope of an investigation. Weight is also about one item of evidence's relationship to the other evidence presented and its relative importance for the concrete assessment, as well as which standard of proof is used. Weight is furthermore about the details or particulars of an item of evidence, which is demonstrated through the use of the simple additive model and fuzzy logic on the truth criteria.

Evaluation of evidence in practice is difficult to investigate because there are few studies examining how judges and other legal professionals think about evidentiary issues – at least in Sweden – and because the concepts used are vague. Another troublesome problem is that the Supreme Court uses criteria that have come to be called 'truth criteria', which by and large have little scientific support. In this book I have questioned where these criteria come from, and argued that they are cultural and have their origin in an idealized perception of what characterizes a true testimony. The ideal testimony meets these criteria, but that this testimony should be true could just as well be a myth.

Because fuzzy logic addresses the uncertainty arising from vague and imprecise information, it presents itself as a realistic theory in a legal context where vagueness is often a problem. Fuzzy logic is inviting, but must be used with good judgement. Its use must be combined, as far as possible, with nonfuzzy sets. The assessor should not for convenience haphazardly say that the witness's testimony has a high degree of membership to 'true testimonies' and be satisfied with that. Clarification is required by breaking down the sets into several subsets.

Due to the fact that fuzzy logic presupposes crisp or nonfuzzy sets, one may ask if it really could remedy the vagueness in a legal context. If a witness says that she observed a 'tall' person, we do not know what the witness means by that. The witness can then be asked what she means by 'tall'. If the witness says that in her opinion, a 'tall' person is someone over 185 cm, is fuzzy logic then needed? No, perhaps not in this case, but there are other situations in which witnesses speak of, for example, moods and attitudes, which cannot be defined as easily as height or weight. 'They seemed stressed and defensive and nonchalantly ignored many of the objections raised by the company's representatives.' People can be slightly stressed or very stressed and a bit defensive or extremely defensive and a touch nonchalant or completely nonchalant. The fuzzy logic says here that they were members of the set 'very stressed people' and the set 'defensive people'. We cannot know exactly what this means, but because the witness perceived the situation in this way, the description has to be considered. The witness paints a picture of the people's membership in these sets and that the degree of membership was perceived as high.

The uncertainty that vagueness brings into the evaluation of evidence is primarily associated with the fact that sentences of experience are as a rule vague, which sometimes is due to the vagueness of the language. Uncertainty may also be due to something that is difficult to define or investigate, such as mental illness. If a doctor is asked to give a statement on whether a crime was committed under the influence of mental illness, she does not say that the accused when the crime was committed had a certain degree of membership in the set of mentally ill people, but the conclusion can have this purport if it is translated to fuzzy logic.

As is shown from the preparatory work of 36 AvtL and what has been developed in doctrine (to return briefly to the agreement example in section 4.4), reference points for the assessment have been provided through various examples in order to give some guidelines for the application of the provision. Regarding the concrete assessment under 36 AvtL, it is thus clear from the preparatory work and doctrine that modification can be considered if, for example, there is a 'disparity between the parties' contractual benefits', or if certain terms 'favour one party' and 'disadvantage' the other party. It is furthermore important what legal consequences ensue if there is a breach of contract. If a party is responsible for an 'immaterial breach of contract', which does not entail 'any considerable damage' for the other party, it can generally not be considered acceptable that the other party claims breach of contract in order to revoke the contract. Instead, the contract could be modified.

The quoted expressions above are part of natural language. It is not possible to further clarify these into purely descriptive statements that consist of simple facts suited to strict probability-based reasoning. The evaluation of evidence will instead be based on more or less vague linguistic expressions. It is, for example, not possible to define the exact point at which there is a 'disparity' between the parties' performances or what 'favours' or 'disadvantages', and so on. Of course there is a basis for the decision, most often in a contract, but even this contains linguistic terms, variables that are vague. As regards 'poor language skills', which the preparatory works mention as a reason for modification, one might ask how this could be proven.[65] In this case, just as in many others, fuzzy logic could be used. The individual's language skills are part of a fuzzy set. The fringe areas most people could agree on: A has obviously poor language skills/A has very good language skills, but in-between these, the borders are blurry. An individual's degree of membership in the set 'individuals with poor language skills' can therefore often be only roughly estimated.

Furthermore, is it possible to prove a 'disparity between the parties' contractual benefits' or a claim that a breach of contract is 'immaterial'? Or is it all about legal subsumption? Can this be determined at all? Looking at the above described models for the evaluation of evidence – the evidentiary value method and the evidentiary theme method – the premise for the use of these is that the evidentiary theme is descriptive (as simple facts as possible), for example a car's speed or that a person was at a certain place and the existence of applicable sentences of experiences that make it possible to connect evidentiary facts with the evidentiary theme. And yes, sometimes it is possible to clarify. But in by far the most cases, vagueness remains, albeit reduced. This vagueness is, as indicated above, not necessarily due to our lack of knowledge on the context of reality but to the fact that the natural language is vague – that the linguistic variables used as connection stations lack precision.

When, for example, 'poor language skills' are indicated in the preparatory work as a factor for the assessment, this factor must in some way be defined in order to make it possible to prove 'poor language skills'. Sometimes it can be immediately determined that a person has 'poor language skills', sometimes a language test is required to more precisely determine the language skills. The results of a language test, however, do not in themselves say if a result is 'good' or 'poor'. The results must be assessed against a norm that indicates what is 'good' or 'poor'. If, on the basis of a language test, it should be asserted that the evidentiary value for 'poor language skills' is 0.75, this obviously has another meaning than that the evidentiary value that a person was at a certain place was 0.75. Language skills can furthermore be sufficient for a certain purpose but insufficient for another. Such an assessment is of the same nature as school marks in a certain subject. For a legal assessment pursuant to 36 AvtL, however, a position must be taken on the question of whether the language skills should be considered so poor that the agreement should be modified, and this depends on the legal context. Ten errors on a language test may not be decisive for the answer to this question. The agreement in general must also be taken into account. It is doubtful that a court would order

---

[65]  See section 1.4.2, above.

expert investigation into determining language skills, particularly because the legal significance of 'poor language skills' would anyway depend on an overall assessment of the contract situation.

The question of whether fuzzy logic can be used for interpretation and application of law is a matter that in any case should initially be kept separate from the evaluation of evidence. 'Disparity between the parties' contractual benefits', as well as if certain terms 'favour one party' and 'disadvantage' the other party, are according to the preparatory work, typical examples of things that could be 'unreasonable'. A certain situation could be a member of the set 'disparity between the parties' or the set 'contractual benefits' and have a certain degree of membership in it. This is usually considered to belong to subsumption or rather subordination and can thus be attributed to the application of law. Fuzzy logic, on the other hand, belongs to the probability. Because it handles vagueness, it can move or shift the boundaries between questions of facts and questions of law so that what is in the prevailing basic ethos a question of law is transformed into a question of facts. Yes, with fuzzy logic, most issues would probably belong to questions of law. However, how much and how fuzzy logic shifts the boundaries between questions of facts and questions of law will not be examined in this book. The key questions, however, are not how much and how, but rather if this would be acceptable and perhaps even preferable, at least in some situations.

# Bibliography

Adlercreutz A and L Gorton, *Avtalsrätt* (Norstedts Juridik 2011).

Andersson T, D Schum and W Twining, *Analysis of Evidence* (2nd edn Cambridge University Press 2005).

Arnoldi J, *Risk. An Introduction* (Polity Press 2009).

Arvind TT and L Stirton, 'Explaining the Reception of the Code Napoleon in Germany: a fuzzy-set qualitative comparative analysis' (2010) LS (1).

Audi R, *The Good in the Right. A Theory of Intuition and Intrinsic Value* (Princeton University Press 2004).

Baldwin T, 'The Three Phases of Intuitionism' in P Stratton-Lake (ed.) *Ethical Intuitionism. Re-evaluations* (Clarendon Press 2006).

Belton V and T Stewart, *Multiple Criteria Analysis. An Integrated Approach* (Kluwer 2002).

Belton V and T Stewart, 'Problem Structuring and Multiple Criteria Decision Analysis' in M Ehrgott, JR Figueira and S Greco (eds), *Trends in Multiple Criteria Decision Analysis* (Springer 2010).

Bengtsson B, R Hager and A Victorin, *Hyra och annan nyttjaderätt till fast egendom* (8th edn Norstedts Juridik 2013).

Betsch T, 'The Nature of Intuition and its Neglect in Research on Judgment and Decision Making' in H Plessner, C Betsch and T Betsch (eds) *Judgment and Decision Making* (LEA 2008).

Blomberg K, *Värt att veta om personuppgiftslagen* (Studentlitteratur 2012).

Bolding PO, *Bevisbördan och den juridiska tekniken* (Uppsala 1951).

Bolding PO, *Går det att bevisa?* (Norstedt 1989).

Boserup H, *Mikrostyring i mediation* (Uppsala universitet 2015).

Bylund T, *Tvångsmedel I,* (Iustus 1993).

Christiansson S-Å and M Ehrenkrona, *Psykologi och bevisvärdering. Myter om trovärdighet och tillförlitlighet* (Norstedts Juridik 2011).

Clermont KM, 'Conjunction of Evidence and Fuzzy Logic', (2012) Cornell Legal Studies Research Paper No 12-58. Available at SSRN: <http://ssrn.com/abstract=2115200> retrieved 21 July 2016.

Clermont KM, 'Death of Paradox: The Killer Logic Beneath the Standards of Proof' (2013) Cornell Law Faculty Publications. Paper 585. <http://scholarship.law.cornell.edu/facpub/585> retrieved 21 July 2016.

Cohen L, *The Probable and the Provable* (Clarendon Press 1977).

Cooper BS, D Griesel and M Ternes (eds) *Applied Issues in Investigative Interviewing, Eyewitness Memory and Credibility Assessment* (Springer 2013).

Datainspektionen, <http://www.datainspektionen.se/press/nyheter/2013 ny-kameraovervakningslag-fran-1-juli/> retrieved 15 August 2014.

Datainspektionen, <http://www.datainspektionen.se/documents/faktabro schyr-intresseavvagning.pdf> retrieved 5 October 2014.

Diesen C, *Bevisprövning i brottmål. Teori och praktik* (Norstedts Juridik 1993).

Diesen C and M Strandberg, *Bevisprövning i tvistemål. Teori och praktik* (Norstedts Juridik 2012).

Dodgson JS and others, 'Multi-criteria Analysis: A Manual' <http:// eprints.lse.ac.uk/12761/1/Multi-criteria_Analysis.pdf> accessed 21 July 2016.

Eckhoff T, *Tvilsrisikoen* (Tanum 1943) 11.

Eckhoff T, 'Temametode och verdimetode i bevisvurderingen' (SvJT 1988) 321.

Eckhoff T and NK Sundby, *Rettsystemer: Systemteoretisk innføring i retts-filosofien* (2nd edn Tano 1991).

Edwards W, 'How to use Multiattribute Utility Measurement for Social Decisionmaking' (1977), IEEE Transactions on Systems, Man, and Cybernetics, SMC-7, 326.

Ekelöf PO, *Kompendium över civilprocessen,* del II (Juridiska föreningen Uppsala 1948).

Ekelöf PO, 'Teleological Construction of Statutes' (1958) 2 *Scandinavian Studies in Law* 75.

Ekelöf PO, *Rättegång IV* (4th edn P A Norstedt & Söners Förlag 1977).

Ekelöf PO and R Boman, *Rättegång IV* (6th edn Norstedts Juridik 1992).

Ekelöf PO, T Bylund and R Boman, *Rättegång III* (6th edn Norstedts Juridik 1994).

Ekelöf PO and H Edelstam, *Rättegång I* (8th edn Norstedts Juridik 2002).

Ekelöf PO, H Edelstam and L Heuman, *Rättegång IV* (7th edn, Norstedts Juridik AB 2009).

Eklund H, *Inhibition* (1998 Iustus).

Elster J, *Reason and Rationality* (Princeton University Press 2009).

Ewerlöf G, T Sverne and A Singer, *Barnets bästa: om föräldrars och sam-hällets ansvar* (5th edn Norstedts Juridik 2004).

Gärdenfors P, 'Evidentiary Value' in P Gärdenfors, B Hansson, N-E Sahlin and S Halldén (eds) *Evidentiary Value: Philosophical, Judicial and Psychological Aspects of a Theory. Essays Dedicated to Sören Halldén on His Sixtieth Birthday* (C.W.K. Gleerups 1983).

Gigerenzer G, P Todd and the ABC Research Group, *Simple Heuristics That Make Us Smart* (Oxford University Press 1999).

Goldsmith RW and SI Andersson, 'Bevisvärdemetoden versus temametoden vid juridisk bevisvärdering' (TfR 1978) 72.

Goodwin P and G Wright, *Decision Analysis for Management Judgment* (4th edn Wiley 2012).

Gräns M, *Decisio Juris* (Iustus 2013).

Grönfors K and R Dotevall, *Avtalslagen. En kommentar* (4th edn, Norstedts Gula Bibliotek 2010).

Hall PG, *Great Planning Disasters* (University of California Press 1982).

Halldén S, 'Indiciemekanismer' (TfR 1973) 56.

Heck P, *Das Problem der Rechtsgewinnung. Gesetzeauslegung und Interessenjurisprudenz: Begriffsbildung und Interessenjurisprudenz.* Redigert von Roland Dubischer (Verlag Gehlen 1968).

Heuman L, 'Avvägningsrekvisit och möjligheten för en domstol att avvisa en fastställelsetalan när käranden kan föra en fullgörelsetalan' (2006–07) JT.

Hollatz J, *Analogy Making in Legal Reasoning with Neural Networks and Fuzzy Logic* (1999) 7(2–3) *Artifical Intelligence and Law* 289.

Holmqvist L and R Thomsson, *Hyreslagen. En kommentar* (10th edn Norstedts Juridik 2010).

Huber F, 'Belief and Degrees of Beliefs' in F Huber and C Schmidt-Petri (eds) *Degrees of Belief* (Springer 2009).

Huemer M, *Ethical Intuitionism* (Palgrave Macmillan 2005).

Ishizaka A and P Nemery, *Multi-Criteria Decision Analysis: Methods and Software* (Wiley 2013).

Joyce JM, *The Foundations of Causal Decision Theory* (Cambridge University Press 1999).

Kahneman D, *Tänka snabbt och långsamt* (Månpocket/Fakta 2014).

Kaldal A, *Parallella processer. En rättsvetenskaplig studie av riskbedömningar i vårdnads- och LVU-mål* (Jure 2010).

Källström K, 'Arrendators ersättningsrätt vid uppsägning av anläggningsarrende. Om ändamålstolkning av avvägningsnormer' (1988) SvJT 622.

Kaplan S, 'The Words of Risk Analysis' (1997) 17 *Risk Analysis* 407.

Keeny RL and H Raiffa, *Decisions with Multiple Objectives: Preference and Value Tradeoffs* (Cambridge University Press 1993).

Keynes JM, *A Treatise on Probability* (Macmillan 1973).

Kilgour MD, Y Chen and KW Hipel, 'Multiple Criteria Approaches to Group Decision and Negotiation' in M Ehrgott, JS Figueira and S Greco (eds) *Trends in Multiple Criteria Decision Analysis* (Springer 2010).

Knobe J and B Fraser, 'Causal Judgment and Moral Judgment: Two

Experiments' in W Sinnott-Armstrong (ed.) *Moral Psychology, Volume 2, The Cognitive Science of Morality: Intuition and Diversity* (The MIT Press 2008).

Lainpelto K, *Stödbevisning i brottmål*, (Jure 2012).

Larichev OI and HM Moskovich, 'Unstructured Problems and Development of Prescriptive Decision Making Methods' in PM Pardalos, Y Siskos and C Zopounidis (eds) *Advances in Multicriteria Analysis* (Kluwer Academic Publishers 1995).

Lindblom PH, Review of Stenings dissertation 'Bevisvärde' (SvJT 1977) 280.

Lindblom PH, *Miljöprocess, Del 1* (Iustus 2001).

Lindell B, *Sakfrågor och rättsfrågor. En studie av gränser, skillnader och förhållanden mellan faktum och rätt* (Iustus 1987).

Lindell B, 'Insolvensbedömningen' (SvJT 1989) 131.

Lindell B, 'Några bevisrättsliga frågor' (Tfr 1989) 237.

Lindell B, *Civilprocessen – rättegång samt skiljeförfarande och medling* (Iustus 2012)

Lindell B, 'Sweden', in P Talman (ed.) *International Encyclopaedia of Laws: Civil Procedure* (Kluwer Law International 2013).

Linköpings universitet, *Multikriterieanalyser vid prioriteringar inom hälso- och sjukvården – kriterier och analysmetoder* (2013:2), Prioriteringscentrum.

Litowitz D, *Postmodern Philosophy & Law* (University Press of Kansas 1997).

Lootsma FA, *Multi-Criteria Analysis via Ratio and Difference Judgement* (Kluwer Academic Publisher, 1999).

Løvlie A, *Rettslige faktabegreper* (Gyldendal Juridisk 2014).

Mabin V and M Beattie *A Practical Guide to Multi-Criteria Decision Analysis. A Workbook Companion to V•I•S•A* (5th edn, Victoria University of Wellington 2006) <http://www.victoria.ac.nz/som/researchprojects/publications/Multi-Criteria_Decision_Analysis.pdf> (retrieved 5 July 2016).

Malczewski J, *GIS and Multicriteria Decision Analysis* (Wiley 1999).

March JG and C Heat, *A Primer on Decision Making. How Decisions Happen* (Simon & Schuster Ltd 1994).

McNeill D and P Freiberger, *Fuzzy Logic. The Revolutionary Computer Technology That Is Changing Our World* (Touchstone & Schuster 1993).

Mead GRS, *Bergson's Intuition* (Kessinger Publishing 2010).

Mendoza GA, P Macan and others, *Guidelines for Applying Multi-Criteria Analysis to the Assessment of Criteria and Indicators* (1999, The Criteria and Toolbox series, Center for International Forestry Research) <http://

www.cifor.org/livesinforests/publications/pdf_files/toolbox-9c.pdf > (accessed 22 July 2016).

Mousseau V, 'Eliciting Information Concerning Importance of Criteria' in PM Pardalos, S Yannos and C Zopounidis (eds) *Advances in Multicriteria Analysis* (Kluwer Academic Publishers 1995).

Mukaidono M, *Fuzzy Logic for Beginners* (World Scientific Publishing Co Pte Ltd 2004).

Nagel SS and MK Mills, *Multi-Criteria Methods for Alternative Dispute Resolution. With Microcomputer Software Applications* (Quorum Books 1990).

National Research Council (U.S.), Committee on Risk and Decision Making, *Risk and Decision Making Perspectives and Research* (2010) National Academies 13.

Nguyen H T and EA Walker, *A First Course in Fuzzy Logic* (3rd edn, Chapman & Hall/CRC/Taylor & Francis Group 2006).

Nilsson J, *Introduktion till riskanalysmetoder*, (2003) Rapport 3124, Lunds universitet, brandteknik, 11.

Nord L and J Strömbäck, 'Hot på agendan: En analys av nyhetsförmedling om risker och kriser'. KBM:s Temaserie (2005) (7) 12.

Nordh R, *Talerätt i miljömål: Särskilt om vattenrättsliga ansökningsmål samt talan rörande allmänna intressen* (Iustus 1999).

Nygaard N, 'Overviktsprinsippet ved bevis for faktisk årsakssammenheng' i Festskrift til Torstein Eckhoffs 70-årsdag (Tano 1986).

Odelstad J, *Intresseavvägning. En beslutsteoretisk studie med tillämpning på planering* (Thales 2002).

Olivecrona K, *Bevisskyldigheten och den materiella rätten* (Uppsala 1930).

Olivecrona K, *Rätt och dom* (Norstedt 1966).

Otway HJ and D von Winterfeldt, 'Beyond Acceptable Risk' (1982) 14 *Policy Sciences* 247.

Ourdane W, N Maudet and A Tsoukiàs, 'Argumentation Theory and Decision Aiding' in M Ehrgott, JS Figueira and S Greco (eds), *Trends in Multiple Criteria Decision Analysis* (Springer 2010).

Persson J, 'Risk fara och riskobjekt' in Persson J and Sahlin N-E (eds) *Risk and Risicio* (Nya Doxa 2008).

Raiffa H, *The Art and Science of Negotiation.* (Belknap/Harvard 1982).

Ramberg J and C Hultmark, *Allmän avtalsrätt* (Norstedts 2000).

Ring P, 'Risk and the UK Pension Reform' (2003) 37(1) *Social Policy Administration* 65.

Rödig J, *Die Theorie des gerichtlichen Erkenntnisverfahren: die Grundlinien des zivil-, straf- und verwaltungsgerichtlichen Prozesses* (Springer 1973).

Roger Jang J-S and N Gulley, *Matlab, Fuzzy Logic Toolbox, User's guide,*

*Version 1* <http://andrei.clubcisco.ro/cursuri/5master/ciblf/Artificial_
Intelligence_-Fuzzy_Logic_Matlab.pdfIntroduction> (retrieved 11 July
2016).

Roy B, *Multicriteria Methodology for Decision Aiding* (Kluwer Academic
Publisher 1996).

Savage L, *The Foundations of Statistics* (New York: Dover 1954).

Schelin L, *Bevisvärdering av utsagor i brottmål* (Norstedts Juridik 2007).

Schuyler J, *Risk and Decision Analysis in Projects* (2nd edn Project
Management Institute 2001).

Seniuk GT, 'Credibility Assessment, Common Law Trials and Fuzzy
Logic' in BS Cooper, D Griesel and M Ternes (eds) *Applied Issues in
Investigative Interviewing, Eyewitness Memory and Credibility Assessment*
(Springer 2013)

Simon HA, *Models of Bounded Rationality. Empirically Grounded
Economic Reason* (The MIT Press 1982).

Simon HA, *Administrative Behaviour. A Study of Decision-Making
Processes in Administrative Organization* (4th edn The Free Press 1997).

Singer A, *Barnets bästa. Om barns rättsliga ställning i familj och samhälle*
(6th edn Norstedts Juridik 2012).

Sinnott-Armstrong W, 'Framing Moral Institutions' in W Sinott-
Armstrong (ed.) *Moral Psychology, Volume 2, The Cognitive Science of
Morality: Intuition and Diversity* (The MIT Press 2008).

Skånér Y, *Läkartidningen* (1999) (96) 4190.

Sokal A and J Brichmont, *Fashionable Nonsense. Postmodern Intellectuals'
Abuse of Science* (Picador 1998).

Stening A, 'Konflikt mellan två bevismodeller' (SvJT 1979) 295.

Stening A, *Bevisvärde* (Acta Universitatis Upsaliensis, Studia Juridica
Upsaliensia 1975).

Stirling A and S Meyer, 'Rethinking Risk: A Pilot Multi-Criteria
Mapping of a Genetically Modified Crop in Agricultural Systems in
the UK' (1999) <http://users.sussex.ac.uk/~prfh0/Rethinking%20Risk.
pdf> (accessed 20 July 2016).

Strandberg M, 'Bevisrettens sannhetsmålsetning' in S Andersson and
K Lainpelto (eds) *Festskrift till Christian Diesen* (Norstedts Juridik
2014).

Strandberg M, *Beviskrav i sivile saker. En beviskravsteoretisk studie av den
norske beviskravslaerens forutsetninger* (Fagbogforlaget 2012).

Strutin K, *Calculating Justice: Mathematics and Criminal Law* <http://
www.llrx.com/features/calculatingjustice.htm> (retrieved 8 July 2016).

Sutorius H and C Diesen, *Bevisprövning vid sexualbrott* (2nd edn Norstedts
Juridik 2013).

Swedish Environmental Protection Agency (2009), 'Multikriterieanalys för hållbar efterbehandling: Metodutveckling och exempel på tillämpning'. Rapport 5891.

Tanaka K, *An Introduction to Fuzzy Logic For Practical Applications* (Springer 1997).

Tolhurst W, 'Moral Institutions Framed' in W Sinnott-Armstrong (ed.) *Moral Psychology, Volume 2, The Cognitive Science of Morality: Intuition and Diversity* (The MIT Press 2008).

von Neumann J and JO Morgenstern, *Theory of Games and Economic Behaviour* (Princeton University Press 1944).

von Post C-R, *Studier kring 36 § avtalslagen med inriktning på rent kommersiella förhållanden* (Jure AB 1999).

Wahlgren P, *Legal Risk Analysis. A Proactive Legal Method* (Jure 2013).

Welamson L and J Munck, *Processen I hovrätt och Högsta domstolen* (4th edn Norstedts Juridik 2011).

Westberg P, *Det provisoriska rättsskyddet I tvistemål. En funktionsstudie över kvarstad och andra civilprocessuella säkerhetsåtgärder*, Bok 1 (Jurisförlaget i Lund 2004).

Westerlund S, *Proportionalitetsprincipen: verklighet, missförstånd eller nydaning* (1996) Miljörättslig tidskrift (2) 254.

Wetherell M and J Potter, 'Discourse Analysis and the Identification of Interpretative Repertoires' in C Antaki (ed.) *Analysing Everyday Explanation. A Casebook of Methods* (Sage Publications Inc 1988).

Wild KW, *Intuition* (Cambridge University Press 1938).

Willén RM and LA Strömwall, 'Offenders Lies and Truths: An Evaluation of the Supreme Court of Sweden's Criteria for Credibility Assessment' (2012) 18(8) *Psychology, Crime & Law* 745.

Winslade J and GD Monk, *Narrative Mediation. A New Approach to Conflict Resolution* (Jossey Bass 2000).

Wolf W (herausgeber) *Festschrift für Fritz Baur*, Zetschrift für Zivilprozess (1978).

Zahle H, *Om det juridiske bevis* (Jurisforbundets forlag 1976).

Zahle H, *Bevisret, Oversigt* (DJØF 1994).

# Index